SOVIET POLICY
IN THE
FAR EAST

SOVIET POLICY
IN THE
FAR EAST
1944–1951

By

MAX BELOFF

NUFFIELD READER IN THE COMPARATIVE
STUDY OF INSTITUTIONS IN THE
UNIVERSITY OF OXFORD

Issued under the auspices of the
Royal Institute of International Affairs

OXFORD UNIVERSITY PRESS
LONDON NEW YORK TORONTO
1953

Oxford University Press, Amen House, London E.C.4
GLASGOW NEW YORK TORONTO MELBOURNE WELLINGTON
BOMBAY CALCUTTA MADRAS KARACHI CAPE TOWN IBADAN
Geoffrey Cumberlege, Publisher to the University

PRINTED IN GREAT BRITAIN

PREFACE

THIS book is an expansion of a paper which I was invited to contribute to the Conference of the Institute of Pacific Relations held at Lucknow in October 1950. Mr. W. L. Holland, Secretary-General of the Institute of Pacific Relations, suggested that a more detailed and documented study of the subject would be of wider interest and I am grateful to him and to the Institute of Pacific Relations for the suggestion and for the assistance given to the project. I also owe a real debt of gratitude to the Royal Institute of International Affairs for making its resources available to me at all stages in the preparation of the book, and in this connexion in particular to Miss Margaret Cleeve, O.B.E., Research Secretary of the Institute.

I have had the assistance of Dr. Joseph Frankel in broadening the basis of the research for the study by undertaking a full analysis of Soviet and other press materials for the period. He has also contributed the chapter on South East Asia, an area of which he has made a special study. I must, of course, take full responsibility for the final form in which the material is here presented and for the conclusions drawn from it.

Various experts on the Far East in this country and the United States have been kind enough to comment on the separate chapters, and I wish to take this opportunity of thanking here: Mr. G. F. Hudson, Mr. B. R. Pearn, Dr. F. C. Jones, Sir George Sansom, Dr. Victor Purcell, Mr. A. S. B. Olver, Professor Owen Lattimore, Mr. P. Langer, Professor Leland Goodrich, Mr. O. E. Clubb, Mr. R. C. North, Mrs. X. Eudin, and Mr. R. N. Carew Hunt. It is more than usually necessary to state that none of them is responsible for any errors of fact or opinion.

I wish to thank the members of the staff of the Royal Institute of International Affairs who have given their assistance in the preparation of the book, and in particular Miss Hermia Oliver, whose work in checking references and in other ways has gone well beyond what is usually understood by preparing a manuscript for the press. In conclusion I must thank my wife for preparing the index.

MAX BELOFF

NUFFIELD COLLEGE
OXFORD
July 1952

CONTENTS

NOTE ON SOURCES AND ABBREVIATIONS

SINCE the material for a book of this kind must inevitably be found mainly in official publications and in newspapers and periodicals, it has not been thought necessary to include a bibliography. Full information about books used is given in the first footnote in which they appear. References to articles in the Soviet press are usually, though not invariably, given to the original Russian source. In the case of *Pravda* and *Izvestia* translations are often available in the *Soviet Monitor* or in *Soviet News*, and some references have been given to these.

The following abbreviations have been used in the footnotes:

Beloff, i, ii.	Max Beloff, *The Foreign Policy of Soviet Russia, 1929–1941* (London, Oxford University Press for RIIA, 1947–9), 2 vols.
CSM	*Christian Science Monitor*
For a Lasting Peace	*For a Lasting Peace, for a People's Democracy* (the Cominform Journal)
FES	*Far Eastern Survey*
MKiMP	*Mirovoe Khozaistvo i Mirovoe Politika* (World Economics and World Politics)
NCDN	*North China Daily News* (Shanghai)
NCNA	*New China News Agency*
NYHT	*New York Herald Tribune*
NYT	*New York Times*
Relations with China	United States, Department of State, *United States Relations with China, with special reference to the period 1944–1949* (Publication 3573, released August 1949).
SCMP	*South China Morning Post* (Hong Kong).

I

Introduction

THE primary purpose of this book is to provide an account of the development of Soviet policies in East and South East Asia from the negotiations concerning eventual Soviet participation in the war against Japan culminating in the Yalta Agreement on the terms of entry of 11 February 1945, to the San Francisco Conference on the Japanese Peace Treaty in September 1951. The major events of the period in the Far East were the defeat of Japan and its replacement by the United States as the major Power in the Western Pacific, and on the mainland, the unification of China under Communist rule. It was marked, once victory over Germany and Japan had been won, by a rapid deterioration in relations between the Soviet Union and the Western Powers with whom it had recently been allied, a phenomenon which had its repercussions throughout the globe but in no area more than in the Far East.[1]

The policies of the Soviet Union both as causes and as consequences of these events can only be fully understood in the light of the policies of the other Great Powers, and of internal developments in the Asiatic countries themselves. Although the ideological basis of Soviet foreign policy, with its fundamental antagonism to 'capitalism' and 'imperialism' and its fundamental belief in the inevitability of an ultimate world revolution, provided a general framework within which Soviet policy continued to be formulated, it would be wrong to jump from this to postulating the existence of a single master-plan conceived in advance for expanding the area of Soviet control to cover the entire Far East.[2] An element of opportunism was

---

[1] No full historical account of these years was available at the time of writing though one will be provided in the projected volumes of the *Survey of International Affairs* published by the Royal Institute of International Affairs. The volume for 1947–8, published when the present work was substantially complete, contained valuable chapters on the Far East by F. C. Jones, and on South East Asia by Peter Calvocoressi. See also RIIA, *Documents on International Affairs, 1947–8*, ed. M. Carlyle.

[2] For a statement of the general point of view from which this book has been written see Max Beloff, *The Foreign Policy of Soviet Russia, 1929–41* (London, Oxford University Press for RIIA, 1947–9), ii. 385–95.

inevitable; Soviet statesmen were as likely to make mistakes in their appreciation of concrete situations as their Western competitors, and in some respects more likely to do so. Neither the success of Communism in China during this period, nor its failure in Japan can, for instance, be understood simply in the light of Soviet policies towards these countries.

On the other hand one must be careful not to underestimate the Soviet role in such events because such an underestimation is all too likely to arise anyhow from the very nature of the materials on which the historian of Soviet foreign policy must in the first instance necessarily rely. The main Soviet sources—official statements and speeches, and commentaries upon them in the Soviet press—tend, it will be found, to deal very largely and in some vital respects almost exclusively, with the policies of other Powers, and to treat the Soviet Union as though it were merely a distant and disinterested spectator of the events in question. The Soviet Union is often pictured as the ultimate target of the aggressive plans allegedly harboured by the 'imperialist' Powers (in the period here treated, by the United States) and with increasing frequency as the model and inspiration for 'peace-loving' and freedom-seeking peoples and movements. But its actual policies, whether designed to discourage the former, or assist the latter, are normally passed over in silence. This is particularly the case where relations between the Soviet Union and Communist movements abroad are concerned, or even, particularly since the disappearance of the Communist International, between the Communist Party of the Soviet Union and Communist parties in the non-Communist world. There is, for instance, hardly any material from the Soviet side to illustrate the relations between the Soviet Union and the Chinese Communists in the post-war period until the formal recognition in October 1949 of the Chinese People's Government.

It is possible from the Soviet sources alone to produce what one writer using such a method has called 'approximately the picture which the Soviet people themselves have of this part of the world scene', that is to say in this case of the Far East.[1] But this in itself is insufficient for estimating the purposes of the

[1] Harriet L. Moore, *Soviet Far Eastern Policy, 1931–45* (Princeton University Press for IPR, 1945), p. xv.

Soviet Government, and the student is bound to seek additional information from both official and unofficial sources of a different provenance.[1] In doing so, however, it is obviously necessary to be on one's guard against producing a wholly external account by overlooking the fact that Soviet policy must presumably be formulated independently at some point in the Soviet hierarchy, and that one must expect it to have its own inner logic and coherence. For however strained and indeed fantastic may seem to the Western observer the shadow world inside which Soviet leaders appear to carry on their thinking on international affairs, their prophecies, fears, and apprehensions are in themselves important political realities. And some of their most characteristic attitudes, and in particular their insistent attacks on all forms of Western 'colonialism' and 'imperialism' find a ready echo in Asiatic countries that are in other respects outside the Soviet orbit.[2] Indeed in resisting the spread of Communism in post-war Asia the Western Powers have been continually handicapped by the widespread belief that they were building up an artificial Communist bogey in order to have an excuse for continuing or reimposing colonial rule.[3] An understanding of the element of 'colonialism' inherent in the Soviet system itself and in the relations between the Soviet Union and its satellites is still far from being widely appreciated.[4]

It has, of course, often been conjectured that these illusions about the external world and its ineradicable wickedness and hostility are not in fact entertained by the highest stratum of Soviet rulers, and indeed that it is precisely 'this freedom from the content of their own ideologies which characterizes the

[1] It is curious to see writers by no means friendly to the Soviet Union deliberately excluding from consideration all non-Soviet sources, presumably with the idea that this guarantees their impartiality and will get them a better hearing. See e.g. Walter Kolarz, *Russia and her Colonies* (London, Philip, 1952), p. v.

[2] For a typical Soviet approach to the period from this point of view see the publication of the Pacific Institute of the Soviet Academy: E. M. Zhukov and others, *Krisis Kolonialni Sistema: Natsionalno-Osvoboditelnaya Borba Narodov Vostochnoi Asii* (The Crisis of the Colonial System: the National-Liberation Struggle of the Peoples of Eastern Asia; Moscow, Akademia Nauk, 1949). This publication is subsequently referred to as *Krisis Kolonialni Sistema*.

[3] cf. C. A. Fisher, 'West New Guinea in its Regional Setting', *Year Book of World Affairs, 1952* (London, Stevens, 1952), p. 206.

[4] See for some study on this point, Kolarz, *Russia and her Colonies*, and the important article by M. Holdsworth, 'Soviet Central Asia, 1917–1940', *Soviet Studies*, January 1952, vol. 3, no. 3.

highest rank of the totalitarian hierarchy.'[1] But the arguments for this partially comforting view are in the case of the Soviet Union at least not very convincing. Events such as the conclusion of the Nazi-Soviet pact of 1939 that have sometimes been adduced as evidence of the Communist leaders' cynicism about their own ideology would seem rather to refer to that ideology as filtered through the minds of liberal-intentioned Western sympathizers than to the version held by the genuine adherents of the Leninist-Stalinist creed.

The printed record available to the historian gives him little encouragement to believe that the Soviet leaders mean other than what they say. The tone of the Soviet press naturally differs at the various levels into which it is divided for more effective propaganda in the highly stratified society of the contemporary Soviet Union.[2] But even at the highest level the fundamental attitudes are identical with those of the journals intended for the masses.[3] Thus a paper read to the meeting of the Pacific Institute of the Academy of Sciences in March 1948 expounded the thesis that American policy in the Far East during the war against Japan and since then had been devoted entirely to establishing the economic and political domination of the United States over China, and that it had been inspired by directly anti-Soviet motives. When the paper was reprinted in 1949 it was followed by one on the relation of American imperialist aims to the agreement between the Kuomintang and the Communists of 10 January 1946 and to the subsequent breakdown of that agreement.[4] The postscript to a general work published in 1951 on international relations in the Far East between 1870 and 1945, dealing with the period after the Second World War, is likewise largely concerned with tracing the history of alleged American aggressiveness.[5] Finally, of

[1] Hannah Arendt, *The Burden of Our Time* (London, Secker & Warburg, 1951), p. 374.

[2] On the structure of the Soviet press, see Alex Inkeles, *Public Opinion in Soviet Russia* (Cambridge, Mass., Harvard University Press, 1950).

[3] See my articles on the Soviet *Diplomaticheskii Slovar* (Diplomatic Dictionary; Moscow, Gospolitizdat, 1948–50): 'Russian Diplomacy', *Listener*, 23 August 1951; 'The Theory of Soviet Foreign Policy', *Soviet Studies*, April 1952, vol. 3, no. 4.

[4] *Uchenie Zapiski Tikhookeanskogo Instituta* (Scientific Papers of the Pacific Institute), vol. 3 (Moscow, Academy of Sciences, 1949), articles by G. V. Astafev and V. I. Nikoforov.

[5] E. M. Zhukov, ed., *Mezhdunarodnye Otnosheniya na Dalnem Vostoke* (International

course, the fact that the Soviet Union invariably acts upon the assumption that it is the object of universal hostility tends in its turn to provoke actions that can indeed be interpreted as evidence of the hostility that has previously been assumed.

But it must be repeated that the adherence of Soviet statesmen to a closed system of thought does not, and cannot, eliminate the element of the contingent and accidental in their policy. The possibilities of the expansion of either the power of the Soviet State or of world Communism are directly related to the balance of forces not merely in the area in question but particularly in more recent years to that in the world at large. It may give one's picture a more sharply defined outline to present the Soviet Union at all times and under all circumstances in the character of a single-minded aggressor taking up once more the Asiatic expansionism of the Tsars with the new ideology as an additional reinforcement.[1] But this can only be done at the sacrifice of some accuracy of definition and appraisal. Furthermore, to seek to impose a too rigid pattern upon events is liable to distort the handling of the material and to make the writer accept too readily that which fits in with his own preconceptions. In particular, the reports appearing from Oriental sources in the Western press cannot always be taken at their face value, for it is clear that over the last few years in the Far East it has often been to the advantage of one side or the other to spread false news. And there has been a tendency in some quarters, even official ones, to accept as ascertained fact what is only the product of rumour at best. As far as Communist China is concerned, the régime itself has done its best to cut off the normal flow of information from the area under its control, and although this has not so far been equally effective throughout the country, there are important points, and in particular the whole question of the role of the Russians in Manchuria and in Communist China generally, upon which it is impossible to be dogmatic with safety.

While the study of Soviet policy in the Far East should make

Relations in the Far East), *1870–1945* (Moscow, Gospolitizdat, 1951). This publication is subsequently referred to as *Mezhdunarodnye Otnosheniya*.

[1] An element of over-simplification of this kind is the main weakness of the otherwise very valuable pioneer works of D. J. Dallin, *The Rise of Russia in Asia* and *Soviet Russia and the Far East*, published in New Haven by the Yale University Press in 1949 and 1948 respectively.

its contribution to a general understanding of the nature of the Soviet approach to international relations, this policy itself has of course been profoundly affected at every stage by events taking place in areas of the globe outside the purview of this study. The Yalta Conference itself, which provides a convenient starting point for a discussion of many of the issues dealt with, was mainly concerned not with Far Eastern questions but with the final stages of the war in Europe. The critical year of the Chinese civil war, 1948, was also the year of the Berlin blockade and of the defection of Yugoslavia from the Soviet camp. Both the Soviet Union and the other Great Powers had to consider the allocation of their resources to the Far Eastern theatre of conflict in relation to the demands upon them made elsewhere.

In view of the crucial importance attached by Communist leaders from Lenin onwards to the 'colonial' and 'semi-colonial' peoples, particularly in Asia, and to their role as the Achilles heel of 'imperialism', not everyone would agree that the Far East was in fact a secondary theatre in the world struggle of ideologies that developed in these years. The primacy of Europe was maintained indeed by the United States Government in the 'great debate' on foreign policy that convulsed America in 1951; and despite its critics, it succeeded in winning the necessary support for its belief that it was not worth trying to save parts of Asia from Communism if the price was to see Soviet power extend to the English Channel and the Atlantic coast.

No such public debate illuminated Soviet policy or strategy. But it would not be difficult to believe that the same priority held good in the Russian case. Despite all the internal reshaping of the Soviet economy before, during, and since the war, it remains true that it is from the West, not from the East that the Soviet Union remains vulnerable. The glacis now formed by the Soviet Union's domination of Eastern Europe must appear in Russian eyes to be a far more precious recompense for the war-time blood and tears than, for instance, the renewed appearance of Russians in Manchuria in the wake of their Tsarist predecessors. Much is made in Soviet propaganda of the enormous numerical accretion to the Communist camp implied by the adhesion of China; but it is doubtful whether the Kremlin in fact regards the allegiance of millions of Chinese peasants as compensation for the failure to establish control over the great industries and advanced proletariats of the Ruhr, of Paris, or of northern Italy. Peking and Shanghai and Canton are great cities; but they are not Berlin or Paris or Rome.

If the leaders of the Soviet Union were in fact to give first place to the West rather than the East in their political and strategic thinking, this would be an indication that in certain respects Tsarist experience does still provide a clue to certain aspects of Soviet policy. One says this with diffidence because some have taken this element of continuity to be so strong as to leave little room for the impact of the new ideology, and this is clearly absurd. Neither in purpose nor in method are Soviet policies anywhere, and least of all in the Far East, identical with those of the Tsarist régime. There have been moments when it has suited the Soviet Government to claim the heritage of the Tsars, as when seeking in Manchuria in 1945 to reverse the decisions of forty years earlier.[1] And the problem of writing the history of Tsarist policies in the Far East to fit in with the new role assigned to the United States as the major imperialist Power has not been an easy one; the solution seems to lie in picturing Tsarist Russia as essentially weak, and therefore as not really a major menace to the independence of the Eastern countries despite its imperialist outlook.[2] But the differences are greater than the similarities.

The truth of the matter lies in the simple reflection that the primary method of forwarding the interests of Communism has come to be either the direct increase in the area of Russian political control, or at least the acquisition of predominant Russian influence through indirect means. Both are predicated upon the survival and strengthening of the Soviet State itself, and since the space occupied by the Soviet Union is roughly identical with that of the Tsarist empire, the lines of advance are substantially dictated by the same geographical factors.

This fact will be as true of areas of relative weakness as of those of greater Russian strength. The period of intensive Russian interest in the Far East that culminated in the Russo-Japanese War of 1904–5 bears a rather forced and artificial air when compared with the permanence of Russian interests in

---

[1] On this point see below, p. 246.
[2] See e.g. *Mezhdunarodnye Otnosheniya*, pp. 703–4.

the Balkans and the Black Sea to which Russia returned after her defeat at the hands of Japan.

For one thing the poverty in men and materials of Russia's own Far Eastern territories and their poor and vulnerable communications with the areas of Russia's strength in the west must be a permanent source of anxiety to her rulers and a check upon her abilities to conduct major military operations.[1] These weaknesses, which are inherent in the geographical factors involved, have not been substantially remedied by the most recent developments in the area.[2]

The area now included under the term the Soviet Far East has been extended by the annexation in 1945 of Southern Sakhalin and the Kuriles, and this has led to an administrative reorganization of the area. In 1947 the Sakhalin oblast (province) was separated from the Khabarovsk territory. In 1948 the Amur oblast was also separated from the Khabarovsk territory and was increased in area by the addition of the north-eastern portion of the Chita oblast. In the same year an area including the port Sovetskaya Gavan (Soviet Harbour) was detached from the Maritime territory and added to the Khabarovsk territory.

The total population of the Soviet Far East seems to have increased from rather more than $2\frac{1}{4}$ million in 1939 to about $3\frac{1}{2}$ million.[3] The population of the town of Khabarovsk is said

[1] On the development of the Soviet Far East before the Second World War see Beloff, i. Appendix B.

[2] In view of the difficulty of obtaining information, it is not surprising that recent geographical studies of the Soviet Union usually include hardly any up-to-date information about this part of the Soviet Union. Theodore Shabad's *Geography of the USSR* (London, Oxford University Press, 1951) does, however, contain on pp. 308–33 a description of the area which may be taken as authoritative within the limits which Soviet reticence on these matters imposes. In addition to what can be gleaned from the Soviet press there are accounts by recent émigrés who have worked in this area, particularly in the mining enterprises based upon the forced labour of political and other prisoners. Such evidence, which cannot adequately be checked, must obviously be used with the utmost caution; it cannot, however, be ignored. See e.g. E. Lipper, *Eleven Years in Soviet Prison Camps* (London, Hollis & Carter, 1951) and V. Petrov, *It Happens in Russia* (London, Eyre & Spottiswoode, 1951).

[3] Shabad, *Geography of the USSR*, p. 314. An indication of the growth of population is to be found in the increase in the representation of the two Far Eastern territories in the Supreme Soviet. Each got an additional deputy in 1946, which should mean an increase of population of about 300,000. (A. Steiger, 'Industrialisation of Siberia', *FES*, 27 February 1946.)

to have increased from just under 200,000 in 1939 to about 300,000 in 1947, and that of Komsomolsk from about 70,000 to about 150,000.[1] Nevertheless the economic development of the Far East does not seem to have been on a scale comparable with that of other parts of Siberia.

Difficulties of communication are an important element in the situation. There have been reports by former Soviet citizens of the completion of the projected northern trunk railway, the Baikal–Amur–Magistral, but there is no confirmation of this in official sources.[2] It seems more likely that, apart from the section known to have been completed between Tayshet and Bratsk (or possibly Ust'-Kut), the construction of this line was abandoned during the war in favour of more urgent projects. It was not listed among major construction projects in the fourth five-year plan (1946–50). Certain lesser railway lines have, however, been completed: between Komsomolsk and Sovteskaya Gavan and between Skovorodino and Tyndinskiy.[3] Developments in aviation connecting the Far East with western Siberia and European Russia and with China are of importance: and in view of the significance of propaganda in the Far East, the construction of powerful radio transmitters particularly at Khabarovsk and Komsomolsk also calls for notice.

On the industrial side, oil production was perhaps the most important sphere of development. Shortly before the German attack, the Soviet press announced that the output of oil in Sakhalin had been doubled, and that the 1942 target had been set at 1,200,000 tons. Post-war production has included that of the previous Japanese concessions which used to produce 300,000 tons a year. It is therefore estimated that the Soviet Union receives from this source between 1 and 1½ million tons of oil a year.[4] The Amurstal steel works at Komsomolsk, which had a reputed capacity of 600,000 tons a year, worked during the war years largely on scrap. Some new consumer-goods industries were also brought into operation.[5]

The discussion of the future development of Siberia by the

[1] Shabad, p. 314.
[2] H. Schwartz, *Russia's Soviet Economy* (London, Cape, 1951), p. 335.
[3] Shabad, pp. 88 and 298.
[4] Steiger, *FES*, 27 February 1946; cf. Werner Leimbach, *Die Sowjet-Union: Natur, Volk und Wirtschaft* (Stuttgart, Frankh'sche Verlagshandlung, 1950).
[5] Steiger, *FES*, 27 February 1946.

geographer V. F. Vasyutin in a paper read in October 1949 revealed that 'in the Far East emphasis is to be placed upon developing metallurgical industry, both ferrous and non-ferrous; expanding forestry activity; and making this area more nearly independent and self-sufficient with regard to food.'[1] The weakness of the area in agricultural potentiality remains, it would seem, the major impediment to its economic and demographic growth. Despite whatever use may have been made of the 'war booty' collected by the Soviet occupation troops in Manchuria, there are obvious limits to the extent to which the Soviet Far East can be built up into an independent power-unit.[2] The fulcrum of power on the mainland in the Far East still lies in Manchuria and the nature of Soviet policy in the whole area can only be understood in relation to this often overlooked fact.

The special importance of Manchuria to Russia is only the most important aspect of the general consideration that Russia's relations with China, and perhaps also with Korea, are influenced not merely by her long-range policy, but also by the specific assistance which could be made by certain parts of the Chinese Empire and Korea to solving particular problems in regard to natural resources and means of communication. The strained relations between the Soviet Government and the Kuomintang after 1927 were due not only to the latter's profound enmity to Communism but also to Russia's territorial encroachments in Outer Mongolia and Sinkiang. China could never be confident that Russia really wished to see the emergence of an independent and united China as a new Great Power in the Far East.

It may also be doubted whether the emergence of such a China even under Communist rule formed part of the original Soviet plan for the post-war Far East. Not only were the Soviet statesmen probably as surprised as were people in the West by the rapidity of the Japanese collapse, particularly since, although as we now know they were informed by their agents of all stages in the manufacture of the atomic bomb, they could not know when or in what circumstances it would be used, but in addition it seems likely that they completely underestimated the strength of the Chinese Communists. As a recent and highly

[1] Schwartz, *Russia's Soviet Economy*, pp. 552–3.
[2] For the 'war-booty' and reparations issues, see below, pp. 38 ff.

competent historian of the Chinese Revolution has put it, Russia's actions in Manchuria in 1945

do not support the simple belief in a world Communist conspiracy planned years ahead, and foreseeing every turn of the world situation. Russia's post-war policy in the Far East, like that of her rivals the Americans and Western democratic powers, suggests inadequate knowledge, shortsighted measures of supposed national advantage, and improvisation in face of a rapidly and unexpectedly developing situation.[1]

The evidence provided by events in Manchuria for views of this kind will be considered later in this book.

Soviet writers themselves cannot, of course, admit either improvisation or attempts to reap national advantages from their policies. Either would be in disharmony with the supposed 'scientific Marxist-Leninist' foundations of Soviet foreign policy. For these writers, the post-war history of the Far East is dominated by two main developments. In the first place there has been a general weakening everywhere in Asia of Western 'imperialism' in terms of its classical formulation by Lenin.[2] A single quotation may serve to set the scene as a Soviet historian now views it:

It is undeniable that the results of the Second World War have brought about a serious alteration in the concrete contents of Pacific problems and not only in the sense that the relation of strength between the principal competitors struggling for the division of 'spheres of influence' in the Pacific—the United States, Japan, and Britain—have become different. The strengthening of democracy and socialism on a world-wide scale, the struggle of the two camps—the camp of democracy and the camp of imperialism—have to such an extent 'complicated' the struggle between the imperialists for 'spheres of influence' and colonies, in particular in the Far East, that the whole question has taken on a completely new aspect.[3]

In the second place there has been the effect of the growth in power of the Soviet Union whose role as the inspiration of the 'anti-imperialist' elements is given full credit:

The USSR—the greatest Pacific Power—has always unchangeably stood in defence of peace, freedom, and the independence of peoples, has frustrated the plans of the imperialists and unmasked

---

[1] C. P. Fitzgerald, *Revolution in China* (London, Cresset Press, 1952), p. 93.
[2] See *Krisis Kolonialni Sistema*, especially the introductory chapter by E. M. Zhukov.   [3] *Mezhdunarodnye Otnosheniya*, p. 625.

their provocations and intrigues. The active role of the USSR as
the greatest factor for peace, counteracting aggressive imperialism,
multiplied many times as a result of the collapse of the fascist Powers
in the Second World War.[1]

It might be added that orthodox Communist historiography
claims the major share in the defeat of Japan as well as of
Germany for the armed forces of the Soviet Union.[2]

When these generalities are translated into concrete terms it
will be found that Soviet policies have of course been affected by
the different conditions of the countries concerned and that the
results from the Soviet point of view have been highly unequal.

The Soviet picture of an attempt to secure a genuine 'coalition' in post-war China, frustrated only by the determination of
American reactionaries to give absolute power to the Kuomintang as a puppet of American imperialism, can only be properly
interpreted in the light of what has happened in coalitions
elsewhere between Communist and non-Communist elements.[3]
And the history of China itself in the nineteen-twenties is not
without its lessons in this respect.[4] On the other hand, it is not
possible to treat the Chinese Communists as mere agents of
Soviet purposes, on the analogy of certain European countries,
where Communism was installed in power after 1945 despite
the virtual absence of indigenous support.[5]

Recent studies of the development of Chinese Communism
have stressed the genuine appeal of Marxism for important
elements in Chinese society and in Chinese tradition:

> The fact that anarchism with its fear of state power, per se, was to
> remain an exotic growth in China, while Marxism-Leninism, with

---

[1] *Mezhdunarodnye Otnosheniya*, p. 625.   [2] ibid. p. 622.

[3] See on European experience in this sphere Hugh Seton-Watson, *The East
European Revolution* (London, Methuen, 1950).

[4] See e.g. Beloff, i. 211–17 and references.

[5] 'Neither in background nor in the social system is there any resemblance.
China was not, before the Communists came to power, a small succession State
only recently liberated from a long period of foreign rule: her social system included,
besides a large impoverished peasantry, an extensive class of literates who were not
aristocratic landowners or city bourgeois, but members of a widespread small land-
owning class, a class which had for many generations provided the officials of the
Civil Service by which the Empire was governed. Few of these were rich, few had
hereditary wealth, almost all depended on their career for a living. There was
thus no striking change of personnel when the Communist Government took over.
Members of the educated class who had become Communists replaced members of
the same class who had not' (Fitzgerald, *Revolution in China*, p. 228).

its confidence that state power 'in the proper hands' could lead man
to the good society, was to win wide and lasting acceptance, may
perhaps itself reflect the abiding influence of Confucian habits of
thought in Chinese life.[1]

Furthermore, as well as this ideological predisposition, there is
the fact that the Chinese Communists after the débâcle of 1927
were forced to work out very much on their own the lines of their
recovery. It was done by abandoning for the time being all
attempts to rebuild the party upon the foundation of the Chinese
proletariat as fundamental Marxist doctrine would have
insisted was necessary. Instead, a peasant base was revealed as
sufficiently strong for a political leadership substantially recruited from intellectuals to rest upon, and to provide the
recruits for the armies upon which survival and eventual
triumph depended. 'The Maoist strategy', as an acute historian
has observed, essentially 'involves the imposition of a political
party organized in accordance with Leninist principles and
animated by faith in certain basic tenets of Marxism-Leninism
on to a purely peasant mass base.'[2] Perhaps we may even go so
far as to admit with the same historian that 'it would have been
most difficult for Moscow to take the initiative in granting the
leadership of the movement to men who were quite satisfied to
see Chinese Communism completely isolated from its supposed
urban proletarian bases', and must conclude therefore that
'Moscow's recognition of the Mao Tse-tung leadership was
essentially in the nature of an acquiescence to a *fait accompli*.'[3]
But it would be a mistake to jump from this too readily to the
idea that the Chinese Communist record in foreign policy was
likely to be one of complete independence of the Soviet view.
Indeed the Chinese Communists had during their period of
isolation in the north-west shown themselves perfectly ready
to accept a lead from Moscow whenever one was definitely
offered. It is not clear what is meant by saying that in 1940 the
united front against Japan in which the Communists participated did not 'fit Moscow's foreign policy'.[4] In the first place
the embroilment of Japan in China was one of the principal

---

[1] Benjamin I. Schwartz, *Chinese Communism and the Rise of Mao* (Cambridge,
Mass., Harvard University Press, 1951), p. 33.
[2] ibid. p. 189.   [3] ibid. p. 187.
[4] Fitzgerald, *Revolution in China*, p. 83.

guarantees against a Japanese attack on the Soviet Union itself, and in the second place, the Soviet version of Chinese Communist policy in this period shows clearly how well it fitted in with Soviet needs once the 1935 decision had been taken in favour of a popular front—a decision taken in Moscow.[1] If the Russians were unwilling in 1945 to stake everything upon the Communist card, there seems little reason to think that this was due to mistrust of Mao Tse-tung's attitude towards the Soviet Union in which his own faith had been proclaimed in thoroughly acceptable terms.

In Japan no such opportunity for Soviet manoeuvre was given as in war-torn and divided China. It was made clear at an early stage that whatever the other Allies might think of their contributions to Japan's defeat, from the United States point of view the future of the country was a matter of purely American concern. The main diplomatic activity of the Soviet Union was a series of futile protests against most of what was being done. These became more vociferous as events progressed in the direction that the Soviet spokesmen had prophesied, namely, towards the re-emergence of an independent Japan in close political and military alignment with the United States. The Japanese Communist Party was at no time strong enough to act as more than a subsidiary arm of Soviet propaganda.

In Korea, where military considerations had led to a division of the country for occupation purposes, the intention of the Russians to see that their zone at least was under full Communist control was evident from a very early stage. Korea found herself indeed as she had half a century earlier, at the meeting point of the different lines of force converging on the Far East. Although political events in North Korea were of course presented as expressive of the will of the Korean people, Soviet historians claim that credit should be given to the active support received by the 'democratic' forces of North Korea from the USSR and the Soviet occupation forces.[2]

In South East Asia, a sector where Russia had taken no part in the war, and concerning which no Russian demands had been put forward, there were no obvious Russian purposes other than those involved in the general weakening of the hold of the

---

[1] See *Krisis Kolonialni Sistema*, chapter on China by G. V. Astafev, pp. 40 ff.

[2] *Mezhdunarodnye Otnosheniya*, p. 655.

former imperial Powers, Great Britain, France, and Holland. In this respect what had changed was not Russian interest, which had been considerable, particularly in relation to Indonesia, but, rather, the blow that had been given to the former régimes in the area by the very fact of the Japanese victories and occupation. On the other hand Soviet historians could treat the rise of the nationalist movements as due in great measure to the inspiration of the Soviet victories:

The world-historic victories of the Soviet Union over the dark forces of fascism in Europe and Asia forced the capitalist world in the Far East substantially to contract—and new people's governments arose. The Democratic Republic of Viet Nam grew up through struggle and strengthened itself. And struggles developed also in other countries of East Asia. The peoples of Burma, Malaya, the Philippines, and Indonesia, encouraged by the defeat of fascism, the victories of the Soviet Union, and the achievements of the democratic forces in China, developed on an unprecedented scale an armed struggle against their oppressors, the imperialists.[1]

Soviet propaganda took the familiar form in these countries of encouraging nationalist movements against the existing or former colonial Powers and of the growth of the Communist element within such movements. In the case of Malaya, indeed, the two were almost synonymous from the first. Elsewhere, however, this basic Soviet strategy clearly raised problems similar to those which had confronted Soviet agents in China between 1923 and 1927. They were met, to some extent at least, by the fact that there now existed for each of these countries a varying number (often it is true very small) of persons thoroughly indoctrinated with the Communist creed and schooled in the full range of Communist tactics. But their rise to power within these movements and the internal history of the movements generally is a side of the whole story for which much basic material is still obviously lacking. In many cases it is necessary to judge of intentions by results.

It is even harder for the historian of any part of Asia to be

[1] ibid. pp. 622-3. It is worth noting that the Soviet work *Krisis Kolonialni Sistema* contains accounts of developments not merely in China, Indonesia, Indo-China, Burma, the Philippines, and Korea, but also in India and Ceylon. Thus nominal political status is ignored and all these countries are treated as witnessing similar 'national-liberation' movements with a difference in the degree of success achieved as the only distinguishing characteristic of each of them.

certain of the precise difference to its post-war evolution that has resulted from the presence on the scene of parties inspired in this way by the Soviet Union and partly led by men trained and indoctrinated within the Soviet Union itself. It is sometimes assumed that the countries concerned would, if left to themselves, have followed a course of emancipation and democratization leading to the establishment of parliamentary régimes of the Western type. Such views tend to overlook, or at least to minimize, the differences in the economic and social structure no less than in inherited tradition of these countries when compared with those in which parliamentary government has proved a success. It has yet to be shown that parliamentary government as understood in the West can work in countries without a firm industrial foundation and a consequently large commercial, managerial and professional class.

It seems more likely that the development of political consciousness in the so-called underdeveloped countries would be bound to lead to popular clamour for an improvement in economic and social conditions, since the idea of social progress itself was one of the most powerful ferments introduced by the period of close contact with the West. The new indigenous Governments would be almost certainly unable to live up to the expectations created by the nationalist movements; and political leadership would tend to slip into the hands of those who promised most. If the Indian sub-continent appeared to prove a partial exception to this rule within the first few years of the Second World War, there were special factors including some measure of industrialization and a longer political apprenticeship to account for this fact; and, as has already been seen, the Russians did not distinguish in theory between the position there and that in other parts of Asia.

It is not without interest that Japan, which has come nearest so far to establishing a State on the Western model (whatever view one may take of its current democratic pretensions), is also the Asiatic country whose economy is least unlike that of the Western countries. And it is here that the Communist Party is both most genuinely 'proletarian' and least effective. Nor is this simply the result of the United States occupation. For the relative ineffectiveness of Japanese Communism was true of an earlier period. It is too often forgotten that Russo-Japanese antagonism, despite some dramatic episodes, is not necessarily a permanent factor in Far Eastern politics. The Revolution interrupted a period in which Russia and Japan were working together on the basis of a series of secret treaties having as their object the partition of Manchuria into spheres of influence to the exclusion of all other Powers, particularly those likely to dominate the Chinese market if open competition were permitted. Soviet denunciations today of the American policy of the 'open door' perhaps still reflect this recognized inability to compete with Americans on the purely economic terrain.[1]

After the Japanese evacuation of eastern Siberia, the Soviet Government attempted for a time a rapprochement with Japan, of a fairly intimate kind.[2] But this produced no dividends in the shape of an advance of Communist influence comparable to what was going on in China. With the Japanese occupation of Manchuria in 1931, relations became strained once more and the Russian response was largely one of appeasement for the sake of keeping a free hand to deal with the threat from Europe. The sale of the Chinese Eastern Railway in 1935 marks the culminating point of this policy. And after the border fighting in 1938–9, this policy was reverted to in the Soviet-Japanese neutrality pact of April 1941. The Soviet Union in dealing with Japan has had to follow to a much greater extent than elsewhere in Asia the pattern of Tsarist diplomacy because it was unable to exert an influence upon the course of internal politics comparable with that available to it in China from an early date, and in South East Asia at least since the Second World War.

Clearly then, the internal history of each individual country as well as its relations with the Soviet Union are of importance in dealing with the development of East Asia as a whole. But this is not to minimize the importance of the co-ordinating centre of world Communism at Moscow, or the relevance of the question—opened up by the activities of the Chinese Communists in Korea and the assistance given to Communist forces in Indo-China by the presence of a Communist China on the border—as to whether Peking may not by 1951 have come to be regarded as an alternative and independent source of

---

[1] See the remarks by Astafev in *Uchenie Zapiski Tikhookeanskogo Instituta*, iii. 36.
[2] Beloff, i. 76–77.

inspiration. Since all these movements in Asia receive a special tinge from the elements of race and colour consciousness, and from a general tendency to suspect and reject what comes from Europe or North America, it might be thought that in any conflict of allegiances the Chinese would be in a strong position, quite apart from the fact that in many of the countries concerned there are considerable Chinese elements.

Against this, it must be admitted that the Russians seem on the whole in China to have been able to dissociate themselves from the general antipathy attaching to other Europeans, partly because of their own genuine lack of colour prejudice. And if one cannot take at face value the emphasis laid by Chinese Communist leaders on their claim that Russians working in China do not demand the higher standards of living expected in the past by other European specialists, it is clear how the argument in their favour runs. It might almost seem as though the Russians were acquiring the ability which has eluded other advanced peoples, that of transmitting their own technical and cultural achievements to others without incurring universal opprobrium in the process. Were this the case, and were the Russians quite free to exploit this important factor in their favour, the chances of Asiatic Communism would seem extremely bright. But it is obvious at the same time that the Soviet State itself puts limitations upon the ability of its representatives abroad to go the whole way in pursuing the needs of the peoples of the countries in which they work. For the Soviet State needs, as has been seen, more immediate achievements which may make claims upon resources which these countries would otherwise devote to their own purposes. They may find it easier and prefer to supply ready-made military equipment, as they do to the Chinese in Korea, than to lay the foundations of an independent industrial economy. Furthermore, the Soviet insistence on complete ideological conformity, and the general attitude of suspicion towards foreigners which the Soviet system engenders at home, are obstacles to close and open collaboration with foreign Communists.

It cannot, however, be too strongly emphasized how slender is our stock of hard information on the inside working of the relationships between the Russians and the indigenous Communist movements. To the most important questions there are no properly substantiated answers, and the disagreement on some of these questions between students of equal competence and equal good faith is striking indeed, and is of course reflected in the differing policies hitherto adopted by the main Western countries concerned. This fact tends to force the historian to restrict his narrative very largely to externals and to Soviet comment upon them. And the best he can hope for is to provide some sort of structural framework within which it is possible to discuss the nature of these profounder but more intangible developments. It is with this very limited ambition in mind that the subsequent chapters of this work have been compiled.

II

Soviet Policy in China
1945–6

THE YALTA AGREEMENT AND THE SINO-SOVIET TREATY OF 1945

THROUGHOUT the war in the West, the Soviet Union remained neutral in respect to the conflict being waged in Asia. Its relations with Japan were governed by the Soviet-Japanese neutrality pact of 13 April 1941. It was obviously in the interest of the Russians to keep the Japanese forces occupied in areas remote from the Soviet border, just as it was the American view that the Russians should if possible be drawn into the Far Eastern war, so as to shorten its duration and minimize the heavy loss of life that was expected to be the price of the final assault on the Japanese home islands. Cordell Hull had his first interview with Litvinov after the latter's appointment to the Washington Embassy on 8 December 1941, and raised with him the possibility of the United States being granted bases on the Russian Pacific Coast. When Litvinov saw Hull again on 11 December, he replied that his Government had informed him that it was not then in a position to co-operate with the Allies against Japan: the Russians were too heavily engaged against the Germans to incur the risk of a Japanese attack.[1] The matter was raised again by Harriman when he accompanied Churchill to Moscow in August 1942. Stalin seems to have told Harriman on this occasion that Japan was Russia's historic enemy and that her final defeat was essential to Russia. He suggested by implication that although the existing circumstances were unfavourable to Soviet participation in the Far Eastern war, the Russians would eventually come into it.[2]

At the Anglo-American Quebec Conference in August 1943,

---

[1] *Memoirs of Cordell Hull* (London, Hodder & Stoughton, 1948), ii. 1111–12.
[2] John R. Deane, *The Strange Alliance* (New York, Viking Press, 1947), p. 226.

the Americans insisted on the importance of Russian assistance.[1]
In October 1943 Stalin gave a definite undertaking on the
subject to Cordell Hull during the Moscow meeting of Foreign
Ministers. According to the United States Secretary of State,
'the Marshal's statement of his decision was forthright, he made
it emphatically, it was entirely unsolicited, and he asked nothing
in return'.[2] The question of the settlement of the Far East after
Japan's defeat was discussed by Roosevelt, Churchill, and
Chiang Kai-shek at the Cairo Conference in November, and
the 'Cairo Declaration' of 30 November promised the return to
China of all the territories stolen from her by Japan—such as
Manchuria, Formosa, and the Pescadores.

At the Teheran Conference in November–December 1943,
Stalin again declared that he welcomed the Allied successes
against Japan, but explained that since the Soviet forces in the
Far East were sufficient for defensive purposes only, they would
have to be tripled before an offensive was possible. This could
not be done until victory in Europe had been secured. In
principle, however, Soviet assistance was once more promised.
Requests made by the Americans that their Army Air Force
should eventually be granted bases in Eastern Siberia for the
bombing of Japan and that preliminary joint planning for the
employment of Soviet forces against Japan should begin were
unanswered at the Conference. But bases were promised by
Stalin to the Americans on 2 February 1944.[3]

Not much attention was seemingly devoted to the post-war
problems of the Far East, though it has been stated that it was
at Teheran that Roosevelt put forward the idea of making
Dairen a free port.[4] On the more general side, Stalin indicated
that he did not share the general American tendency to rate

---

[1] R. L. Sherwood, *The White House Papers of Harry L. Hopkins* (London, Eyre &
Spottiswoode, 1948–9), ii. 745.

[2] Hull, *Memoirs*, ii. 1310. A four-Power declaration (including China) was
published on 1 November, pledging a united conduct of the war against the
Powers with whom the signatories were severally engaged and co-operation in
establishing a post-war security system.

[3] W. D. Leahy, *I Was There* (London, Gollancz, 1950), p. 248; R. Dennett and
J. E. Johnson, eds., *Negotiating with the Russians* (Boston, World Peace Foundation,
1951), Ch. 1 by J. R. Deane, pp. 19–20. Roosevelt also suggested that Soviet ports
might be used for American naval forces. See A. Harriman's statement to Senate
Committee on Armed Forces and Foreign Relations on 13 July 1951 in *Congressional
Record*, vol. 97, App. pt. 14, pp. 5410–16; Sherwood, *White House Papers*, p. 774.

[4] Sumner Welles, *Seven Major Decisions* (London, Hamilton, 1951), pp. 139, 152.

China very highly and that he did not visualize for that country a very important role in the post-war world.[1] Despite Stalin's promise in February, no progress was made with the project for securing bases for American aircraft in the Far East. But the flow of lend-lease goods continued and the Russians surreptitiously released American airmen who had made forced landings on Soviet territory.[2]

Soviet interest in Far Eastern matters quickened with the successful progress of the war in Europe in 1944 and in September of that year Stalin pointed out to Harriman that the report of the second Quebec Conference (of September 1944) did not mention Russia's eventual participation in the war against Japan:

He asked Harriman if the President still considered it essential that Russia should join the war against Japan. He appeared to be somewhat surprised that after the assurances he had given the President at Teheran, we had not taken Soviet participation into account in our planning. Stalin said that there had been no change in the Russian attitude, but if the United States and Great Britain preferred to bring Japan to her knees without Russian participation, he was ready to agree.[3]

It is not easy to take this remark of Stalin's at its face value. Everything would seem to indicate that the Russians had decided that they would have to participate in the Far Eastern fighting in order to secure their own objectives, and that they would in all probability have entered the war even without a preliminary agreement with their allies. But they were naturally concerned to present their decision to enter the Far Eastern conflict as a sacrifice on their part for the sake of their allies for which they ought to be adequately compensated.

The question was raised again during Churchill's visit to Moscow in October 1944. Stalin proved highly forthcoming about Soviet co-operation with the Allies. He once more accepted the view that the Americans should be granted air bases in the Soviet Far East and went into some detail on their probable location and on the projected operations generally.[4] It was made clear that the Soviet Union would undertake the

[1] Sherwood, *White House Papers*, p. 781.
[2] Deane, *Strange Alliance*, Chs. XII–XVI.   [3] ibid. p. 240.
[4] Dennett and Johnson, eds., *Negotiating with the Russians*, pp. 20–24.

offensive against Japan three months after the defeat of Germany, but this was made conditional on the United States helping to build up the necessary supplies and on a clarification of the political aspects of the matter. This point seems to have referred to the securing of Chinese agreement to the claims that the Soviet Union proposed to make on Japan after victory. Stalin now estimated that the Russian forces in Siberia would have to be increased from thirty to sixty divisions before the Soviet Union entered the war. He refused to put the agreements reached into writing, giving it as his reason that the secret might get out and so precipitate a Japanese attack before the Russians were ready. But since he did hand over a seven-page typewritten list of supplies that he needed in Siberia, the Americans not unnaturally concluded that his real object was to make certain of his political claims before committing himself.[1]

Once the American supplies began to arrive, Soviet enthusiasm for intimate co-operation with the United States in the Far East appeared to wane. In December 1944 General Deane was informed by the Soviet Chief of Staff, General Antonov, that the requirements of the Soviet air force made it impossible to grant air bases to the Americans; and when in January 1945 the American officers at last met the Soviet officers with whom they were to undertake joint planning, it became clear at once that the Russians were not in earnest. At the Yalta Conference in February, Stalin gave another undertaking about air bases; but this too came to nothing.[2]

The full scope of the Soviet ambitions in the Far East was not revealed by Stalin to Harriman until December 1944.

He said that Russia's position in the East should be generally re-established as it existed before the Russo-Japanese war of 1905. The lower half of Sakhalin should be returned to the Russians, as well as the Kurile Islands, in order to protect Soviet outlets to the Pacific. The Russians wished again to lease the ports of Dairen and Port Arthur and to obtain a lease on those railways in Manchuria built by the Russians under contract with the Chinese, specifically, the Chinese Eastern Railway, which was the direct line from the

---

[1] Deane, *Strange Alliance*, pp. 247-8.

[2] Dennett and Johnson, eds., *Negotiating with the Russians*, pp. 24-26; Leahy, *I Was There*, pp. 361, 365; Harriman, *Congressional Record*, vol. 97, App. pt. 14, pp. 5410-16.

Trans-Siberian Railway through to Vladivostok, and the South Manchurian Railway making a connection to Dairen. He stated that the Soviet Union would not interfere with the sovereignty of China over Manchuria. In addition Stalin asked for the recognition of the status quo in Outer Mongolia. I pointed out to Stalin that the talks at Teheran had envisaged internationalization of the Port of Dairen rather than a lease. Stalin replied that this could be discussed. I immediately reported Stalin's proposals to President Roosevelt and they became the basis of the discussions at Yalta.[1]

The matter of Russia's entry into the Far Eastern war was finally concluded in the talks between Roosevelt and Stalin at Yalta—talks from which Churchill was excluded. The conclusions reached were, however, embodied in the secret agreement concerning the entry of the Soviet Union into the war against Japan which was signed by all three leaders on 11 February 1945. The accounts of the discussions themselves are all from the American side, and they show that the dominant consideration in the mind of Roosevelt was the military necessity of securing Soviet aid.[2] It is clear, however, that Roosevelt also felt that a direct agreement with Stalin on Far Eastern matters would be of great assistance to his general plans for a post-war settlement centred on the United Nations, and that his ready suspicions of British, French, and Dutch 'imperialism' were largely dormant where the Russians were concerned.[3]

Roosevelt had already approached Chiang Kai-shek with the object of securing an understanding between the Chinese leader and the Russians. Chiang had indicated to Henry Wallace on 23 June 1944 that he was prepared to see Dairen become a free port provided the Soviet Union would co-operate with China in the Far East, and provided there was no impairment of Chinese sovereignty.[4]

Although the agreement signed at Yalta was not published

---

[1] Harriman, *Congressional Record*, vol. 97, App. pt. 14, p. 5411.

[2] James F. Byrnes, *Speaking Frankly* (London, Heinemann, 1947), p. 43; Harriman, loc. cit.; Edward R. Stettinius, *Roosevelt and the Russians* (New York, Doubleday, 1949), pp. 92–98; Sherwood, *White House Papers*, ii. Ch. 34; Leahy, *I Was There*, Ch. 18; cf. H. L. Stimson and McGeorge Bundy, *On Active Service in Peace and War* (New York, Harper, 1948), p. 637. On American optimism about future Soviet policy see *The Forrestal Diaries*, ed. Walter Millis (New York, Viking Press, 1951), pp. 35–36.

[3] cf. Chester Wilmot, *The Struggle for Europe* (London, Collins, 1952), Ch. 32.

[4] *Relations with China*, p. 558.

until a year later, it is of such importance that it must be reproduced in full at this point:

Agreement concerning the Entry of the Soviet Union into the War against Japan, signed at Yalta February 11, 1945, released simultaneously in London, Moscow and Washington, February 11, 1946.[1]

The leaders of the three Great Powers—the Soviet Union, the United States of America and Great Britain—have agreed that in two or three months after Germany has surrendered and the war in Europe has terminated the Soviet Union shall enter into the war against Japan on the side of the Allies on condition that:

1. The *status quo* in Outer Mongolia (The Mongolian People's Republic) shall be preserved;

2. The former rights of Russia violated by the treacherous attack of Japan in 1904 shall be restored, viz:

(a) the southern part of Sakhalin as well as all the islands adjacent to it shall be returned to the Soviet Union,

(b) the commercial port of Dairen shall be internationalized, the pre-eminent interests of the Soviet Union in this port being safeguarded and the lease of Port Arthur as a naval base of the USSR restored,

(c) the Chinese-Eastern Railroad and the South-Manchurian Railroad which provides an outlet to Dairen shall be jointly operated by the establishment of a joint Soviet-Chinese Company it being understood that the pre-eminent interests of the Soviet Union shall be safeguarded and that China shall retain full sovereignty in Manchuria;

3. The Kurile Islands shall be handed over to the Soviet Union.

It is understood, that the agreement concerning Outer Mongolia and the ports and railroads referred to above will require concurrence of Generalissimo Chiang Kai-shek. The President will take measures in order to obtain this concurrence on advice from Marshal Stalin.

The Heads of the three Great Powers have agreed that these claims of the Soviet Union shall be unquestionably fulfilled after Japan has been defeated.

For its part the Soviet Union expresses its readiness to conclude with the National Government of China a pact of friendship and alliance between the USSR and China in order to render assistance to China with its armed forces for the purpose of liberating China from the Japanese yoke.

J. V. STALIN. FRANKLIN D. ROOSEVELT. WINSTON S. CHURCHILL.

[1] Cmd. 6735 (1946).

The gains that the Russians were to receive were confined, with the exception of the provision about Outer Mongolia, to territories under Japanese occupation. But almost all of them were of direct concern to China as well. Later attacks upon the American President for bartering away China's rights were concentrated on the phrase that the claims of the Soviet Union would 'unquestionably be fulfilled'. For this could be held to suggest an obligation on the signatories to enforce these claims upon China itself, should the Chinese Government refuse to implement any of them. Roosevelt did in fact offer to obtain China's concurrence, but he agreed not to take the matter up with Chiang Kai-shek until requested to do so by Stalin, in view of the latter's continued insistence on the need for secrecy. Stalin told the American Ambassador Hurley when he passed through Moscow on his way to Chungking in April that he wished to delay discussing the Yalta Agreement with Chiang for about two months longer.[1]

Stalin explained at Yalta that it was necessary for him to pitch the Russians' demands so high because only in this way could he persuade the Russian people that to enter the Far Eastern War would be worth the sacrifices involved. In fact Russian public opinion was not intensively prepared before the event, and it was only after the campaign was over that the Russian gains were made much of in internal propaganda. Stalin again expressed his lack of confidence in China's ability to fulfil the role of a world Power and he deplored the inability of the Chinese to form a united front against Japan. He still declared that he considered Chiang Kai-shek the most suitable person for national leader but maintained that he ought to include some Communist representatives in his Government.[2]

In May 1945 Harry Hopkins visited Moscow as a special envoy from President Truman and discussed among other subjects the agreement reached at Yalta for the Soviet Union to enter the Far Eastern war. On 28 May Stalin told Hopkins that the Red Army would be ready for action by 8 August, that is to say at the expiration of the three months' delay after Germany's defeat that had been agreed upon in October 1944. He repeated the argument that he had already put forward at

---

[1] Harriman, *Congressional Record*, vol. 97, pt. 14, p. 5411.
[2] Sherwood, *White House Papers*, ii. 855–7.

Yalta, namely that he must be able to offer his people some adequate reason for assuming the new burdens involved, and that this depended upon the willingness of the Chinese to accept the Yalta Agreement. He would, he said, take the matter up directly with the Chinese Foreign Minister T. V. Soong and would have him come to Moscow for the purpose before 1 July. He told Hopkins that he agreed with America's 'open door' policy and 'went out of his way to indicate' that the United States was the only Power with resources available for helping China economically after the war. The Soviet Union's resources would for many years to come be absorbed by internal claims upon them. Stalin declared categorically that he had no territorial claims against China, mentioning Manchuria and Sinkiang specifically in this connexion. He would do what he could to promote the unification of China under the leadership of Chiang Kai-shek. No Communist leader was strong enough for the task. He stated that he would welcome representatives of Chiang Kai-shek to be with his troops on their entry into Manchuria in order to facilitate the organization there of Chinese administration.[1]

At this point the negotiations with the Americans and the projected talks with the Chinese clearly involved some Soviet decision on the future role of the Chinese Communists and their armed forces. The temporary cordiality between the Chinese Nationalists and the Communists which had existed in 1937-8 had vanished as a result of subsequent events and had been replaced by extreme tension between them.[2] According to official American sources a large proportion of the best nationalist troops was kept from the front in order to prevent the further expansion of Communist-controlled territory; and this in turn immobilized large Communist forces which was a serious impediment to the prosecution of the anti-Japanese struggle.[3] Nationalist troops were in fact deployed against the citadel of Communist power in Shensi, which may have hindered the southward expansion of Communist strength from this province. But struggles were also going on both within the area under Kuomintang rule and behind the Japanese lines. The Communists themselves also had a front with the Japanese.

---

[1] Sherwood, *White House Papers*, ii. 891–2.   [2] Beloff, ii. 315–19.
[3] *Relations with China*, pp. 59–61.

After an earlier period of complete silence, the Russian press began, in the summer of 1943, to comment on the Chinese internal situation, and for the first time to give independent mention to the anti-Japanese activities of the Chinese Communist forces; but criticism of Chiang Kai-shek's leadership was very restrained, and it was still asserted that the main condition for Chinese successes was 'a real unification of all national forces in the fight for freedom and independence'.[1] Similar Russian articles in the subsequent months presented the argument that the anti-Communist activities within the Kuomintang were largely the result of Japanese instigation. It was typical of the Soviet approach that mention of the successes of the Chinese Communists and of the shortcomings of the Kuomintang were substantiated from American sources.[2] More important perhaps was the fact that in September 1944 a similar article appeared in *Bolshevik*. This made a special appeal to those elements within the Kuomintang who were alleged to wish to see the implementation of the agreements previously arrived at with the Communists.[3] Even as late as the spring of 1945 Chiang Kai-shek himself was not personally attacked and was quoted as being still hopeful of bringing about national unity.[4]

The Chinese Communists themselves continued to stress their close ideological alignment with the Russians. When announcing the dissolution of the Comintern on 23 May 1943, Mao Tse-tung declared that this organization had not intervened in the internal affairs of the Chinese Communist Party since 1935. But on 1 July, in a speech commemorating the sixth anniversary of the outbreak of the Sino-Japanese war, he said that if it had not been 'for the Soviet Union, its Red Army, its people, its leader Stalin, and the decisive victory of Stalingrad, the destiny of mankind would still be an unknown factor', and went on to stress the scientific truth of Marxism-Leninism.

    [1] See the article by the Soviet correspondent V. Rogov in *War and the Working Class*, no. 5, August 1943.
    [2] See, for example, I. Alexandrovich, 'The Situation in China', *War and the Working Class*, 15 July 1944. Alexandrovich attributed the Japanese successes in 1944 to Chiang Kai-shek's retaining about 400,000 of his best troops to watch the Communist special areas.
    [3] B. Grigoriev, 'China in the Eighth Year of War', *Bolshevik*, nos. 17–18, 1944.
    [4] B. Avarin, 'Whither China?', *War and the Working Class*, 15 July 1945.

The party manifesto on the same occasion also stressed the decisive importance of the Stalingrad battle, although it recorded in addition the contributions of the Western Allies to the war effort.

At this time, Chiang Kai-shek himself seems to have believed it possible that he could retain or rather renew close relations with the Russians. There were also reasons why he should believe such an improvement of relations with Russia desirable. In the first place, there were indications that the German venture in Russia had failed and that Russia was going to emerge successfully from the war. At the same time Chiang Kai-shek's American advisers, General Stilwell and the Ambassador Gauss, were pressing for policies which were uncongenial to the Generalissimo. His internal position was also not of the strongest, quite apart from the direct Communist challenge. Finally there were particular difficulties in the local situation in Sinkiang. His bargaining position all round might thus be strengthened by an improvement in his relations with the Soviet Government. And from the time of the Cairo Conference in December 1943, Chiang began to seek American mediation to bring about such a rapprochement.

In a conversation with the American Vice-President, Henry Wallace, on 23 June 1944 Chiang Kai-shek suggested that the United States should bring about a meeting between Soviet and Chinese representatives.[1] The American Ambassador Patrick Hurley reported that Chiang now believed that the Chinese Communists were not receiving support from the Soviet Government and that they could be bargained with directly. Such a settlement with them need not involve 'foreign entanglements'.[2] The Americans themselves seem to have considered the possibility that if they were to co-operate directly with the Chinese Communists it might serve to draw them away from exclusive dependence on Soviet support.[3] And this was the political basis for Roosevelt's attempt in 1944[4] to place all the Chinese forces, including the Communist troops, under the

---

[1] *Relations with China*, p. 558.
[2] ibid. p. 73.   [3] ibid. p. 65.
[4] J. W. Stilwell, *Papers*, arr. and ed. by T. H. White (New York, Sloane, 1948), pp. 323 ff. According to one account, Mao offered to put all his troops under Stilwell's command (J. Alsop, 'The Strange Case of Louis Budenz', *Atlantic Monthly*, April 1952).

command of the American General Joseph W. Stilwell. Hurley
and other members of the American Embassy opposed the idea
of dealing with the Communists and when, in January 1945,
the Communist military leader Chu Teh made a request for a
loan, they recommended that no American arms or equipment
should be sent to any authority in China other than the National
Government.[1] Although the Americans were favourable to the
idea of a direct approach by Chiang Kai-shek to the Soviet
Government, they did not wish to take the responsibility of
acting as mediators or even as advisers.[2]

In April 1945 Hurley had an interview with Stalin. He
reported that Stalin had spoken with approval of the policy of
pursuing Chinese unification that was being followed by the
United States, and of Chiang Kai-shek himself, but that he had
declared that there was corruption among certain Nationalist
officials.[3] The optimism which this interview created in Hurley's
mind was not shared by the American expert on Russian affairs,
George Kennan, who was then serving in the Moscow Embassy.
On 23 April Kennan telegraphed to Washington as follows:

Actually I am persuaded that in the future Soviet policy respecting
China will continue what it has been in the recent past: a fluid
resilient policy directed at the achievement of maximum power with
minimum responsibility on portions of the Asiatic continent lying
beyond the Soviet border. This will involve the exertion of pressure
in various areas in direct proportion to their strategic importance
and their proximity to the Soviet frontier. I am sure that within
the framework of this policy Moscow will aim specifically at: (1)
Reacquiring in substance, if not in form, all the diplomatic and
territorial assets previously possessed on the mainland of Asia by
Russia under the Czars. (2) Domination of the provinces of China
in central Asia contiguous to the Soviet frontier. Such action is
dictated by the strategic necessity of protecting in depth the
industrial core of the USSR. (3) Acquiring sufficient control in all
areas of north China now dominated by the Japanese to prevent
other foreign powers from repeating the Japanese incursion. This
means, to the Russian mind, the maximum possible exclusion of
penetration in that area by outside Powers including America and
Britain.[4]

This more cautious attitude was shared by Averell Harriman,

---

[1] *Relations with China*, pp. 86–88.   [2] ibid. pp. 92–93.
[3] ibid. pp. 95–96.   [4] ibid. p. 97.

the American Ambassador in Moscow, and was the one which seemed most acceptable in Washington.[1] Early in July 1945 Hurley reported from China that in his view the Chinese Communists, whose support and strength he believed to be exaggerated, would come into an all-China Government if they were convinced by a treaty between the Soviet Government and Chiang that the Russians were not supporting them.[2]

It seems from these accounts that while the Chinese Communist Party was satisfied that it had full Russian support for its opposition to an agreement with the Kuomintang, which might prejudice its tenure of an independent territorial base and its control of independent military forces, the Russians themselves were still of the opinion that the main source of resistance to Japan must continue to be provided by the Nationalist army, which was also the sole recipient of external aid. The Russian support for Chinese unity under Chiang Kai-shek was expressed firmly enough to satisfy at least some Americans, though it was not of a nature to discourage the Communists from believing that their own time would come.

In Hopkins's view it was desirable that the Americans should participate in the proposed Sino-Soviet negotiations because of the magnitude of Russia's claims. The contents of Stalin's statement to Hopkins were told to Soong by President Truman on 14 June.[3] On the following day Hurley informed Chiang Kai-shek about the decisions reached at Yalta and about the assurances given by Stalin on the question of China's sovereignty in Manchuria and the acceptance by him of the principle of the 'open door' in China. Chiang Kai-shek's reaction to this communication made it obvious that the Russians had already informed him of the terms of the Yalta Agreement. It is possible that the Russians believed that this direct approach would prevent the Americans interfering to limit their demands.[4]

Direct negotiations with Soong began in Moscow in the first week of July.[5] The Chinese were in a weak bargaining position. They were committed to the Yalta provisions and were anxious to arrive at an agreement with Stalin before Russia actually

[1] ibid. pp. 97-98.   [2] ibid. pp. 99-100.
[3] ibid. p. 116. Leahy speaks of a meeting between Soong and Truman on 9 June (*I Was There*, p. 445).
[4] *Relations with China*, p. 116.
[5] Aitchen K. Wu, *China and the Soviet Union* (London, Methuen, 1950), pp. 291-7.

entered the Far Eastern war, so that Russia would be bound by a treaty negotiated with the Chinese Government, and not simply by the Yalta Agreement, to which China was not a signatory. The demands made by the Russians were—first that they should have a controlling interest in the Chinese Eastern Railway and the South Manchurian Railway; second, that the boundaries of the Port Arthur naval base should be those which obtained prior to the Russo-Japanese war of 1904; and thirdly, that the Chinese should recognize the complete independence of the Mongolian People's Republic (Outer Mongolia). In connexion with the last demand, it may be noted that Stalin had conferred with Marshal Choibolsan, the Prime Minister of Outer Mongolia, in the first week of July.[1]

Soong complained to President Truman that these demands exceeded the terms of the Yalta Agreement; and in replying, the Secretary of State telegraphed to him not to go beyond them.[2] Soong received through Harriman, on 10 August, further assurances of American support for considering the Yalta Agreement as the limit of Chinese concessions; and in thanking Harriman later, Soong told him it was this support which had enabled him to refuse some of the demands made.[3] On 13 July these negotiations were adjourned so as to allow Stalin and Molotov to go to the Potsdam Conference; they were resumed in August and the agreements were finally signed on 14 August—the day on which Japan surrendered. Thus the rapid advance of Russian troops into Manchuria must have forced the hand of the Chinese negotiators. The first of the agreements was a treaty of friendship and alliance directed against the possibility of a renewal of Japanese aggression.[4] In an exchange of notes relative to the treaty, the Soviet Government pledged itself 'to render to China moral support and aid in military supplies and other material resources, such support and aid to be entirely given to the National Government as the central Government of China'. It also reaffirmed 'its respect for China's full sovereignty over the Three Eastern Provinces' [Manchuria] and recognized their territorial and administrative integrity. In connexion with the unrest in Sinkiang, the

[1] *Izvestia*, 6 and 8 August 1945.
[2] Harriman, *Congressional Record*, vol. 97, pt. 14, p. 5415. Byrnes, *Speaking Frankly*, p. 205.
[3] *Relations with China*, pp. 116–18.   [4] The texts are in ibid. pp. 585–96.

Soviet Government also confirmed that it had no intention of interfering in China's internal affairs.

The Russians did not claim a revival of extraterritoriality or of the other concessions which they had renounced in 1919 and 1920, and which had not been restored in the treaty of 1924; although Soong had feared that they would do so. There was a dispute over the meaning to be attached to the Yalta Agreement in so far as Outer Mongolia was concerned. The Russians interpreted the relevant clause as signifying a full recognition of Mongolian independence, whereas the Chinese claimed that it merely meant a return to the pre-war position, a guaranteed autonomy for Outer Mongolia combined with a formal recognition of Chinese overlordship. Harriman persuaded Soong to agree to the Soviet demand for a plebiscite, which meant accepting the Soviet position, since such a plebiscite was certain to result in giving legal sanction to the existing position of *de facto* independence of China.[1]

The other agreements concerned Manchuria. The Chinese Eastern Railway had been sold to 'Manchukuo' in 1935. Subsequently the Japanese had invested much capital and energy in the development of the CER, as well as of the South Manchurian Railway which Japan had owned since 1905. Now, the two railways were combined under the name of the Chinese Changchun Railway. The new system was to be jointly operated, like the Chinese Eastern Railway under the agreement of 1924. The new railway would have a board of directors with ten members—half of them Chinese and half Russian. The Chinese Government would appoint a chairman and the Soviet Government a vice-chairman. One of the Russian members of the board was to be a manager of the railway, with one of the Chinese members as his deputy. These provisions were widely held to mean that the railway was to be directed in fact by the Russians; for under the 1924 agreement the differences that had arisen between the Chinese and the Russian members of the board had resulted in the actual control being exercised by the manager.[2]

The Soviet Union also received an additional concession in the extension of the duration of the agreement to 1975, since the old agreement would have expired in 1961. On the other

[1] ibid. p. 117.   [2] Dallin, *Rise of Russia in Asia*, p. 255.

hand, in some respects the agreement seemed more favourable to China than the old one by which the Russians had actually had a majority on the board. Even more important was the provision that China would be responsible for the security of the railway; the previous allocation of this responsibility to the Russians had enabled them to introduce considerable military forces into Manchuria. The new agreement also provided that the transport of Soviet troops on the railway would be permitted only during hostilities with Japan.

These provisions for ownership and operation were to extend to all lands acquired and subsidiary lines built during the Russian and Sino-Russian administration of the Chinese Eastern Railway and the Russian administration of the South Manchurian Railway. The lines built by the Japanese after 1905 remained in the hands of the Chinese. On the other hand, 'the subsidiary enterprises built during the said periods and directly serving these railways' were to be included in the joint system. The importance of this arose from the fact that both railway companies had engaged in commercial activity outside the ordinary scope of railway operations. Thus in 1935, when the Chinese Eastern Railway was sold to the Japanese, it operated among other enterprises forest concerns, coal mines, power stations, various industrial plants, and health resorts.[1] The other Manchurian railway had even more numerous auxiliary enterprises, and although most of these had been constructed by the Japanese, some had been built up as enlargements of Russian enterprises in existence before 1905. An example was the coal mines of Fushun, which were now of considerable importance. Such enterprises could be claimed for joint ownership.

The naval base of Port Arthur was to be used jointly by China and the Soviet Union; and for this purpose a military commission of three Russians and two Chinese was to be set up. The civil administration of the whole Port Arthur area, which was approximately that of the area leased by Russia before 1904, was to be under Chinese civil administration, though the Chinese were to carry out suggestions of the Soviet military command in defence matters. In the town of Port Arthur the

[1] Raymond Dennett, 'The Sino-Soviet treaty and Reparations', *FES*, 28 August 1945.

civil administration was to be appointed and dismissed by the Chinese Government by agreement with the Soviet military command. This agreement was for thirty years.

The commercial port of Dairen was to be made a free port, open to all countries, but the principal interests of the Soviet Union were to be safeguarded by the leasing to her of docks and warehouses, and by the provision that a Soviet citizen should be appointed to the post of Harbour Master. This seems to have exceeded what the Americans intended by the Yalta provisions. The final agreement dealt with the relations between the Soviet forces which had now successfully overrun Manchuria and the Chinese National Government, to whose civil administration it was to be handed over. In this connexion Stalin was asked by the Chinese to give a time limit in which the Russian troops would be withdrawn. He declined to include any statement on this point in the written agreements, but said that the Soviet forces would begin their withdrawal within three weeks after Japan's capitulation, and that, in his opinion, evacuation would be complete within two months. On a further question being put he confirmed that three months would be the maximum period required.[1]

Soviet comment on these agreements was to the effect that they were proof of 'the self-evident fact that the Soviet Union's entire foreign policy is based on the principle of unqualified respect for the national sovereignty of its neighbours and of all peace-loving nations, both large and small.'[2] The ratification of the treaty led to complimentary telegrams between the leaders of the two countries, emphasizing their traditional friendship. An editorial in *Pravda* described the agreements as an appropriate manifestation of the Sino-Soviet friendship that Sun Yat-sen had stressed in his death-bed message.[3]

Chiang Kai-shek and other important Chinese figures expressed their satisfaction with the agreements.[4] It appears probable that it was not so much their terms as the fact that they were concluded with the Chinese National Government, with no attempt by the Russians to bring in the Chinese

[1] 'Minutes of the 5th meeting between Stalin and Soong, 11 July 1945', *China Handbook, 1950* (New York, Rockport Press), p. 331.
[2] *New Times*, 1 September 1945, p. 1.
[3] *Soviet Monitor*, 27 August 1945.
[4] *Relations with China*, pp. 120-1.

Communists, that caused this satisfaction.[1] It was taken to suggest that the Soviet leaders expected the Chinese National Government to remain in power; and this view is borne out by Russian comment on the Chinese domestic situation. For instance *New Times* in the editorial on the agreements already quoted said:

It is no secret that China's progress has hitherto been hampered in no small degree by the disagreements between the Kuomintang and the Chinese Communist Party. There are plenty of dubious well-wishers abroad who every now and again raise the cry that civil war in China is inevitable. There is no doubt that such a war would be disastrous for the country which now needs peace above all, in order to repair the devastating consequences of the long years of Japanese occupation. All sincere friends of China look forward to closer co-operation between all the progressive and democratic forces of the Chinese people.[2]

In so far as one can deduce the Russians' policy from their actions, it would appear that the Soviet Government genuinely believed that the Communists could not gain power by themselves and were concerned to secure their participation in some form of coalition. In such a coalition the Communists would be able to bring pressure upon the Chinese Government to give the Russians further concessions in Manchuria, beyond those stipulated in the treaties. Otherwise a situation might arise there in which the presence of the Russians, along the railways and in the ports, would subject them to pressure from the Chinese in the rest of the country. This would reproduce substantially the same situation as existed between 1924 and 1929. In pursuit of their policy the Russians were prepared to go as far as they could, so long as it did not provoke, or provide an excuse for, American intervention. This interpretation of their intentions would seem to fit in with what is known of their local policy in Manchuria itself.

After the signature of the agreements of August 1945, Chiang Kai-shek gained confidence and felt able to adopt a much firmer attitude towards the Chinese Communists. The Com-

---

[1] The statement made in 1949 by Kan Chieh-hou that Chiang Kai-shek had failed to reach an agreement with the Russians in 1945 because of their demand for a neutrality pact and for the inclusion of the Communists in a Chinese coalition government does not seem to be borne out by any other evidence (*NYT*, 24 August 1949).

[2] 1 September 1945.

munists themselves now showed themselves willing to reopen negotiations.[1] On 28 August Mao Tse-tung flew to Chungking for this purpose. The American Embassy in Moscow agreed with the view that the agreements had weakened the bargaining power of the Chinese Communists but pointed out in a telegram on 10 September that the Russian assurances to the Chinese Government had in another way benefited the Communists, for they had removed any excuse for American intervention against them. Indeed critics of Russia's role in the Far East now found themselves disarmed.[2]

EVENTS IN MANCHURIA 1945-6

The Russians probably had about seventy divisions in Manchuria when the campaign began on 9 August, against about thirty to forty on the Japanese side.[3] But they had to overcome considerable natural obstacles, and faced difficult problems of supply.[4] On the first Far Eastern front an offensive was developed from Vladivostok into northern Korea and eastern Manchuria; on the second Far Eastern front the Soviet forces penetrated into northern Manchuria in the direction of Harbin; while on the trans-Baikal front the main Soviet force under Marshal Malinovsky converged from the north-west towards the same point. Mongolian cavalry to the number of about 80,000 under Marshal Choibolsan advanced on its right flank.[5] The Soviet advances covered considerable distances in a short space of time and were supported by intensive bombing of the enemy's rail centres. On 11 August Russian marines, under the protection of the Russian Pacific fleet, captured the Japanese naval base at Rashin, in northern Korea. At the time of the Japanese capitulation on 14 August Russian forces had penetrated deeply into Manchuria. Fighting did not stop at once and on the 16th a Soviet communiqué actually reported a Japanese counter-offensive. On the same day Malinovsky ordered the Japanese Kwantung army to surrender by 20

---

[1] CSM, 14 August 1945; The Times, 28 August 1945.
[2] Relations with China, pp. 122-3.
[3] Byrnes, Speaking Frankly, p. 217. For the diplomatic antecedents of the campaign, see below, Ch. VI.
[4] NYT, 19 August 1945.
[5] Outer Mongolia declared war on Japan on 10 August.

August; and this order was obeyed. Fighting stopped on that
date, and Russian troops occupied the major Manchurian
cities—Harbin, Mukden, and Changchun. On 10 September
the Russians reported the final results of the campaign. They
claimed a total of 594,000 prisoners including 148 generals, and
estimated the Japanese killed, excluding naval casualties, at
80,000; the weapons captured included 925 aircraft and 369
tanks.[1] According to the Soviet press, the Russian troops were
welcomed by the Chinese inhabitants of Manchuria, who were
reported as glad to shed the Japanese yoke.[2] On the other hand
foreign witnesses asserted that the behaviour of the troops soon
created widespread resentment, and that no distinction was
made by them between Japanese and Chinese nationals.[3]
Furthermore, from early September the Soviet command began
to carry out a deliberate policy of stripping the country of its
industrial equipment. Japanese technicians and Chinese labour
were used for the purpose as well as Red Army forces. Foreign
observers of this process were not numerous.[4] American and
British prisoners of war found in Manchuria were repatriated,
and the mass of the Japanese Kwantung army interned. Some
Germans and a few Russian émigrés were arrested as war
criminals and sent to Russia; other Russians were offered Soviet
citizenship if they would return to the 'Russian motherland'.
American officials only arrived in Mukden in March 1946 after
the Soviet withdrawal. It became clear that the Soviet Government intended to secure important economic concessions as a
result of the presence of its troops in Manchuria. According to
a later Chinese account, on 24 November 1945, Slatekovsky,
the economic adviser to Marshal Malinovsky, approached
Chang Chiangau, the chairman of the Economic Commission
of the Chinese Government's headquarters in Manchuria, with
the proposal that 80 per cent. of Manchuria's heavy industry
should be placed under joint Sino-Soviet operation. On 4
December Chang Chiangau declined to enter into economic
discussions before the evacuation of the Soviet troops from
Manchuria. On 7 December Slatekovsky again raised this sub-

---

[1] This summary of the campaign is based on the official communiqués published in the *Soviet Monitor* and the *NYT*.
[2] *Izvestia*, 17 August 1945; *Pravda*, 23 August 1945.
[3] F. C. Jones, *Manchuria since 1931* (London, RIIA, 1949), p. 225.
[4] *NYT* and *NYHT*, 13 October 1945; *CSM*, 6 November 1945.

ject, declaring that all industrial enterprises in Manchuria could be regarded as war booty. This view was naturally dissented from by Chang Chiangau. In further discussions Marshal Malinovsky declared his inability to predict the date of the withdrawal of Soviet troops until this question had been decided.[1] These local negotiations led to no result and after a protest from the Chinese Government a reply from the Soviet Government was handed in at Chungking on 21 January 1946. This declared that all the equipment removed was 'war booty', and this term in the Russian view comprised all those industrial enterprises which had been of use to the Japanese army. The Russians claimed further that they had obtained the consent of the other allies to this interpretation.[2] On 9 February the United States Government protested against the removals, in notes to both the Chinese and Soviet Governments. The grounds of the protest were both the excessively broad Soviet interpretation of war booty, and the fact that the Soviet Government was taking unilateral action with regard to Japanese assets. On 27 March a formal Soviet proposal was handed to the Chinese Foreign Minister whereby the main industrial and mining enterprises and the airfields of the principal cities of Manchuria were to be under joint Sino-Soviet administration. A joint company was to be formed for each enterprise with each Government holding 50 per cent. of the stock, and with a Chinese chairman and Soviet vice-chairman, and a Soviet manager and Chinese deputy manager. This formula was obviously intended to secure Soviet control. The joint stock companies were to operate for thirty years, after which period the enterprises were to be returned to China without compensation. The remaining enterprises were to be returned to China immediately. These proposals were also unacceptable to the Chinese Government.[3] In May and June a reparations commission, under the chairmanship of Edwin Pauley, investigated industrial conditions in Manchuria on behalf of the United States. His report stated: 'Upon their

[1] Statement by F. T. Tsiang to the First (Political) Committee of the UN General Assembly, 4th Session, 25 November 1949.
[2] The legal aspects of the Soviet claim are discussed in Daniel S. Lew, 'Manchurian Booty and International Law', *American Journal of International Law*, vol. 40, July 1946.
[3] Tsiang's statement, loc. cit. pp. 344-5; *Relations with China*, pp. 596-8.

arrival, the Soviets began a systematic confiscation of food and
stock piles and in early September started the selective removal
of industrial machinery.' It was, Pauley believed, intended to
complete these removals by 3 December 1945—the date origin-
ally fixed for the withdrawal of the Soviet military forces.
Pauley estimated the damage to Manchurian industry at $858
million and the cost of replacement at $2,000 million. Since
80 per cent. of Manchuria's industry was concentrated in the
south outside the fighting zone, its equipment should have been
intact, and the damage must have been the result of the Russian
removals.[1] According to other observers much of the damage
was due to other causes, such as the removal of equipment by
Chinese guerrilla forces when retreating before the Kuomintang
troops and looting by the mob in the intervals of occupation by
the different armies.[2] Finally, some equipment was probably in
a poor state, since at the end of the war the Japanese had to
'cannibalize' some plant in order to keep the rest going when
spares became unobtainable.[3]

According to Pauley, the Russians restricted their removals
to certain categories of materials: stock piles, certain complete
installations, a large part of the valuable generating and
electrical equipment, and the best machine tools. Less valuable
material was left or, as at the Mukden arsenal, destroyed. In
addition to the damaged buildings, this removal of key equipment resulted in a heavy decline in production. In the mines
irreparable damage was done by flooding. The Russians also
confiscated about $3 million in gold and $500 million in local
currency. They circulated nearly 10,000 million yuans of
occupation currency, thereby almost doubling the note issue.[4]
The value of the equipment actually removed by the Russians
was thus obviously only a fraction of the total loss to Manchuria's
economy. It could therefore be held that Soviet policy had the
additional purpose of destroying, for some time to come, the
industrial and military potential existing there. And this suggests that the Russians did not expect Manchuria to be in
friendly hands once their own troops had been withdrawn.

[1] *Department of State Bulletin*, 22 December 1946.
[2] Jack Chen, 'Manchurian Tragedy', *United Nations World*, June 1947.
[3] Everett Hawkins, 'Manchuria's Post-war Economy', *FES*, 12 February 1947;
Jones, *Manchuria since 1931*, pp. 229–30.
[4] *Department of State Bulletin*, 22 December 1946, pp. 1144–5.

These matters were not mentioned in the Soviet press in 1945 or 1946. To the Russian public a different picture was given, one of Soviet assistance in the rehabilitation of the Manchurian economy, and particularly in the restoration of its railway system. On 27 January 1947, however, *Izvestia* published an article which protested against the American decision to apportion Japanese reparations without Soviet consent—a decision caused by disagreement over the 'war booty' question. The writer claimed that the Soviet concept of booty had been agreed on by the other allies in the armistices concluded with Rumania, Hungary, and Bulgaria, and also that the estimate of the value of the removals made by Pauley was much too high. The Russians put it at only $97 million. The reported industrial destruction was attributed to Japanese and Kuomintang troops, and to American bombing raids, which, it was claimed, had been strategically unnecessary.[1]

The problem of the withdrawal of the Soviet troops from Manchuria was thus connected with the negotiations with the Chinese for economic concessions. It had been agreed, as has been seen, that the Soviet troops would not stay in Manchuria for longer than three months at the outside, after the Japanese capitulation; that would have given the date of 3 December. On 1 October, however, the Soviet radio stated that the evacuation had already begun.[2] The Chinese Government clearly wished to avoid the appearance of suspecting the Russians' good faith, and on 15 October Chiang Kai-shek declared that he 'felt sure that Soviet forces in Manchuria would be withdrawn in accordance with the Sino-Soviet pact'.[3]

The eagerness of the Chinese Government to secure the evacuation of the Russian troops was connected with the situation in the north of China. On 11 August four Communist army groups had been ordered to march into the provinces of Chahar, Jehol, Liaoning, and Kirin. These succeeded in blocking the main roads into the country by land before the Kuomintang armies could reach them. Large numbers of Chinese Communist troops were in control in important areas of

[1] G. Astafyev, 'China's Economic Problems', *New Times*, 12 April 1950; Wu Min, 'Industry in People's China', *For a Lasting Peace*, 17 November 1950.

[2] *Soviet News*, 1 October 1945. In February 1946 the Russians stated that they had only begun to evacuate in November (*Soviet Monitor*, 26 February 1946).

[3] Dallin, *Soviet Russia and the Far East* (London, Hollis & Carter, 1949), p. 254.

Manchuria within two or three months after this date, and many of them were armed and equipped from the material left by the Japanese after their surrender. Kuomintang sources make it clear that the Russian withdrawals were timed in such a way as to facilitate the Communist advances and their seizures of materials.[1]

Chiang Kai-shek sent a military mission to Changchun to discuss with the Russians the conditions for the entry of his troops into the country through the seaports or by air. But the Russians made various legalistic excuses for objecting to the proposals, such as that Dairen was a commercial port and therefore unsuited for the entry of troops. As the occupying force, the Russians were responsible for seeing that the proper authorities were placed in control of the civil administration. There were insufficient Communists to have prevented the Kuomintang taking over without Russian connivance in obstruction.

In October the American fleet under Vice-Admiral Daniel Barbey was ordered to escort Government troops to Manchuria, but found all the seaports closed to them. Hulutao had been turned over to the Communists, and there a launch from the Admiral's flagship was fired upon by them. On 29 October Marshal Malinovsky agreed that the troops could enter through Yingkow and that the Soviet troops would evacuate the port by 10 November. But on 6 November the Americans learnt that the Russians had evacuated the port five days ahead of the proposed date, thus allowing it to fall into the hands of the Chinese Communists, who threatened to open fire on the troop convoy. Eventually the Chinese were landed at the port of Chinwangtao, which is inside the Great Wall, so that they had to make their journey into Manchuria by the long land route, which gave the Communists plenty of time to establish themselves before the Government forces arrived.[2] Some troops were actually landed at some time at Yingkow, but found that the rolling stock had been removed from the railway so that they could not readily proceed inland.

During November the Chinese Government, according to the Russians, actually asked them to keep their troops in Manchuria

---

[1] See Tsiang's statement to the United Nations, cited above, p. 39.
[2] George Moorad, *Lost Peace in China* (New York, Dutton, 1949), pp. 91–92; Dallin, *Soviet Russia and the Far East*, p. 252.

for some time longer.[1] Other sources suggest that the Russians
took the initiative in asking for a postponement of the evacuation
on the grounds of the continued presence in China of the
American marines. It is said that Chiang Kai-shek agreed to
this on condition that the Soviet forces assisted the Kuomintang
troops in taking over the Mukden area.[2] In fact, again according to the Chinese Nationalist account, the Russians gave direct
assistance to the Communist troops, who for some time succeeded
in blocking the entry of the Kuomintang forces into Mukden.[3]
In Changchun itself, and in several other places, the National
Government's administration functioned under the protection
of the Russian forces. The formal Russian attitude continued
to be that the National Government was the only legitimate
authority in China, and that the agreements concluded with it
in August still held good. The Russians' policy in this period
was no doubt affected by the increased tension in their relations
with the other Allies, particularly the Americans. Their obvious
reluctance to show an open partiality for the Chinese Communists may have been largely due to an unwillingness to provide an
excuse for American intervention in China on a larger scale.
But there is no reason to believe that they estimated very
favourably the prospects of an immediate large accretion of
strength to the Chinese Communists. And military events in
November and December, when the Nationalists finally
launched a full-scale attack upon the Communists, showed that
there were good grounds for such scepticism.[4]

It is in fact very difficult to estimate to what extent there had
been definite Soviet assistance to the Chinese Communists prior
to this offensive; the Soviet command refused a formal offer of
co-operation from General Chu Teh, which was made on 11
August. Chinese Nationalist spokesmen repeatedly alleged that
the Russians had handed large quantities of arms and equipment to the Communists. But the Communists and the Russians
both maintained that the arms had been obtained from dumps
in towns where no Russian troops were stationed. Since the
Soviet Command had by inter-allied agreement the sole right

[1] *Soviet Monitor*, 29 November 1945; *Soviet News*, 1 December 1945.
[2] Dallin, *Soviet Russia and the Far East*, p. 252.
[3] Tsiang's statement to the United Nations, cited above, p. 39.
[4] 'Chinese Revolution', *The World Today*, June 1950.

to take the surrender of the Japanese in Manchuria, large dumps of arms could not have fallen into Communist control except through Japanese officers defying their orders, which is unlikely, or through Russian collusion. Certain local forces were raised, it seems, under Russian auspices, for service on the spot.[1] There are other American press reports on the position which confirm this general picture although they vary in detail.

The Russians used their presence in Manchuria to seize, try, and convict various Russian émigrés who had taken a prominent part against the Bolsheviks in the civil war.[2] According to Soviet sources, a very large number of Russian exiles in Manchuria took up the offer made to them of Soviet citizenship, and some appear to have left for the Soviet Union when the Russian troops finally withdrew.[3] The Nationalist offensive against the Communists which has already been referred to was the climax of increasing friction. The negotiations between the Kuomintang and Communist leaders which began in August under the auspices of the American Ambassador Hurley had had the express approval of the Russians.[4] At the end of September, Moscow Radio stated that under an agreement reached between Chiang Kai-shek and Mao Tse-tung a central unified Government would be set up. It was claimed that the Sino-Soviet agreements had been an important factor in bringing this about.[5]

These talks had averted a major clash for the time being, but fighting had continued on a minor scale as the Communist troops spread through Inner Mongolia and along the Manchurian border. The assistance given by the Americans to Chiang Kai-shek in connexion with the surrender of the Japanese armies and their disarmament led to isolated clashes between Americans and the Chinese Communists. The Communists began to voice forceful demands for the total withdrawal of the American forces, and from early November the Russian press began to

[1] A. T. Steele in *NYHT*, 16 January and 15 March 1946; Jones, *Manchuria since 1931*, p. 232.

[2] *Soviet Monitor*, 28 and 29 August 1946.

[3] ibid. 14 February 1946; Dallin, *Soviet Russia and the Far East*, pp. 317–18.

[4] *Red Star*, 31 August 1945; radio Khabarovsk quoted in *NYT*, 1 September 1945.

[5] *NYT*, 29 September 1945. According to information given in 1951 to the American journalists Joseph and Stewart Alsop by Yugoslav Communists, Stalin actually ordered Mao to enter a coalition Government on Hurley's terms but was persistently defied on this point by the Chinese leader (*NYHT*, 25 July 1951).

exhibit concern on this subject.[1] An American official statement immediately pointed out that plans for withdrawing the
marines were in hand, but that no details could be given since
this was a military matter.[2]

The matter was broached by Molotov at a meeting of the
Moscow Conference of Foreign Ministers on 16 December 1945.
The American Secretary of State made a statement about the
number of American troops in China, and claimed that they
were solely employed in disarming the remaining Japanese.
They would be withdrawn, he declared, as soon as this task was
completed. Molotov, however, repeatedly raised the question;
and Byrnes eventually discussed it with Stalin himself. Stalin
stated, according to Byrnes, that his Government had recently
recognized the Chinese National Government as the central
Government of China and had concluded agreements with it.
He did not object to the presence of American troops in China,
but wished to be informed about their activities. He was concerned lest the Chinese Government should lose its prestige
with its own people because of its apparent dependence on
foreign support. Byrnes also raised the question of the hindrances
put in the way of the Chinese National Government's taking
over Manchuria, but Molotov refused to discuss the matter.
The official communiqué of the Conference summed up the
discussions on China in Section IV:

The three Foreign Secretaries exchanged views with regard to the
situation in China. They were in agreement as to the need for a
unified and democratic China under the National Government, for
broad participation by democratic elements in all branches of the
National Government, and for a cessation of civil strife. They
reaffirmed their adherence to a policy of non-interference in the
internal affairs of China.

Mr. Molotov and Mr. Byrnes had several conversations concerning Soviet and American armed forces in China. Mr. Molotov
stated that the Soviet forces had disarmed and deported Japanese
troops in Manchuria but that the withdrawal of Soviet forces had
been postponed until 1 February, at the request of the Chinese
Government. Mr. Byrnes pointed out that American forces were in
north China at the request of the Chinese Government, and referred
also to the primary responsibility of the United States in the implementation of the terms of surrender with respect to the disarming

---

[1] *Izvestia*, 6 November 1945.   [2] *The Times*, 8 November 1945.

and deportation of Japanese troops. He stated that American forces would be withdrawn just as soon as this responsibility was discharged or the Chinese Government was in a position to discharge the responsibility without the assistance of American forces.

The two Foreign Secretaries were in complete accord as to the desirability of withdrawal of Soviet and American forces from China at the earliest practicable moment consistent with the discharge of their obligations and responsibilities.[1]

No information is available about the negotiations leading up to the formulation of this part of the communiqué, but it implies that continued support for the National Government was contingent, from the Russian point of view, on the participation of what they called democratic elements in all branches of that Government, and on the ending of the civil war which was now again raging. The vague wording of the undertaking to evacuate both the Soviet and the American troops suggests only a superficial agreement on this issue. This Moscow Agreement was, however, important, being, as it turned out, the last formal one that the Allies managed to reach on Chinese affairs; and later on, Russian criticism of the Americans frequently referred to their alleged breaches of this statement.

At the beginning of 1946 the Americans made their major effort at securing a united China under Chiang Kai-shek's leadership through the mission of General Marshall. The Russians at first gave their approval to General Marshall's efforts, and the descriptions of the early negotiations given by Soviet and American sources are almost identical.[2] At the beginning of February it seemed that a considerable measure of agreement had been reached between the contending Chinese factions, but on 18 February there was an apparently coordinated attack on the Soviet Union by the Chungking press; and this was followed by various anti-Russian demonstrations. These demonstrations were provoked by the continued presence of Russian troops in Manchuria, the economic demands made by the Soviet Union, and the alleged assistance given by it to

[1] Text in RIIA, *United Nations Documents* (1946), pp. 263–4; see also Byrnes, *Speaking Frankly*, pp. 226–70 and U.S. Department of State, Moscow Meeting of Foreign Ministers, Dec. 16–26, 1945, *Report by J. F. Byrnes . . . and Soviet-Anglo-American Communiqué* (Dept. of State publication, 2448).
[2] A. Perevertailo, 'The Struggle for National Unity and Democracy in China', *New Times*, 15 February 1946; *Relations with China*, pp. 133–43.

the Chinese Communists. What, in fact, had happened was that Russian pressure had made Chiang Kai-shek more and more intransigent, and more and more convinced that he could rely on American support. It had also strengthened within the Kuomintang those elements which were unhesitatingly anti-Soviet as compared with those which still wished to try and achieve a bargain with both the great Powers.[1] The Russians took up the issue of the non-evacuation of their troops from Manchuria, and Malinovsky's Chief of Staff, Trotsenko, made a statement declaring that the withdrawal had been twice postponed as a result of Chinese requests, the second time until 1 February. The withdrawal, he claimed rather disingenuously, had actually been resumed in mid-January, but had been delayed by the slow arrival of the Chinese troops, by inadequate transport facilities, and by the operations of groups of bandits and remnants of the Japanese and 'puppet' forces. Trotsenko's statement went on: 'The Soviet command in Manchuria reckons on completing the withdrawal of Soviet troops from Manchuria earlier than the time within which the American command can withdraw the American troops from China, or at least not later.'[2] In Washington the Russian Embassy also protested against the anti-Soviet demonstrations.[3] And these demonstrations led to a decisive breakdown in the Kuomintang-Communist negotiations.

On the other hand there was no overt breach between the Soviet and Chinese Governments. The Chinese Government was only indirectly blamed for the anti-Soviet manifestations. Early in April 1946 the chief of the Chinese military mission at Changchun was informed of the new timetable of the withdrawals. According to Russian sources he asked that small garrisons be left in some towns until the Nationalists arrived. But the Russians refused to prolong their stay after the end of April.[4] The Soviet press also publicized a reception held at Changchun by the Chinese in honour of the Red Army in Manchuria.[5] The Russians officially notified the Chinese

[1] The Times, 19 February 1946; Guenther Stein in CSM, 23 February 1946; 'Cloud over Manchuria', The Economist, 23 February 1946.

[2] Soviet Monitor, 26 February; Pravda, 27 February 1946.

[3] Red Star, quoted by Information Bulletin of the Soviet Embassy (Washington), 28 March 1946; Dallin, Soviet Russia and the Far East, p. 316.

[4] Soviet News, 8 April 1946.   [5] Pravda, 10 April 1946.

Government on 23 May that the evacuation of their troops was complete, although Chinese official sources cast some doubt upon the truth of this claim.[1] As early as 10 April, the Russian press on its side was beginning to express impatience with the attitude of the Chinese Government. It was made clear that despite the treaty between the two Governments facts which the Russians regarded as contrary to Soviet-Chinese friendship would not be overlooked, and there was particular criticism in *Izvestia* of the 'campaign of lies directed against the Soviet Union'.[2]

A cease-fire which had been arranged by General Marshall on 10 January had not been extended to Manchuria, and there had been some severe fighting there, as a result of the continued Communist infiltration. Russian troops evacuated Changchun on 14 April 1946 and on 18 April it was captured by the Communists.[3] The position was, in fact, that although some of the cities and the railway lines were already held by Government troops, they had to fight for any extension of their authority into the rural areas, where the Communists held sway.[4]

The controlling position which the Communists thus had acquired in so much of Manchuria, at a time when Russian forces were still present, might seem to have called for some formal co-operation with the latter, at least on a local basis.[5] In fact, however, relations were on the surface very distant.[6] The assistance received from the Russians, whether in the securing of arms from the Japanese dumps or the holding up of Nationalist forces so as to give the Communists an opportunity of establishing themselves at key-points, was so unobtrusive as to make it difficult to challenge the Russians with any overt breach of their agreements. As for Russian supplies, Chou En-lai stated on 1 February 1946 that Yenan had received nothing from the Soviet Union, except two plane-loads of medical supplies.[7] And there was a rather roundabout Soviet denial of

[1] *Soviet News*, 23 May 1946.

[2] cf. Evgenyev, 'Who is Hampering the Unity of the Chinese People?', *Red Star*, quoted in *Soviet Monitor*, 26 April 1946.

[3] *Relations with China*, p. 149.

[4] For an account of the military operations see ibid. pp. 313–23.

[5] Guenther Stein, *CSM*, 18 May 1946.

[6] See the account by Tillman Durdin of his visit to the Communist-held areas on the Manchurian border, *NYT*, 5 November 1945.

[7] *NYT*, 2 February 1946.

rumours that Mao Tse-tung and other Communist leaders had visited Moscow, and made agreements granting the Russians a long-term control of Manchuria.[1]

On the other hand whatever irritation the Chinese Communist Party may have felt at its being kept officially at arm's length, and whatever local friction the conduct of the Soviet troops may have caused, there seems no reason to doubt that the fundamental loyalty of the party to Moscow remained unshaken. The party leadership seems to have been successful in explaining away any grievances voiced by the rank and file about the rights acquired by the Russians, by saying that there would be new negotiations when China had a new Government.[2] With regard to Soviet removals of 'war booty' Li Li-san, who had returned to Manchuria in September 1945, after ten years' exile in Moscow, and who was reputed to stand high in the counsels of the Communist leaders, declared in a speech at Harbin: 'I feel that the movement of the machinery is not an important problem at all. Of course the Soviet Union moved some machinery, but not a large amount compared with its war losses.'[3]

EVENTS IN CHINA, APRIL–DECEMBER 1946

The Nationalist forces recaptured Changchun on 19 May, and generally speaking the year 1946 was a superficially successful one for the Kuomintang armies. On the other hand, as later became evident, the Chinese Government had miscalculated what it could effectively do in Manchuria. For it had neither the military nor the administrative ability to retain its holdings along the Manchurian railway lines while the countryside remained in the hands of Communist guerrillas, who lived off it, and did not depend, like the Government troops, on supplies from distant bases.[4]

On the political side the remainder of the year was notable for increasingly outspoken criticism by the Communists of American

---

[1] *Tägliche Rundschau* (the organ of the Soviet Military Government in Berlin), 2 April 1946.

[2] Otto van der Sprenkel and others, *New China* (London, Turnstile Press, 1950), pp. 74–75.

[3] *Daily Worker* (New York), 26 July 1946, quoted by Dallin, *Soviet Russia and the Far East*, p. 245.

[4] *Relations with China*, p. 314.

activities in China. They objected, in the spring, to American financial assistance being given to the National Government before it had reorganized itself on 'democratic' lines, and to the role played by the Americans in transporting and training Nationalist divisions. They argued that such aid, by assisting the 'reactionary elements' of the Kuomintang, prolonged the civil war.[1] The American marines came in for special criticism, and in June some of them found themselves within the area of actual hostilities. Although they were assured of immunity by the Communist commanders, there were some small but serious incidents in succeeding months.[2]

In June a truce was arranged by General Marshall. This came into force on the 6th, and was later renewed until the end of the month. An attempt to get it continued was unsuccessful, and in July hostilities spread. At this point the Communists became more overtly anti-American. On 24 June Mao Tse-tung broke a long silence in a speech directly asking that the marines be withdrawn from China.[3] On 7 July the Communists issued a manifesto strongly attacking American policy. On 10 August General Marshall announced the failure of his mission, and five days later the first personal attack upon him appeared in the Chinese Communist press. Henceforth both sides in the Chinese conflict made ever increasing use of accusations about foreign help to their opponents. Such accusations against the Communists were invariably referred to in the Russian press as 'provocative propaganda'. On 7 September Tass denied the accusation that 800 Chinese pilots had completed their training in Russia, and on 14 October *Izvestia* denied that the Russians had transferred to the Communists military aircraft, tanks, and 4 million rifles. The Chinese Communist leaders were similarly emphatic about their independence of Russian aid. In an interview on 8 September Chou En-lai reviewed the relations between the Chinese Communist Party and the Soviet Union. He insisted that the links between them had been severed in 1935,

[1] *NYT*, 3 and 5 April; *CSM*, 14 May 1946. From June 1946 the Americans also came in for criticism from the Nationalist side; both for helping Japan and for allegedly intervening in Chinese affairs to prevent the Nationalists from obtaining an outright victory over the Communists.

[2] *CSM*, 29 May; *NYT*, 16 June, 16 July, 11 August, 5, 7, and 22 October 1946; *Relations with China*, pp. 172 and 709.

[3] *NYT*, 25 June 1946.

after a decision of the Comintern to allow independence of action to the national parties. He added: 'They [the Russians] made too many mistakes for us in the early days. . . . Stalin has a correct impression of the Chinese situation. He believes that the Chinese revolution is a democratic one by nature.' Russian intervention on the Communist side could only increase the degree of American intervention.[1] In October Chou En-lai also denied that there had been any supplies of arms from Russia. The arms of the Communist troops had been captured from the Japanese and their supporters, or from the Nationalists. The Communists themselves manufactured small arms, machine guns, and ammunition.[2] The failure of the Marshall mission led to reports that the Communist leaders had visited Moscow in order to request Soviet mediation in the conflict, but these rumours were denied by Tass on 19 October 1946.

On the other hand, it is possible in 1946 to trace a definite hardening of the Soviet attitude towards the National Government. At the beginning of the year only its 'reactionary elements' had been attacked, but after May it was no longer referred to as the National Government, but as the 'Kuomintang Government' and its army as the 'Kuomintang army'. Reports about the Kuomintang forces were now given only the same prominence as news about the Communist troops, who were called the 'United Democratic Army', but Chiang Kai-shek was still not personally criticized, and importance was still attached to the alleged remnants of Japanese influence among the Kuomintang 'reactionaries'.[3] On the whole, however, news from China in this period was very scanty, and material from the Communist Sinhua agency was rarely reproduced. For a long period there seems to have been no mention of military operation by the Communists.[4]

---

[1] *NYT*, 9 September 1946.   [2] *CSM*, 2 October 1946.

[3] See the articles by Avarin in *Pravda* quoted in *Soviet Monitor*, 5 July 1946, and by Evgenyev in *Red Star*, 6 July 1946. In *Izvestia* on 6 January 1948 a report of a speech by Mao Tse-tung called the Communist forces 'the National Liberation Army'. It has not been possible to trace references to the Communist forces under either title between these dates.

[4] There is no evidence to support Kan Chieh-hou's assertion in 1949 that in 1946 Chiang Kai-shek told the Soviet Ambassador he was prepared to reconsider the Soviet proposals he had previously rejected (see above, p. 36 n. 1), but refused an invitation to Moscow, and that thereafter Soviet officials were ordered not to co-operate with the National Government (*NYT*, 24 August 1949).

The main attention of the Soviet press was devoted to the question of American intervention, echoing in this respect the complaints of the Chinese Communists. Stress was laid on the alleged co-operation between American and Japanese officers, and on the alleged use of Japanese troops by some Kuomintang provincial governors. Under the terms of the military agreement of 28 June 1946, the Lend-Lease agreement between the United States and the Chinese National Government was extended.[1] The Russian comment on this extension was that it amounted to a removal of the American 'neutrality mask'.[2] The Russians had also noted with concern the arrival at Tsingtao of the American Seventh Fleet. On 7 July, *Pravda*, referring to the bill for military aid to China, which was before Congress at the time, said that this bill amounted to 'pouring oil on fire' and that it was 'equivalent to direct interference in the internal affairs of China', in direct contradiction to the Moscow agreement (of December 1945). The Americans were accused of deliberately delaying the repatriation of the Japanese troops in order to have an excuse for continuing to send arms to China.[3] Criticism of the Americans was also voiced in August, in connexion with a bombing attack on the Communist capital at Yenan, when American equipment was used.[4]

One of the questions put by Alexander Werth to Stalin in September was: 'Do you believe that the earliest withdrawal of all American troops from China is vital to future peace?' Stalin's affirmative reply was given on 25 September, and was no doubt intended as a formal warning to the Americans.[5] During this period the Russians also showed considerable interest in the economic activities of Americans in China. Their main point was that the interests of China traditionally clashed with foreign interests. The United States, they argued, wished to preserve China as a market for America's over-expanded heavy industry, and to encourage the development in China of light industries only. The products of these when sold in other Asiatic countries would be used to pay for the imports of

---

[1] Transfers under this scheme amounted to a total of $781 million by 30 June 1948 (*Relations with China*, pp. 172 and 969).

[2] *Pravda*, 26 June 1946.

[3] *Soviet Monitor*, 7 July 1946; cf. *Pravda*, 15 September 1946.

[4] *Izvestia*, 12 August 1946; *Pravda*, 12 August 1946.

[5] *Soviet News*, 25 September 1946.

American machinery.[1] The real national interest of China lay, on the contrary, in the development of its own heavy industry.[2] Similar arguments were raised by Soviet representatives at the meetings of the Ecafe with regard to the entire Far East. The conclusion on 4 November 1946 of an American-Chinese trade treaty was made an occasion for further comment of this kind.[3] The Chinese were also accused of having diverted Unrra deliveries to strengthen their armies.[4] Thus by December 1946 the connexion between the 'reactionary circles' of the Kuomintang and 'foreign imperialists' had become a stock phrase of the Russians. An article in *Izvestia* on 8 December stated: 'American policy in China is inspired by those reactionary circles in the United States who want to turn China into a semi-colony and a military-strategical jumping-off ground in the Far East.' The Chinese Communists were a step ahead of the Russians, since it was Chou En-lai who early in December launched the first personal attack on Chiang Kai-shek.[5]

The formal relations between the Soviet and Chinese Governments also deteriorated. Late in November 1946 the Russians decided to evacuate their railway personnel from Mukden. Chinese sources reported that this decision had been taken after 'repeated consultation between the Chinese Government and the Soviet authorities'; but a communiqué from the Soviet Embassy at Nanking on 28 November declared that the withdrawal had been made because the Chinese had made working and even living conditions unbearable.[6]

---

[1] Maslennikov, 'The Problems of the Economic Development of China', *MKiMP*, no. 7. 1945 ('American Trade Policy in China', *Pravda*, 14 July 1946); N. Vaintsvaig, 'The Economic Plans of the United States in China', *MKiMP*, nos. 10 and 11, 1945.

[2] cf. *Diplomaticheskii Slovar* (Diplomatic Dictionary), vol. 1, 1948, p. 67.

[3] *Soviet Monitor*, 29 November 1946.

[4] *The Times*, 15 December 1946.

[5] *NYT*, 15 December 1946.   [6] *The Times*, 30 November 1945.

III

The Soviet Union and the Chinese Civil War

January 1947–April 1949

AFTER the final breakdown of General Marshall's efforts at mediation, the Kuomintang convened a National Assembly, which met on 15 November 1946. The Communists refused to recognize the authority of this body or of the Constitution which it produced on 25 December 1946. The Constitution was on the face of it a more democratic document than that of 5 May 1936, which it replaced, but General Marshall himself was sceptical as to what would actually happen when it came to be put into operation.[1]

General Marshall's mission finally ended with his recall on 6 January 1947. As the newly appointed Secretary of State it fell to him to announce the American withdrawal from the Committee of Three set up with the National Government and the Communists.[2] Further efforts at mediation were undertaken by his successor John Leighton Stuart, but these broke down in February. The National Government dismissed the Communist mission from Nanking and announced a programme of national reorganization without Communist participation.[3]

Military operations were resumed, and at first went very successfully for the National Government, culminating in the occupation of Yenan in March.[4] But subsequently the Communists began to gain ground steadily, and towards the end of 1947 they not only commanded the railways nearly to Mukden, but had also cut off the Nationalist forces in the remainder of Manchuria.[5]

[1] *Relations with China*, pp. 207, 215. It was promulgated on 1 January 1947 and became effective on 25 December. The text is in *China Handbook*, 1950, pp. 144-55.
[2] *Relations with China*, p. 219.
[3] ibid. pp. 230-2.
[4] On the military operations in China see Gen. L-M. Chassin, *La Conquête de la Chine par Mao Tse-tung, 1945-1949* (Paris, Payot, 1952).
[5] *Relations with China*, pp. 315-18.

The Soviet press gave publicity to a remark made by General Marshall at a press conference at Honolulu on his return journey from China in January 1947, to the effect that there was no evidence whatever to indicate that the Chinese Communists were being supported by Russia.[1] Although during the remainder of the year there continued to be reports of Russian supplies, these were steadily denied by the Soviet Government, and in fact were rarely if ever confirmed.[2] However, an Australian journalist, Michael Keon, who spent six months in the Communist-occupied areas of Shantung, did see small quantities of Russian materials arrive from the port of Chefoo, before its capture by the Nationalists.[3] The large quantity of Japanese arms which fell into the Communists' hands as a result of Russian collusion, and which were infinitely more important than any Russian supplies, could of course not be distinguished from Japanese arms which the Communists had captured themselves as a result of military operations. But it was these arms which must supply the reason why the Communist forces, so poorly armed before the autumn of 1945, appeared to be so well provided in the subsequent campaigns.

On the political side, the Chinese Communists fully acknowledged the finality of the breach between themselves and the Kuomintang, and denounced the American aid to the Nationalists with increasing violence. On 10 January Chou En-lai attacked General Marshall's final statement on his mission and contended that the mission itself had been a cover for American meddling in Chinese affairs. On 1 February the party announced that it would refuse to recognize any international agreements entered into by the National Government after 10 January.[4] These and subsequent Chinese protests against the presence of Americans on Chinese soil and against alleged excesses by American troops were fully reported in the Soviet press. American support for the Chinese National Government

[1] *NYT*, 12 January; *Soviet News*, 16 January 1947.
[2] See e.g. *Soviet News*, 8 January and 20 February; *Soviet Monitor*, 21 June; *Pravda*, 25 June 1947.
[3] *NYT*, 19 October 1947. Another correspondent that summer could find no substantiation of reports of Russian aid for the Communists, and said that a spokesman for the Nationalist high command in Manchuria admitted that he could not prove a single case (ibid. 15 June 1947).
[4] *Relations with China*, pp. 232 and 706–20.

was ascribed to the desire of American capitalists to curb 'the Soviet peril' and to secure economic advantages for themselves.[1] The Soviet press also gave increasing publicity to reports of the deepening financial and economic crisis in the Kuomintang-controlled territories, and to the Chinese Communist Party's protests about the closure of its delegations in Nanking, Chungking, and Shanghai. The Kuomintang was accused of 'accepting American aid in any form and of suppressing all democratic forces including the non-Communist ones'.[2]

During the Conference of Foreign Ministers in Moscow, in March 1947, Molotov proposed the inclusion of the Chinese problem in the agenda. This move was opposed by the American delegation and vociferous support for their objections came from the Chinese National Government. The Chinese Communist Party, however, announced its support for the Russian proposals, but insisted that it should itself be represented when Chinese affairs were under discussion. In view of the American and Chinese Nationalist position, neither the proposal to discuss China at the Conference nor a second Soviet proposal for informal talks outside the Conference could be proceeded with. In a note on 26 March Molotov agreed, on Marshall's suggestion, to exchange written information as to their countries' fulfilment of the Moscow Agreement.[3]

The notes containing this information were duly exchanged and published. General Marshall in his note of 31 March repeated the argument that American forces had been stationed in China solely for the purpose of assisting in the disarmament of the Japanese armies. After the American abandonment of attempts at mediation the marines who had been stationed in China to protect the American mission had been recalled. It was proposed to reduce the total number of American troops in China to 6,180 by June. The letter also expressed concern at the lack of information on what had happened to the 700,000 Japanese who had been taken prisoners by the Russians in Manchuria.[4]

The Russian note declared that the Russian determination

[1] See, for instance, the articles by Avarin in *New Times*, 3 February and 21 March 1947, and by Maslennikov in *MKiMP*, no. 1, 1947.
[2] Marinin, 'Where do the Reactionaries of the Kuomintang lead China?', *Pravda*, 21 April 1947.
[3] *NYT*, 17 and 27 March 1947.   [4] ibid. 3 April 1947.

to abide by the Moscow Agreement had been proved by the completion of the withdrawal of Russian forces on 3 May of the previous year.[1]

During the remainder of 1947 Russian reactions to American policies in China formed only part of an increasing Russian concern over the general Far Eastern policy of the United States, in which, it was alleged, the reinstatement of Japan as a military Power played a dominant part.[2] General Wedemeyer's mission to the Far East in August 1947 attracted special attention in this respect, as did the movements of American troops and ships in the Far East, and evidence of American interest in Formosa.[3] The signing at Nanking, on 27 October 1947, of an agreement providing relief for China was also denounced, on the grounds that, although ostensibly economic, this relief was clearly of military importance. In this connexion, the Soviet press struck a new historical note by references to the traditionally aggressive nature of American Far Eastern policy, beginning with the clauses stipulating extraterritorial rights in the 1844 treaty with China, and Perry's expedition to Japan, and continuing with the annexation of Hawaii and the Philippines.[4]

Prominence was also given to such events in Chinese internal affairs as the expression of opinions in Kuomintang circles favourable to a resumption of negotiation with the Communists, and the severe treatment meted out by the authorities to all those suspected of Communist sympathies. Towards the end of the year, the Russians began to give more space to the military progress of the Communist forces and to the increasing difficulties in which the Nationalists found themselves. But the Communist victories were dealt with in a factual form, and both the reports upon them and the comments of Soviet military

[1] *Pravda*, 7 April 1947. The last American marines left Shanghai in May 1949.
[2] See e.g. the article by Markov, 'American Policy in the Far East', *New Times*, 11 April 1947.
[3] It is now known that Wedemeyer formulated a plan for a five-Power guardianship or a United Nations trusteeship over Manchuria which was rejected by the United States Government. But it was from this point, it seems, that the United States Government began to formulate a new programme of direct aid to Chiang Kai-shek, which culminated in the China Aid Act of April 1948 (*Relations with China*, pp. 249–71).
[4] V. Avarin, 'A new stage in American intervention in China', *New Times*, 12 November 1947.

experts preserved an objective tone and refrained from political invective.

In China, the end of the year 1947 was marked by a statement by Mao Tse-tung, on 25 December, which contained a vitriolic attack on the United States as the Power responsible for the continuation of the civil war.[1] At the same time, the increasing precariousness of the Kuomintang's position led to the emergence of significant elements in the party, who thought that something might still be preserved by an agreement with the Communists through Soviet mediation. On 20 December 1947 General Chang Chih-chung, who had played an important part in the negotiations with General Marshall, informed the American Ambassador that he had approached the Soviet Embassy in Nanking with a request for mediation. He believed that he had impressed the Russians with his warning that China could never be won over to support Russia against the United States, and with his statement that in aiding China, the United States had no ulterior anti-Soviet purposes. He stated that Chiang Kai-shek had permitted him to make these approaches, though refusing personally to take any initiative. Subsequently Chiang Kai-shek's private secretary informed the Ambassador that the Russians had offered to mediate but that Chiang Kai-shek himself had not given his approval to Chang Chih-chung's approaches, and that he did not believe a settlement with the Communists either possible or desirable.[2] There is no information on these talks from the Russian side, and Russian commentators treated reports that the Kuomintang might seek a compromise as indicating merely a wish on the part of its leaders to use this as a threat to extort more supplies from the Americans.[3]

In 1948 the military position of the National Government became increasingly unfavourable, and in April Yenan was recaptured by the Communists. This event and subsequent successes by the Communists led to another stream of reports that they were receiving aid from the Russians. Indeed, in his New Year message Chiang Kai-shek had declared that the Communist menace in China came as much from without as

[1] *Relations with China*, pp. 265–7.
[2] ibid.
[3] Avarin, 'Economic Disintegration in China', *New Times*, 7 April 1948.

from within. In July his Vice-President Li Tsung-jen declared that the Chinese Communists were 'part of the international communist front'.[1] Such reports were denied as usual by the Russians as well as by the Communists themselves. Later in the year, Mao Tse-tung said to an American journalist that although Chinese Communists were fully in sympathy with Russia, they were not dependent on the Soviet Union, and that even their staunchest enemies did not claim that they were.[2]

American policy towards China was considerably revised during 1948. Although President Truman and the Secretary of State still talked of the creation of a broad-based Government, it was made clear by the President at a press conference on 11 March that this did not mean that the Americans wanted Communists in the Chinese Government or anywhere else.[3] There were no direct exchanges between the Soviet Union and the United States during this period, but in his 'open letter' to Stalin in May, Henry Wallace suggested, among possible contributions to peace, the withdrawal of troops from China and Korea. In his reply, Stalin commented favourably on Wallace's proposals.[4]

The scepticism which had developed in American Government circles was not shared by a majority in Congress and, in order to secure support for its general policies, the Administration was forced to give some heed to their wishes. A programme of aid for the Chinese economy, to extend over fifteen months, was placed before Congress by the Department of State, and the China Aid Act was passed on 2 April. The Act included provision for the payment of a sum of $125 million to be used at the discretion of the Chinese Government. It was generally understood that this sum would be used for the purchase of arms and ammunition.[5] Owing to the Administration's lack of enthusiasm, however, no arms allocated under the Act were actually shipped for eight months after its passage. During the

[1] *NYT*, 1 June and 25 July 1948.
[2] *Combat*, 8 November 1948. At the beginning of 1948 the American correspondent Tillman Durdin investigated reports that the Chinese Communists were sending to Siberia large quantities of soya beans and other produce which were exchanged for captured Japanese equipment. He verified the report of an exchange of goods but could find no evidence for the supply of arms from the Soviet side (*NYT*, 2 February 1948).
[3] *Relations with China*, pp. 271–3.
[4] *NYT*, 18 May 1948.   [5] See *Relations with China*, ch. 8.

first half of 1948 increased publicity was given in the Soviet press to pronouncements from the Chinese Communist leaders. Interest extended not only to the military and diplomatic situation, but also to the organization of the 'liberated regions' under Communist control and to the administrative and economic reforms in these areas.[1] Nevertheless there was still no overt breach between the Soviet Union and the National Government. On 25 February A. Petrov was replaced as Ambassador by N. V. Roshchin. On 21 February 1948 *Pravda* referred to the fact that the Soviet-Chinese non-aggression treaty of 1937 had not been denounced within the prescribed period and was, therefore, automatically prolonged for another two years. When, in April, a member of the Foreign Affairs Committee of the National Assembly demanded that the Chinese Government should denounce the treaty of August 1945, a commentator in *Pravda* vigorously attacked this suggestion, declaring that the agreement was cherished by the Chinese as a guarantee against Japanese aggression.[2]

In the summer of 1948 the military and economic disintegration of Kuomintang China continued. There were many reports, throughout the civil war, about alleged divergences between those Chinese Communist leaders who were thought to express a more specifically pro-Soviet viewpoint and those whose outlook was more national. But most of these rumours seemed to lack any confirmation sufficient to make them worth chronicling. On the other hand, the unexpected speed of the Kuomintang's débâcle in 1948 clearly called for a revision of Soviet expectations and Communist policy. There is thus reason to accept as probably well founded a report that major decisions were taken at a conference to determine strategy for the coming campaign held in July in southern Hopei. This report suggested that the Soviet view was that the Communists should continue to wage war on a guerrilla basis, and that no all-out offensive should be undertaken. The Russians would thus secure a weakening of the United States by forcing her to continue to pour military aid into China. They argued that the 'Third

---

[1] *Pravda*, 6 and 30 January 1948; *New Times*, 24 March and 16 June 1948.

[2] *Pravda*, 25 April 1948. In April 1948 a dispute arose over the shooting down of a Chinese plane which, according to the Russians, crossed the boundary of the Port Arthur military zone and refused a demand to land. But this was an isolated incident without consequences (*Soviet Monitor*, 5 April 1948).

World War' was not imminent and that the Chinese Communists could afford a waiting game. The opposite view is said to have been expounded by Chou En-lai. He is believed to have pointed out that China was exhausted by invasion and civil war and that the Kuomintang was on the verge of collapse. The Communists should exert all their strength now that victory was within reach. He was not convinced that a new world war could be avoided. If it were to come, the Americans would use China as a battlefield and the Communists would be pushed back again into the hills. He therefore urged an immediate offensive directed towards the conquest at least of the whole of north China, and if possible of the rest of the country as well. If such a disagreement did take place, it is clear that it was Chou En-lai's strategy which was accepted; and presumably Moscow placed no obstacles in the way of its execution.[1]

American policy towards China was now uncompromisingly anti-Communist. Marshall made it clear in a dispatch to the United States Embassy in China on 12 August that the United States Government had decided not to attempt any further mediation between the Kuomintang and the Communists and would not support bringing the Communists into any coalition government that might be established.[2] Soviet suspicions were continually on the alert for signs of active American intervention. At the end of August 1948 the former President of the Executive Yuan, Chang Chun, went to Tokyo, where he spent three weeks of what was declared to be a private visit. During his stay he was received by General MacArthur and met Japanese leaders. The Soviet press interpreted this visit as an attempt to form a close military and political combination between Nationalist China, Japan, and South Korea under American auspices.[3]

The fall of Mukden to the Communists on 1 November 1948 was a military event of great importance. Hundreds of thousands of Kuomintang troops were lost, and a mass of American supplies. It meant the establishment of Communist control over all Manchuria and the probability that this would

[1] 'The Chinese Revolution', *The World Today*, June 1950; cf. Fitzgerald, *Revolution in China*, pp. 103 ff.
[2] *Relations with China*, pp. 279–80.
[3] *Pravda*, 30 August and 27 September 1948.

soon extend to north China proper. The balance between the two conflicting forces in China was decisively tilted in the Communists' favour.

The Soviet press devoted only short reports to these resounding Communist victories of the autumn, which included the capture of Changchun, Mukden, and Kalgan. And curiously little attention was paid to the increasing disintegration of the Nationalists. In his speech on the thirty-first anniversary of the Russian revolution Molotov, while referring to the general growth of the 'liberation movements' in Asia, made no specific mention of the Chinese Communist successes. This gives support to the view that the Russians were still contemplating a settlement in which the Kuomintang would be left in control of a part of the country.

In November 1948 new Chinese appeals for American military assistance were rejected, since the American military representatives in China considered that the régime could not be saved.[1] As a result of this, the pro-Russian trends in the Kuomintang got their opportunity. Some Kuomintang politicians, notably Sun Fo and Cheng Chi-tien, openly admitted that if there were to be no more large-scale American help, the Chinese Government would have to seek for other ways out of its predicament. In December Sun Fo formed a Cabinet and there were rumours of the presence within it of supporters of a compromise settlement and of mediation by the Russians. On 4 January 1949 Tass referred to rumours of such mediation, admitting that the Soviet Ambassador had been approached, but denying that he had expressed willingness to consider an official request for mediation. The Kuomintang Government, however, continued its efforts in this direction, and on 8 January its Foreign Minister officially requested the American, British, French, and Soviet Governments to act as intermediaries with a view to attempting a restoration of peace. The United States declined this request.[2] On 17 January the Soviet Deputy Minister for Foreign Affairs, Vyshinsky, handed the Russian reply to the Chinese Ambassador in Moscow. It was to the effect that the Soviet Government abode by the principle of

[1] *Relations with China*, pp. 286–8. The last American marines left China in the middle of May 1949.

[2] *Relations with China*, pp. 290–1, 922–3.

non-intervention in the internal affairs of other countries, and did not, therefore, consider it expedient to undertake the proposed mediation.[1] On 19 January *Pravda*, which three days earlier had announced, without comment, the Communist occupation of Tientsin, published the eight conditions of peace which Mao Tse-tung had made public. In subsequent issues it repeated Chinese Communist claims that Chang Kai-shek was not genuinely desirous of concluding peace, but was only seeking a breathing-space in which to reorganize his armies.

On 21 January Chiang Kai-shek resigned, and the Vice-President, General Li Tsung-jen, became acting President. Editorial comment in the Soviet press suggested that this retirement of the Chinese leader was not genuine. General Li Tsung-jen seems to have entered into some form of negotiations with the Soviet Embassy, although accounts of what took place vary. According to the American account, he informed the Americans that he had reached a tentative agreement which was to be taken to Moscow by the Soviet Ambassador. The three main points were: (*a*) strict Chinese neutrality in any future war; (*b*) the elimination of as much American influence in China as possible; and (*c*) the establishment of a 'basis of real co-operation' between China and the USSR. It is stated that Li had agreed to these conditions and had asked for a statement of United States support which would strengthen his hand in further negotiations. The Department of State immediately replied that it considered it 'incredible that Li Tsung-jen should seek a United States statement indicating support for the purpose of strengthening his position while at the same time arranging a tentative agreement with Russia calling for elimination of American influence from China.'[2] When this account was published in the American White Paper of 5 August 1949 (*Relations with China*), Li Tsung-jen's representative in Washington, Kan Chieh-hou, issued a comment in which he maintained that Li had not agreed to the Soviet conditions referred to, and would not have asked for American support had he done so.[3]

There is as usual no evidence from the Soviet side about these discussions. But even after the capture of Peking by the Communists on 31 January 1949, the Soviet Government continued

---

[1] *Soviet News*, 19 January 1949.   [2] *Relations with China*, p. 293.
[3] *NYT*, 24 August 1949.

to maintain diplomatic relations with the Chinese National Government, and was, in fact, the only Government to send its Ambassador to Canton after the Chinese Government had been forced to retire there. Simultaneously it ostensibly closed its consulates in the Communist-occupied centres, though the staffs remained at work. It even seems to have continued negotiations with the National Government on economic matters, notably with regard to Sinkiang.[1] It is difficult to assess how far a desire to secure an agreement on these matters may have influenced this continued recognition. It may be simply that Soviet policy took time to adjust itself to the new situation which the Communist victories were bringing about. On the other hand it may be that the Soviet Government was even now not convinced that the victories of the Communists in north China could immediately be repeated in the south, and that they still looked forward to drawing a South China Nationalist Government into some form of pro-Russian alignment.

[1] *NCDN*, 23 March 1949; and see the section on Sinkiang, pp. 97–101, below.

IV

The Soviet Union and China
1949–51

THE ESTABLISHMENT OF THE CHINESE PEOPLE'S REPUBLIC

IN April 1949 the official public attitude of the Soviet Union towards the Chinese Communist forces underwent a radical alteration. On 10 April *Pravda* published a Chinese Communist declaration, promising support for the Soviet Union in the event of a world war. On 25 April, five days after the Communist forces crossed the Yangtse, *Pravda* talked of the 'liberation of Nanking' as having put an end to the 'reactionary rule of the Kuomintang', and said that the Kuomintang Government had now ceased to exist. Li Tsung-jen was referred to as the 'so-called Acting President'. From this time references to the 'New China' in the Russian press and in periodical literature became frequent.[1]

Nevertheless, throughout May the Russians maintained diplomatic relations with the Kuomintang, and continued the earlier negotiations about Sinkiang. Finally, the existing aviation agreement was renewed for five years, but the other Soviet demands were refused.[2] The Soviet Ambassador, Roshchin, then returned to Moscow for consultations.[3] He did not return to the Kuomintang capital. It appears that some time during the summer the Soviet consulates in the Communist-occupied territories were reopened; and the Soviet Union was able to use them for establishing diplomatic relations with the Central People's Government after the establishment and proclamation of the new Government of the Chinese People's Republic on 30 September 1949.[4]

Even before this event the Chinese Communist Party had begun to participate again in the activities of the international

---

[1] See e.g. *Oktiabr* from the April number onwards; *Voprosy Istorii*, May 1949; *Bolshevik*, 15 July 1949.

[2] See section on Sinkiang, pp. 97–101 below.

[3] *NCDN*, 31 May 1941. [4] *Soviet Monitor*, 1 October 1949.

Communist movement. This participation could be supervised by Moscow, since all the Chinese delegates to conferences abroad had to travel by land across the Soviet Union. The Chinese Communist Party was represented at the Trade Union Conferences in Moscow in April, and in Warsaw in May–June 1949.[1] In April it was represented by a large delegation at the World Peace Congress in Prague. The Chinese spokesman described the recent Communist victories as an historic event, ranking with the October Revolution and the defeat of Germany and Japan. He assured the Congress that the Chinese Communist Party condemned the defection of Tito from the Cominform and emphasized that it had done this a year earlier. Another delegation appointed to the Congress of the World Federation of Trade Unions, held in Milan in July, was refused entry into Italy; but its report was published in *Pravda*, and a Chinese was elected as one of the vice-chairmen of the Federation's Executive Committee.[2] Possibly in order to demonstrate that there was no foundation for rumours of any form of deviation in the case of the Chinese Communist leaders, the Soviet press began to publish the statements of prominent Chinese Communists, emphasizing their doctrinal orthodoxy.[3] Although Mao himself still made the customary declarations about the willingness of the Chinese people to co-operate with all countries for the establishment of international economic relations, this offer of co-operation was not to be taken as meaning that the Chinese Communists were neutral in the great division in world politics. In an article for the twenty-eighth anniversary of the founding of the Chinese Communist Party, Mao declared:

Unity in the common struggle with the countries of the world which regard us as an equal nation, and with the peoples of all countries! This means alliance with the USSR and with the People's Democracies in Europe and alliance with the proletariat and the masses of the people of the other countries to form an international united front. We are told: 'You incline toward one side'. This is precisely what forty years' experience of Sun Yat-sen and the twenty-eight years' experience of the Communist Party has firmly convinced us of: that in order to achieve and consolidate victory we must follow one side . . . the Chinese people must either side with

[1] *Izvestia*, 19 April, 4 June 1949.
[2] *Pravda*, 15 July 1949.
[3] ibid. 7 and 9 June 1949; *For a Lasting Peace*, 1 June, 1 and 15 July 1949.

imperialism or with Socialism. There can be no question of remaining between them, there is no third path. . . . Internationally we belong to the anti-imperialist front headed by the Soviet Union, and for genuine friendly aid we must look to this front and not to the imperialist front.[1]

It was childish reasoning to claim that China needed American and British aid. The motives for supplying it on the part of the Western Governments would not be mutual benefits but capitalist exploitation.

Apart from the ideological alignment the position of the Chinese Communists was such as to make external support very desirable since the Nationalists were blockading the coast. The publication of the American White Paper, *Relations with China*, on 5 August suggested that they might have to reckon with American hostility as well. For the letter of transmittal stated: 'the Communist leaders have forsworn their Chinese heritage and have publicly announced their subservience to a foreign power.'[2] Soviet comment on the White Paper was that it failed to disguise the breakdown of the policy of the United States towards China, the large scale of American intervention, and the fact that the United States was the driving force behind the Kuomintang.[3] The Chinese Communist press made a special attack on the reference to Chinese 'liberals' whom the White Paper hoped would exert a restraining influence on China's relations with Soviet Russia.[4]

The final moves towards establishing the Communist régime in China as a fully fledged Government were taken by the Chinese People's Political Consultative Conference which met at Peking on 21 September 1949. On 29 September it adopted a common programme, and on 30 September, before adjourning, it confirmed the 'basic law' of the Central People's Government, and elected the members of this body. In his declaration on 1 October announcing this event, Mao Tse-tung stated that the Chinese People's Government had decided to inform all foreign Governments that the Government of the Chinese People's Republic was the only legal Government of China and

---

[1] *For a Lasting Peace*, 15 July 1949.   [2] *Relations with China*, p. xvi.
[3] Zaslavsky, 'How Mr. Acheson Gave Himself a Flogging', *Pravda*, 11 August 1949.
[4] *NYT*, 25 August 1949.

that it was prepared to enter into diplomatic relations with any foreign country which was prepared to agree to the principles of equality, reciprocal benefits, and mutual respect for territorial integrity and sovereignty.

This proclamation was handed to the Soviet Consul-General in Peking on the same day, with an accompanying note from Chou En-lai, the Foreign Minister of the new Government, stating that it was essential to establish normal diplomatic relations between the Chinese People's Republic and other countries.[1] On 3 October *Pravda* announced the Soviet decision of 2 October to establish diplomatic relations with the CPR, and to withdraw recognition from the Kuomintang Government. On 5 October the Soviet press reported that diplomatic relations had been established between the Chinese People's Republic and Poland, Czechoslovakia, North Korea, and Rumania. Other countries in the Soviet bloc announced similar intentions. On 10 October Roshchin, the previous Ambassador to the Kuomintang Government, was received by Mao Tse-tung, and on 30 October the first Chinese Communist Ambassador to Moscow presented his credentials.

The international importance of this series of events was stressed in the Soviet press. The Tadjik poet Mirzo Tursun-Zade wrote:

The struggle for independence and national sovereignty, for the reorganization of the world, has begun to burn brightly over the whole East. . . . Now in the East there is not a single country where the banner of struggle does not gleam red and where the toilers are not inspired by the example of the peoples of the Soviet Union.[2]

Millions of people, it was asserted, would now be drawn into the movement for peace.[3] India, Indonesia, Viet Nam, and Burma were among the countries whose peoples would find inspiration in the Soviet achievement.[4]

Such statements became common in Soviet speeches and writings. Reference was frequently made to Lenin's dictum that the outcome of the conflict between capitalism and

[1] *Izvestia*, 2 October 1949.   [2] ibid.
[3] Kovalev, 'A Great Historic Victory of the Chinese People', *Bolshevik*, 15 October 1949. For the 'world peace movement' and its propaganda culminating in the 'Stockholm Peace Appeal', see Donald H. McLachlan, 'The Partisans of Peace', *International Affairs*, January 1951.
[4] *For a Lasting Peace*, 7 October, 1949.

Communism would in the long run be settled by the fact that the overwhelming majority of mankind lived in Russia, India, China, &c.[1] The prediction made by Stalin in 1925 about the future strength of China's revolutionary elements was also often quoted.[2] It was declared that despite the large sums spent by the Americans on aid to the Kuomintang, their plans to use China as the main base for their domination of Asia and the Pacific had been defeated.[3] In the slogans published for the anniversary of the Russian revolution, one was devoted in 1949 to China: 'Fraternal greetings to the great Chinese people, who have won the freedom and independence of their country, and created a State of the People's Democracy. Long live the People's Republic of China.'[4]

On the Chinese side Liu Shao-chi published an article on the 'Inviolable Friendship of the Chinese and the Soviet Peoples', which directly refuted rumours of a 'Titoist' defection of the Chinese Communists.[5] At the same time the Chinese Nationalists published other rumours to the effect that in secret agreements the Chinese Communists had granted vast concessions to the Russians.[6] The report of these alleged agreements was described by the Chinese Communists and the Russians as pure fabrication.[7]

Other unconfirmed reports took up a theme which had been intermittent in Kuomintang propaganda since 1945, namely that the Soviet Union were attempting to set up a puppet régime in Manchuria, irrespective of the form to be taken by the Chinese Central Government. At the end of July 1949 Moscow papers reported the arrival of a trade delegation of the 'Manchurian people's democratic authorities' under the leadership

[1] Lenin, 'Better fewer but Better', *Pravda*, 4 March 1923, trans. in V. I. Lenin, *Selected Works* (London, 1947), ii. 854.

[2] Report to the Fourteenth Party Congress, 18 December 1925, in J. Degras, ed., *Soviet Documents on Foreign Policy* (Oxford University Press for RIIA, 1951-), ii. 74-75.

[3] Malenkov's speech on the 32nd anniversary of the Russian revolution (*For a Lasting Peace*, 11 November 1949). The sum spent by the Americans was usually given by the Russians as 6,000 million and this was specified in detail by G. Astafyev, 'Chinese Economic Problems', *New Times*, 5 April 1950.

[4] *Soviet News*, 3 November 1949.

[5] *For a Lasting Peace*, 21 October 1949.

[6] The texts of two pacts allegedly concluded between them are printed in *China Handbook, 1950*, pp. 278-9.

[7] *Pravda*, 1 February 1950; *NCNA*, 7 February 1950.

of Kao Kang. This delegation concluded a one-year trade agreement by which the Manchurians were to deliver soya beans, vegetables, fats, maize, rice, and other products in exchange for industrial equipment, motor vehicles, petrol, textiles, paper, and drugs. No mention of prices or quantities was made in the announcement.[1] While it is difficult to define the exact status of these Manchurian authorities, the agreement was welcomed by the official news agency of the Chinese Communists.[2] In August a body styling itself the 'People's Congress of the North-East Provinces of China' met at Mukden. In a speech to the Congress, Kao Kang, the secretary of the North-East Bureau of the Central Committee of the Chinese Communist Party, who now became chairman of the People's Government for the North-East (i.e. Manchuria), said:

In order to carry out these historic tasks and speed up reconstruction, it is necessary seriously to study the experience of the Soviet people in their struggle against the imperialists' blockade following the Great October Socialist Revolution as well as their experience in economic construction, the development of technique and administrative methods.[3]

THE SINO-SOVIET NEGOTIATIONS

DECEMBER 1949 TO FEBRUARY 1950

On 16 December 1949 a Chinese delegation, headed by Mao Tse-tung himself, arrived in Moscow. The importance attached to the subsequent negotiations can be judged from the fact that they were, it seems, conducted personally by Stalin. The first meeting between Mao and Stalin took place on the day of Mao's arrival.[4] In an interview on 2 January 1950 Mao stated that the main object of his visit was to negotiate 'on the existing treaty of friendship and alliance between China and the Soviet Union, the question of Soviet credits for the People's Republic of China, the question of trade and a trade agreement between our countries, and other questions.' He added that the visit would last for several weeks.[5] The course of these negotiations naturally remained secret, but on 12 January the American

[1] *Pravda* and *Izvestia*, 3 July 1949.
[2] *NCDN*, 2 August; *NYT*, 4 August 1949.
[3] *NCDN*, 28 August; *Soviet Monitor*, 30 August 1949.
[4] *Soviet News*, 19 December 1949.   [5] *Soviet Monitor*, 2 January 1950.

Secretary of State, Acheson, made a speech in which he claimed that certain fundamental developments were taking place in China:

The Soviet Union is detaching the northern provinces [areas] of China from China and is attaching them to the Soviet Union. This process is complete in Outer Mongolia. It is nearly complete in Manchuria and I am sure that in Inner Mongolia and in Sinkiang there are very happy reports coming from Soviet agents to Moscow. . . . I should like to suggest at any rate that this fact that the Soviet Union is taking the four northern provinces of China is the single most significant, most important fact in the relations of any foreign Power with Asia. . . .[1]

Acheson's accusations were commented on by Angus Ward, the American Consul at Mukden who had stayed in Manchuria with his staff up to the end of 1949 in a state of virtual imprisonment in Communist hands. He stated that he presumed that they referred to the economic detachment of the provinces rather than their political integration into the Soviet Union. He said that the Soviet Government would use the same techniques that it had perfected in Eastern Europe and that no direct political partition would be needed to accomplish its objective, which was the same imperialist expansion towards ice-free ports that had occupied Russian dreams in the past two generations. In addition, Soviet East Asia urgently needed the economic support of Manchuria's rich supplies, to avoid the long haul from the west through some of the world's frostiest country.[2]

In an article published a month later, Ward again stressed the economic importance to the Soviet Union of having a friendly Government in Manchuria. But he now went so far as to state that such a friendly régime could only mean the 'economic if not territorial assimilation of Manchuria in the Soviet Union'.[3] It is not clear to what extent this revision of his views was due to more information about Soviet intentions having come to light.

Vyshinsky made a statement about Acheson's claims which was published on 20 January 1950. He denied that the Soviet Union contemplated any infringement of China's territorial

[1] *Department of State Bulletin*, 23 January 1950.
[2] *NYT*, 15 January 1950.
[3] *The American Journal for Foreign Service*, 26 February 1950.

integrity or sovereignty, and denounced the American Secretary of State for his 'mendacious and crudely slanderous' statement. In particular he denied that Outer Mongolia had been incorporated into the Soviet Union and stated that its existence as an independent State had been specifically recognized in the Yalta Agreement and by Chiang Kai-shek in 1945. As for the remaining territories concerned, he said: 'It is common knowledge and normal people cannot doubt that Manchuria, Inner Mongolia and Sinkiang remain within the territory of China, constituting a component part of it.'[1] Acheson's charges were reiterated on 26 January and the State Department published what was called 'background material' for them. In this document, the situation in Manchuria was summarized as follows:

Manchuria is currently ruled by a Sino-Soviet partnership with the strongest partner in the dominant position. The USSR is utilizing the 1945 Sino-Soviet Treaty to penetrate and extend its economic and strategic domination. Soviet troops occupy Dairen and the Port Arthur Naval base area; Soviet control of the railroads there has reportedly gone much further than was contemplated in the 1945 Treaty, both as regards the railroads themselves and collateral interests.

Soviet influence in the native military forces in Manchuria is generally recognized; Chinese Communists have openly admitted this Soviet participation. Soviet participation in the Manchurian secret police has also been reported.

The USSR has obtained special navigation and fishing rights in Manchuria; operates the only civil air service in Manchuria; controls and operates industrial facilities in Dairen, Harbin and Chia Mussu [Kiamusze]; controls the power transmission from the Yalu hydroelectric plant; controls and operates several coal and gold mines.

The Sha Ho Kon Vehicle Manufacturing Works, the Dairen Shipbuilding Yard and the Dairen Sugar Works are all under Soviet military control. Munitions factories in the area are also reportedly being operated by the USSR. The Soviet Union has placed the richest industrial area of China firmly behind the Far Eastern segment of the Iron Curtain.[2]

The Department of State also alleged that the trade pact of July 1949 between the Soviet Government and the local authorities in Manchuria, under the terms of which agricultural products, amounting reportedly to 60 per cent. of each farmer's

[1] *Soviet News*, 23 January 1950.   [2] *NYT*, 26 January 1950.

produce, were exported to the Soviet Union, was causing severe local shortages and had been concluded without regard to the conditions of famine prevailing in parts of China. In return, Manchuria was receiving, for the most part, industrial equipment and machinery which the Russians themselves had removed from there. Acheson himself said that in addition to this trade agreement there were reported to be two secret agreements between the Soviet Union and the Chinese Communists.[1]

Meanwhile on 21 January Chou En-lai had arrived in Moscow to join in the negotiations. He was accompanied by Li Fi-chun, the deputy Chairman of the Manchurian Government, its deputy Minister of the Department of Industry and Trade, and a delegation from Sinkiang. After two months of negotiations in all, three agreements were finally signed on 14 February and published in the Soviet press on the following day.[2]

The new agreements were based on those concluded in 1945 with Chiang Kai-shek but included some important innovations. The first of them was a 'treaty of friendship, alliance, and mutual assistance'. The title indicated the closer ties now existing between the two countries, since the 1945 treaty had been one only of 'friendship and alliance' with no mention of mutual assistance. In 1945 the object of the treaty had been stated as co-operation in the war against Japan until that country's unconditional surrender. In 1950 the object was to prevent a 'repetition of aggression and violation of peace on the part of Japan or any other State which should unite in any form with Japan in acts of aggression.' Its new wording corresponds closely to that of the treaties concluded by the Soviet Union with the countries of Eastern Europe, and was clearly directed against the United States.

While in 1945 both parties pledged themselves not to conclude a separate peace, in 1950 they undertook 'by means of mutual agreement to strive for the earliest conclusion of a peace treaty with Japan, jointly with the other Powers which were allies during the Second World War.'[3] The 1945 and 1950 treaties are similar in pledging the two parties not to conclude an alliance or take part in any coalition directed against the

---

[1] ibid.
[2] Texts in Appendix below, p. 260 ff.   [3] Art. 2.

other party, but whereas the relevant article of the 1945 treaty mentioned only the common interests of the two countries in defence and economic matters, the corresponding article in 1950 mentioned cultural ties as well. Co-operation was to take place 'in conformity with the principles of equality, mutual interests, and also mutual respect for the State sovereignty and territorial integrity and non-interference in internal affairs.' The only change here is the word State added before sovereignty and it does not seem to have any special significance; but there is a new provision for consultation on 'all important international problems affecting the common interests of the Soviet Union and China.'[1] There could in the new treaty be no reference to the United Nations organization, since Communist China was only just beginning to press her claim to membership in that body.

Both treaties were concluded for thirty years. The 1945 treaty was to remain in force indefinitely thereafter unless denounced, while the 1950 treaty, unless denounced, was to be extended by further five-year periods.

The second agreement dealt with the Chinese Changchun Railway, Port Arthur, and Dairen. The basic principle of the new agreement was the Soviet renunciation of all rights in Manchuria except in Dairen, but the changes envisaged were not to be implemented immediately but only on the conclusion of the peace treaty with Japan, or not later than the end of 1952. In view of the differences between the Great Powers, it seemed fairly clear that the end of 1952 would, in fact, be the crucial date. On the face of it the changes were all to China's advantage; the railway was to be transferred gratis together with all the property belonging to it, and in the interim period the leading posts in its administration were to be filled alternately by representatives of the two sides.[2]

Regarding Port Arthur, the treaty provided for the withdrawal of Russian troops at the expiry of the stated period but also that, on the proposal of the Chinese People's Republic and with the agreement of the Soviet Union, the port could be used again as a joint naval base in the event of either country being

[1] Art. 4.
[2] The railway was formally handed over to China on 31 December 1952 (*The Times*, 1 January 1953).

attacked by Japan, or any State acting in co-operation with Japan. In the interim period the civil administration was to be in the hands of the Chinese Government. Military affairs were to be run by a joint military commission composed of an equal number of members from the two sides, which within three months was to make proposals on the subject for the approval of the two Governments. There was no mention of the military commission set up under the 1945 treaty, upon which the Soviet Union was supposed to have a three to two majority.[1]

The future of Dairen was left to be decided after the conclusion of the peace treaty or the end of 1952. But the Chinese were to receive by the end of 1950 the property provisionally in charge of or under lease to the Soviet Union.

Under the third agreement the Soviet Union was to extend credits to the Chinese People's Republic, to be used for paying for deliveries of equipment and material which the Soviet Union was to supply for the 'restoration and development of the national economy of China'. This credit was fixed at $300 million spread over five years from 1 January 1950. Details as to quantities, prices, and dates of delivery of the equipment and material to be supplied by the Russians were left for later discussion. The agreement provided that the Chinese should pay interest on the loan at the rate of 1 per cent. per annum and that it should be repaid by deliveries of raw materials, tea, gold, and American dollars over a ten-year period, beginning with the end of 1954. This financial arrangement was the least gratifying of the concessions to China, since the sum was very small by comparison, for instance, with the loan of $450 million obtained by Poland from the Soviet Union a year earlier.[2] No mention was made, it will be seen, of many of the subjects upon which it was believed that differences between the Soviet Union and China remained unresolved. Those who believed that the Soviet Union was seeking for a special status for Manchuria were fortified in their views by the fact that the Vice-Chairman of the Manchurian Provincial Government was

[1] By an exchange of notes dated 15 September 1952, the treaty was amended to provide for the retention of Soviet troops in Port Arthur until peace treaties had been concluded between the Soviet Union and Japan, and between the Chinese People's Republic and Japan. (*The Times*, 22 September 1952.)

[2] Its value was diminished by about one-fifth through the revaluation of the rouble on 28 February.

given precedence over the Chinese Ambassador at the concluding banquet, and that he remained in Moscow after the departure of the main party. In the subsequent period there were
numerous reports that the Manchurian Administration and
economy were still kept apart from those of the Chinese People's
Republic proper; Manchuria certainly retained its special currency. On the other hand the dominant personality in Manchuria was Kao Kang, Chairman of the North-Eastern Government and Vice-Chairman of the Central Government and of
the People's Revolutionary Military Council. But quite apart
from these rumours and speculations, it was clear that by post-
poning the implementation of so many of the clauses of the
agreements for nearly two more years the Soviet Union put
itself in a position of being able to see first what policy Mao and
his Government would in fact adopt.

The Sinkiang delegation also remained in Moscow after the
conclusion of the talks, and its visit culminated in the economic
agreements of 27 March 1950.[1]

Needless to say, the Soviet press hailed the treaty with China
as a further proof of the Soviet Union's love of peace and regard
for the independence of other nations. It was pointed out that
the agreements were particularly necessary at a time when the
Americans were converting Formosa into a strategic base against
the new China, and when Japanese reactionaries, under American protection, were openly proclaiming their intention of
seeking revenge.

Molotov commented on the treaty in the course of a speech
to his Moscow constituents:

A lasting anti-imperialist alliance was formed between the Soviet
and Chinese peoples, between the two largest States on earth—the
camp of peace, democracy and socialism has become a most for-
midable force. . . . The treaty of fraternal alliance between the
USSR and the People's Republic of China transformed Soviet-
Chinese friendship into a mighty force for consolidating universal
peace such as has no equal and never had an equal in human history.
. . . After the October revolution in our country, the victory of the
people's liberation movement in China is another tremendous blow
against the whole system of world imperialism and all the plans of
imperialist aggression.[2]

[1] See the section on Sinkiang, pp. 97–101 below.
[2] *Pravda*, 11 March; *Soviet News*, 13 March 1950.

Mao's comments on his visit at his send-off from Moscow had been no less enthusiastic. What he had seen had confirmed the conviction that the Chinese Communists had always had, that the Soviet Union's experiences in economic and cultural construction and in other spheres would serve as an example for the construction of the new China.[1]

The treaty was ratified on 11 April and the instruments of ratification were exchanged on 30 September 1950.[2] This was followed by a declaration that the 1945 agreements were invalid and by the recognition of the independent status of the Mongolian People's Republic.[3]

A short-term trade agreement had been concluded in March 1950. By its terms China was to provide soya beans, tobacco, wolfram, and fats in exchange for textiles, metal products, technical equipment, and chemicals. Other articles mentioned as likely to be exported to the Soviet Union were tin, rice, and tea.[4] There were also rumours that China was to act as an intermediary for the rubber required by the Soviet Union. Before the Chinese delegation left Moscow on 19 April, a trade treaty was signed together with an agreement on the turnover of goods for the year 1950. Under the latter agreement the Soviet Union was to supply manufactured goods and China raw materials. The Chinese also signed an agreement for the supply of manufactures and other goods for the period 1950–2 under the terms of the credit agreement of 14 February.[5]

A new Sino-Soviet Company for the Changchun Railway was formally inaugurated on 25 April. Although the Russians had been supplying the technicians for the railway throughout, they had, it seems, not participated in its management since their evacuation in 1946. Despite the provision now made for filling the chief posts, it appeared that, as in the other joint enterprises, the General Manager was in fact to be a Russian.[6] The agreement provided for the transfer to China of property in Soviet hands in Dairen, and also of property acquired by Soviet State organizations from Japanese owners in Manchuria, and buildings of the previous military establishments in Peking. These

[1] *The Times*, 20 February 1950.   [2] *Pravda*, 8 October 1950.
[3] *Vedomosti Verkhnogo Soveta* (Gazette of the Supreme Soviet), 16 November 1950.
[4] *CSM*, 27 March 1950.
[5] *Soviet Monitor*, 21 April 1950.   [6] ibid. 28 April 1950.

matters were to be dealt with by mixed commissions during 1950. A list of the property transferred to the Chinese by them was published in *Pravda* on 10 February 1951.[1] It is unlikely that this list covered the total property that the Russians had acquired, and it must therefore be presumed that in some form or other a considerable share in the running of the Manchurian economy was still retained by the USSR after this date.

SOVIET RELATIONS WITH OTHER POWERS ARISING OUT OF EVENTS IN CHINA

Soviet propaganda was, as has been seen, directed at demonstrating the aggressiveness of American policy in China, and contrasting with it the disinterested friendliness of the Soviet Union towards the Chinese people.[2] Reports were published of alleged new military agreements with Chiang Kai-shek,[3] and of alleged American espionage.[4]

It was made clear that the Soviet Union would support the Chinese People's Republic in its efforts to establish its rule over Hainan island[5] and Formosa, which had become the last stronghold of the Chinese Nationalists. It was stressed that the return of Formosa to the Japanese, or the continuation of American occupation and a refusal to hand over the island to China would be contrary to the inter-Allied agreements, notably the Cairo and the Potsdam Declarations.[6]

Despite President Truman's statement on 5 January 1950 that the United States had no intention of establishing bases on Formosa or of providing military aid to the Chinese Nationalist Government, the question of Formosa was linked in Russian propaganda with the alleged plans for an American-inspired anti-Communist bloc in the Far East. The Russians regarded with misgiving any efforts at co-ordination between the Asiatic

[1] The list referred to the various buildings comprising the former military cantonment at Peking; to port installations and equipment, and to various factories and power installations at Dairen, as well as a number of dwelling houses and buildings used for cultural purposes; and finally to twenty-one installations in Manchuria, mainly mills and processing plants, as well as dwelling houses and cinemas.

[2] See e.g. an article by Y. Yavorov, *Pravda*, 8 January 1950.

[3] *Pravda* and *Izvestia*, 5 and 6 January 1950.

[4] *Izvestia*, 15 October; *Pravda*, 17 and 22 October 1950.

[5] Hainan fell to the Communists in April 1950.

[6] *Izvestia*, 12 February 1949; *New Times*, 18 January 1950.

countries that were not on a Communist basis, as for instance the New Delhi Conference on Indonesia. Visits in 1949 by Chiang Kai-shek to the Philippines, and by President Quirino to the United States were also commented on unfavourably.[1]

The outbreak of the Korean war on 25 June 1950 and President Truman's order on 27 June to the American Seventh Fleet to protect Formosa against Communist invasion, produced renewed Soviet comment on the dangers presented by the Nationalist forces in that island, in spite of the fact that Truman simultaneously appealed to the Kuomintang forces to refrain from further attacks on the Chinese mainland.[2] The Soviet press printed reports on MacArthur's visit to Formosa and on the arrival there of American arms.[3] Although the Russians noted uneasiness among some Americans and in British circles over certain of MacArthur's actions, they gave no intimation, either at this point or later, that there might be any serious differences of opinion in the United States or Britain as to the policy to be pursued in the Korean war. In fact the conviction that MacArthur was the true spokesman for the intentions of the United States Government found expression even in the comments on his dismissal in April 1951. It is an interesting illustration of the rigidity of Soviet diplomacy and propaganda that no serious effort was made to profit by the obvious differences between the British and the American approach to events in the Far East.

The Russians did their best to convince the Chinese that they had no other friends in the world. If Britain and some other States associated with her had in fact recognized the Chinese People's Republic this was no indication, they argued, of a real desire for friendship with the Chinese people, and was primarily due to the antagonism between British and American capitalists.[4] Britain's real policy was to support the United States in keeping the Chinese People's Republic outside the United Nations.[5] The Soviet press also made the most of minor

[1] *Pravda*, 17 July; *Pravda* and *Izvestia*, 9 and 10 August; *Izvestia*, 16 August 1949.
[2] *Pravda* and *Izvestia*, 30 June 1950.
[3] *Pravda*, 1 August; *Izvestia*, 8 August 1950.
[4] E. Zhukov, 'Historical Significance of the Victory of the Chinese People', *New Times*, 18 June 1950.
[5] Avarin, 'International Significance of the Victory of the Chinese People', ibid. 27 September 1950.

incidents involving Anglo-Chinese friction, for instance some alleged 'arbitrary acts' by the British authorities at Hong Kong.[1]

The question of direct Soviet military assistance for the Chinese People's Republic was still obscure. On 20 March 1950 the Chinese Nationalists announced that their planes had encountered over Shanghai fighter aircraft of types previously not met with,[2] and this announcement was followed by a series of reports that Soviet-type aircraft were now being used by the Communists.[3] On 10 April the Kuomintang delegate to the United Nations complained to the Secretary-General that the Soviet Union had sent to China 'a large number of military aircraft and personnel, including pilots and ground technicians.'[4] Reports of the use of jet aircraft over Shanghai were confirmed by some though not all of the foreign residents evacuated from the city.[5] There is, however, no reliable evidence to support the reiterated claims of the Chinese Nationalists that the Russians had plans for equipping a Communist army for the invasion of Formosa, until frustrated by President Truman's order to the Seventh Fleet.

The Soviet Union, from 1949 when the matter was first mentioned, fully supported the Chinese contention that Tibet was an integral part of the Chinese State, and disputed the claims made in some British circles that Tibet was an independent country. They adduced the argument that the Dalai Lama had become a vassal of Peking in 1652. They claimed that these Chinese rights had not been renounced in the 1914 treaty with Great Britain since, although a Chinese representative had initialed the treaty, it had not subsequently been accepted by the Chinese Government itself.[6] The Soviet press quoted with approval hostile Peking comments on the proposed goodwill mission from Tibet to the United States, Britain, Nepal, and China. What the Tibetans really wanted, it was said, was to enter the great democratic family of China, and a mission to negotiate on these lines would alone be welcome.[7]

When the Chinese Government decided to invade Tibet,

[1] *Pravda*, 26 August, 4 November 1950.   [2] *NYT*, 21 March 1950.
[3] ibid. 27 March; 1, 4, 6, and 9 April 1950.
[4] ibid. 11 April 1950.   [5] ibid. 21 April and 4 May 1950.
[6] 'Sir Basil Gould's Latest Researches', *New Times*, 1 February 1950.
[7] *Pravda* and *Izvestia*, 22 January 1950.

the Soviet press published the order to the Chinese army and the early stages of the campaign were covered by special correspondents and were widely publicized.

THE CHINESE COMMUNISTS AND THE UNITED NATIONS

In the American plans for the post-war world, a non-Communist China had been given an important role. The Kuomintang Government was, therefore, represented in all the international institutions that were set up. The emergence of the Chinese People's Government as the effective Government of the Chinese mainland raised a delicate problem in connexion with China's representation in all these bodies.

In the autumn of 1949 the Kuomintang Government formally raised the issue of what it called the threats to the independence of China, resulting from the Soviet violations of the treaty of August 1945. In spite of Soviet opposition the matter was allowed to come before the First (Political) Committee of the General Assembly on 29 November 1949. Vyshinsky stated that the Soviet delegation supported the point of view expressed in a note from the Chinese People's Republic, namely that the Kuomintang delegation headed by Mr. Tsiang had no right to represent the people and Government of China, and unsuccessfully demanded its withdrawal.[1] When the Political Committee refused to accept the resolution put forward by the Kuomintang delegation and accepted a much milder one, the Soviet press commented that despite the slanderous attacks that had been made on the Soviet Union, even the American clique did not dare to support entirely unsubstantiated charges.[2] On 8 December the General Assembly adopted a resolution which referred the matter for further study to its Interim Committee, the so-called 'Little Assembly'. The Soviet representative, however, had announced on the previous day that the Soviet Union would not participate in any discussions held on the complaint of the Kuomintang delegation, or be bound by any decisions taken.[3] In support of the claim of the Chinese

[1] General Assembly, 4th Session, First Committee, 29 September–6 December 1949, p. 339. Chou En-lai's note to the Secretary-General and the President of the General Assembly had been sent on 15 November.

[2] *Pravda*, 5 December 1949.

[3] General Assembly, 4th Session, Plenary Meetings, 20 September–10 December 1949, p. 565.

People's Republic to be represented, the Soviet delegate to the Security Council announced that he would not participate in its work until the Kuomintang representative had been removed, and withdrew from the sessions of 10 and 13 January 1950. Subsequently, Soviet delegates withdrew from the various bodies of the United Nations in the proceedings of which Kuomintang delegates participated.

On 8 March the Secretary-General, Trygve Lie, proposed a formula for breaking this deadlock, namely that the organs of the United Nations should recognize the Government which exercised 'effective authority' over the country and was 'habitually obeyed by the bulk of the population', without prejudice to the question of its diplomatic recognition by other States. This was supported by the Russians, and there is some reason to believe that American opinion was moving towards a less intransigent attitude on this point than it had shown in the previous discussions.

A further move was made during Lie's visit to Moscow in May 1950. He there made contact with a representative of the Chinese People's Government, and asked him whether his Government would discharge the international obligations contracted by the Chinese Nationalist Government, and whether it would modify its anti-Western attitude.[1] There now appeared a possibility of a solution of the problem of Chinese representation, since many people in the West began to admit that in the long run the continued exclusion of the *de facto* Chinese Government was impossible. The opinion was sometimes expressed that the inclusion of Communist China in the United Nations would in fact lessen her dependence upon the Soviet Union. Some observers even believed that the Soviet Union actually hoped that the exclusion of Communist China would be maintained.[2]

The attitude of the Western Powers towards this question was altered by the outbreak of the Korean war. The expected British support for the admission of Communist China to the United Nations did not materialize, and American opposition to it hardened. Despite these facts, the United Nations action in

[1] *NYT*, 17 May 1950.
[2] Jean Chauvel, principal French delegate to the United Nations, quoted in *Manchester Guardian*, 13 June 1950.

Korea caused the Soviet Union to revise its opinion as to the desirability of absence from its meetings.

On 27 July Malik informed the Secretary-General that 'in accordance with established procedure' (i.e. the monthly rotation in the presidency of the Security Council) he would assume the presidency in August, and on 1 August the Soviet delegation duly returned. As President, Malik proposed the following agenda: (1) the recognition of the Peking delegate as the representative of China; (2) the peaceful settlement of the Korean question.[1] Since the United States would not agree to the admission of China while the Korean issue was undecided, the putting of the proposals in this order was an effective bar to either of them being considered.

Complaints from the Chinese Communists continued to reach the United Nations: on 24 August against the presence of Americans in Formosa, on 31 August against alleged violations of the Manchurian border by United States aircraft. The Soviet proposal that a Peking representative should be admitted to the Council to support his Government's case was not accepted. In September the Soviet Union itself lodged a complaint of American 'aggression' against Formosa.[2]

After this date, the question of admitting Communist China to the United Nations became so much bound up with the general diplomacy of the Korean war that it would be artificial to discuss it separately at this point. The Chinese Communists were excluded from the subordinate organs of the United Nations as well.[3]

THE CHINESE PEOPLE'S REPUBLIC AND INTERNATIONAL COMMUNISM

The role which the Chinese People's Republic might play in the further spread of Communism was obviously an important one, but its exact nature was not at first evident and Soviet comment was guarded. It is likely that, despite the use of the

---

[1] Security Council, 480th meeting, 1 August 1950.

[2] *Pravda*, 27 August, 1, 12, and 30 September 1950.

[3] In the Universal Postal Union, the delegate of the Chinese People's Republic was admitted when the Executive Committee met in May 1950. But early in 1951 the Americans endeavoured to get this decision reversed. Despite Soviet protests Communist China was not invited to the Executive Committee's meeting in May 1951.

term 'People's Democracy' to describe the new régime, China was not regarded as having reached the stage on the road to Communism represented by the People's Democracies of Eastern Europe, let alone the Soviet Union.[1] In October 1949 the Chinese situation was described in *Bolshevik* as that of 'an anti-imperialist régime, also anti-feudal and anti-bureaucratic, transitional to a non-capitalist or more accurately to a socialist development of the country'.[2] Although Soviet leaders, for instance Marshal Voroshilov in his speech at Minsk on 7 March 1950, referred to the importance of Russia's friendly neighbours in the Far East, the Chinese were still not treated as an integral part of the world Communist movement, though the tendency was in that direction, and there was certainly no idea expressed of an evolution in any direction other than that prescribed by Soviet orthodoxy.

No question of admitting China to the Cominform seems to have arisen, although the journal of that organization (*For a Lasting Peace, For a People's Democracy*) gave considerable space to Chinese developments. Instead it was made evident that the proper channel for organizing Asiatic Communism was the World Federation of Trade Unions. On 11 August 1949 the WFTU announced that a Trade Union Conference of the countries of Asia and Australasia would take place in Peking on 16 November. It was attended by 117 delegates representing thirteen countries: the Soviet Union, China, Mongolia, Korea, India, Viet Nam, Burma, Thailand, Indonesia, Ceylon, the Philippines, Malaya, and Persia, as well as by European members of the executive bureau of the Federation. In a report of the activities of the World Federation of Trade Unions in Asia up to that time its secretary, Louis Saillant, described the convening of the Conference in the capital of the new China as one of the most significant acts of the WFTU since its formation, and declared that the Chinese example would have

---

[1] C. P. Fitzgerald points out that Mao uses 'socialism' and 'communism' indifferently to represent the ultimate transformation of Chinese society (*Revolution in China*, p. 171).

[2] E. Kovalev, 'The Great Historic Victory of the Chinese People', *Bolshevik*, no. 18, October 1949. Analysing the programme adopted by the People's Consultative Conference in 1949, a Soviet historian notes that the régime was officially described as a people's democracy 'based on the union of workers and peasants and under the leadership of the working class' (*Mezhdunarodnye Otnosheniya*, p. 691).

tremendous consequences for the future of the whole Far East.[1]
This report gave the following examples of the activity of the
Federation and, by implication, of the Communist movement:
(1) assistance in the organization of trade unions in Persia,
Japan, and both parts of Korea in 1946 and 1947; (2) support
for the Chinese trade union movement and for the rejection of
a compromise between it and the Kuomintang since 1947; (3)
the admission of the central organization of the Indonesian
trade unions in 1947, and thereafter opposition to the Dutch
attempts to retain control over the country; (4) an unsuccessful
attempt in 1947 to send an organizer to Viet Nam; (5) support
for the all-Malayan Federation of Trade Unions; (6) support
for the immediate demands of the Indian trade unions; (7) a
report to the United Nations on alleged encroachments on the
rights of workers in the Far East; (8) endeavours to direct the
work of the Economic Commission for Asia and the Far East
in the direction of recognizing the rights claimed for the Asiatic
peoples; (9) the carrying-out of the decision of the second
WFTU Congress concerning 'the international day of the
struggle for peace'; (10) the reinforcement of the position of the
Federation in the Far East and the renewal of relations with
Burma after this Congress; (11) the welding together of the
workers' movements of the countries in the Far East belonging
to the Federation, that is to say, Viet Nam, Malaya, Thailand,
North Korea, South Korea, the Philippines, Japan, and
Mongolia.[2]

The opening address at the Congress was delivered by Liu
Shao-chi. He said that the World Federation of Trade Unions
would take its place in the struggle against imperialism and
colonial oppression. He analysed the ways in which the Chinese
people had achieved their victory as follows: they had realized
that a coalition of the working class with all other classes
opposed to imperialism was necessary. This united front had
had to be led by and built around the working class, which in
turn had to be centred on the Communist Party, and it had
therefore been essential to build up a Communist Party
'equipped with the theory of Marxism-Leninism, a party
mastering strategy and tactics, a party exercising self-criticism

[1] *NCNA*, 22 November 1949.
[2] *For a Lasting Peace*, 30 December 1949.

and strict discipline and which was closely linked with the masses.'
It had been necessary to set up a people's liberation army led
by the Communist Party, to provide it with bases, and to co-
ordinate the struggles of the masses in the enemy-controlled
territory with the operations of the liberation army.

Moreover [he continued] armed struggle is the main form of
struggle in the national liberation struggle in many colonies and
semi-colonies.

This is the main path followed in China by the Chinese people
in winning their victory. This path is the path of Mao Tse-tung.
It can also become the main path of the peoples of other colonial and
semi-colonial countries for winning emancipation where similar
conditions prevail.[1]

A resolution for the setting up of a permanent liaison bureau
of the Federation, with headquarters in China, was moved by
the Soviet delegate, Solovyov. It was to consist of four members,
representing China, the Soviet Union, India, and Australasia,
with the main responsibility resting with the Chinese representative. Its competence was left very wide, although it was
to be controlled through the World Federation of Trade Unions.
On 1 December 1949 the Conference issued a manifesto to the
workers in Asiatic countries, calling upon them to fight against
imperialist oppression.

An article in the Cominform Journal discussed with approval
the tactics advocated by Liu Shao-chi, the formation of broad
national fronts embodying all classes and parties willing to fight
against imperialism. It also declared that where the necessary
conditions existed, national liberation armies should be organized under Communist leadership and that their formation
was an essential condition of success. The guerrilla activities in
Viet Nam, Malaya, Indonesia, and South Korea were regarded
as examples of such action, and the Indian Communist Party
was urged to greater activity.[2] It seemed that revolutionary
action in Asia was to be based in future on Chinese experience,
while it was of course always made clear that China herself
had been directly inspired by the Russian example.[3]

---

[1] *For a Lasting Peace*, 30 December 1949.
[2] ibid. 27 January 1950.
[3] E. Zhukov, 'Historic Significance of the Victory of the Chinese People', *New Times*, 16 January 1950.

Nevertheless, neither in China nor in Russia was it maintained that China was yet a socialist country. The dictatorship of the proletariat was not yet the dominant force, and in this the Chinese People's Republic differed from the European People's Democracies.[1] It thus represented a less advanced stage of the revolutionary process. But it is precisely because China was still conditioned in the Marxist view by its recent subjugation to imperialism that it could serve so well as an example for other colonial and 'semi-colonial' countries.[2]

At the same time that the Chinese Communists were thus developing their international relations in Asia, they were continuing to support Soviet policy in world affairs.[3] For instance, the Soviet-inspired peace movement, the 'partisans of peace', was fully supported in China, and by November 1950 it was claimed that 224 million signatures had been obtained for the 'Stockholm Peace Appeal'.

RUSSIAN INFLUENCE ON CHINA'S INTERNAL AFFAIRS

The extent to which the Soviet Union played a direct part in assisting the carrying out of the Chinese Communists' domestic programme in the period after the Sino-Soviet treaties of 1950 is extremely uncertain. No reference was made in the published agreements to the use in China of Soviet advisers such as had played so important a role in China proper during the period of Kuomintang-Communist co-operation in the nineteen-twenties or in Sinkiang in the nineteen-thirties. In 1949 the presence of such Soviet advisers was widely reported from Communist-held China. In 1950 such reports grew more numerous and circumstantial though extremely confused as regards the number of Soviet citizens involved and the nature of their employment.[4] Some reports indicated that military

---

[1] On the actual structure of Communist China in the period immediately following the establishment of the Chinese People's Republic, see 'Report on China' in *Annals* of the American Academy of Political and Social Science, September 1951, especially the articles by G. B. Taylor, S. B. Thomas, and K. A. Wittfogel.

[2] Peking radio and the *Peking People's Daily* came out in September 1950 with direct advice to the Japanese Communist Party on the correct way of handling its internal crisis. The Japanese Communists were told to follow the 'sincere suggestions' of the Cominform (*CSM*, 5 February 1941).

[3] In November 1950 the Russians raised unsuccessfully the question of a seat for Communist China on the Allied Council in Tokyo (*The Times*, 8 November 1950).

[4] *NYT*, 21, 24, and 27 March; 1 and 6 April; 4 May 1950.

specialists were involved, such as anti-aircraft gunners. On the other hand the Kuomintang Prime Minister Chen Cheng said, on 24 March 1950, that he doubted whether there were Russian troops in Shanghai and Nanking, as had been suggested, and that he thought that the Russians were only technicians and advisers.[1]

Communist sources admitted only the presence of very small numbers, such as the group of fifteen town-planning engineers at Peking.[2] In his speech to the inaugural conference of the Sino-Soviet Friendship Association on 5 October 1950, Liu Shao-chi stated that the total number of Russian specialists including those in Manchuria was no more than 200—a figure very much lower than that generally accepted as correct in non-Communist circles. He also claimed that, unlike the Western experts previously employed in China, the Russians were willing to work under Chinese direction and to receive the same pay as Chinese of equivalent skill.[3] On the other hand reports reaching foreign observers suggested that Soviet citizens had their salaries fixed in roubles at the Soviet standard rate, that these were then exchanged into dollars at the official rate of exchange, and finally paid out in local currency, or sometimes (presumably only in the early period) in United States dollars.

Western correspondents were inclined to agree that the Soviet advisers, though much more numerous than officially admitted, were not imposed by the Russians but sent at China's own request, and that their functions were technical rather than political, but that they were concerned with Soviet methods of organization rather than with technical instruction in the narrow sense.[4] In the special case of Manchuria, however, the position was clearly different.

The foundations for the economic relations between the Soviet Union and China had been laid down in the 1950 agreements, including that for the $300 million loan. It was not clear to what extent the agreement made with Manchuria

[1] *NYT*, 25 March 1950. It is often argued that the experience of Yugoslavia is suggestive of the probable situation in China; but it is uncertain whether European parallels can be accepted without confirmation, and whether the Russians might not have learned caution from the Yugoslav revolt against their methods of control.
[2] *NCNA*, 13 June 1950.   [3] ibid. 18 October 1950.
[4] Walter Sullivan in *NYT*, 6 July 1950; R. Guillain in *Manchester Guardian*, 7 May 1951.

before the establishment of the Chinese People's Republic was modified, or to what extent this had involved a position for the Soviet Union as favourable as that which it had acquired in Sinkiang in the nineteen-thirties or was now enjoying in the East European 'People's Democracies'.

On 19 February 1951 the Chinese delegation arrived in Moscow for the negotiations for a new agreement. There may have been considerable difficulties encountered in the subsequent talks, since a protocol on the exchange of goods was signed only on 15 June, together with another protocol for the delivery of materials and equipment under the February 1950 credit agreement.[1] The Chinese leaders were obviously aware that the economic assistance to be expected from the Soviet Union was inadequate to meet their needs, but this was justified by Russia's own needs after her war losses.[2] And in connexion with the first anniversary of the treaties of February 1950, China's Minister of Trade announced that the Soviet Union had greatly helped China's economic recovery.[3]

Efforts were also made to improve transport between the Soviet Union and China. An agreement on railway communications was signed on 14 March 1951. The road between Sinkiang and Lanchow, which had been developed for motor transport early in the Sino-Japanese war, was reported to have been repaired and improved.[4] On 27 March an agreement was also reached for the setting up of a joint company for civil aviation.[5] Under the old agreement with the Nationalist Government, effective at least as late as 1943, there was a joint airline in operation from Alma Ata to Hami via Kuldja and Urumchi. By the middle of 1950 reports from Peking mentioned that the line was in operation right up to Lanchow. There was also an airline from Chita through Hailar, Tsitsihar, Harbin, and Mukden to Peking, Taiyuan, and Sian; and there was in addition a proposal for a link between Irkutsk and Mukden, presumably via Urga.[6]

Not only political and economic but also cultural ties with the

---

[1] *Soviet News*, 22 June 1951.
[2] Speech by Mao Tse-tung reported in *Pravda*, 1 October 1950.
[3] *Soviet News*, 16 February 1951.
[4] ibid. 30 March 1951. In October 1952 it was reported that work on a Lanchow–Sinkiang railway was in progress. (*The Times*, 4 October 1952.)
[5] *Scotsman*, 24 July 1950.   [6] *Soviet Monitor*, 2 April 1950.

new China were stressed in Soviet propaganda. During the war there had been a Sino-Soviet friendship association in the areas controlled by the Nationalist Government. After the war a series of such societies under Communist control was established first in Manchuria and then elsewhere in China. In October 1949, at the inaugural conference already referred to, the Sino-Soviet Friendship Association took on a more formal aspect as the major channel of cultural co-operation between the Soviet Union and China. The Soviet Academy of Sciences reorganized its Institute of Oriental Studies, which engaged in the preparation of new Chinese dictionaries. In November 1950 and February 1951 the special sessions of the Institute were devoted to China and to the various achievements credited to the Chinese Communist Party.[1]

There were also publications of documents and materials bearing on the establishment of the Chinese People's Republic, an exhibition of Chinese art, and various visits from Chinese personalities and groups. It was perhaps even more important that Soviet literature was being widely distributed in China and that classes in the Russian language were being held in the large cities. Scientific delegations from the Soviet Union toured China and reported on their experiences. The Russians began to exercise a perceptible influence in Chinese education, and Russian teachers and experts were engaged at the University of Peking in June 1950. It was reported in the same year that 700 Chinese students had been selected to go to Russian towns to study Communist doctrine.[2] On the other hand it is not possible to say to what extent former students at Russian educational institutions for Asiatics were influential in Chinese circles. Developments in China pointing to an adoption of Soviet methods in education, administration, and labour relations were greeted with approval in the Soviet press.[3]

[1] 'Current Tasks of Historians in the Orient', *Voprosy Istorii*, 12 December 1950. Cf. *Literaturnaya Gazeta*, 2 November 1949; *Pravda*, 13 November 1950; *Izvestia*, 2 November 1950; *Vestnik Akademii Nauk SSSR*, February–March 1951. See also K. E. Priestley, 'The Sino-Soviet Friendship Association', *Pacific Affairs*, September 1952.

[2] *CSM*, 17 March 1950; *NYT*, 8 October 1950. Cf. K. E. Priestley, 'Communist Education', *Manchester Guardian*, 9 May 1952.

[3] *For a Lasting Peace*, 9 June 1950; *Izvestia*, 24 June 1950 and 20 February 1951; *Pravda*, 29 April 1950; *Literaturnaya Gazeta*, 8 April 1950; *Professyonalnie Soyuzy*, nos. 7 and 10, 1949.

V

The Soviet Union and the Chinese Border-lands

THE MONGOLS

THE Chinese provinces bordering on the Soviet Union were historically inhabited by non-Chinese peoples, although the composition of their populations has been altered particularly in comparatively recent times by the advance of Chinese settlement. The most important of these peoples are the Mongols, separated by the barrier of the Gobi desert in Outer Mongolia and Inner Mongolia, and extending also into western Manchuria. One branch of this people, the Buriat Mongols, lives within the confines of the Soviet Union itself.[1] Another, the Kalmuks, previously lived between the Don and the Volga, but were deported *en masse* to Siberia after the retreat of the Germans from the Caucasus. In Sinkiang (Chinese Turkestan) the Turki-speaking Moslem majority of the population is also closely affiliated to peoples within the Soviet frontiers.[2] The building of the Trans-Siberian and Turksib railways has meant that both Outer Mongolia and Sinkiang are more accessible from the Soviet Union than from China. This factor has been of assistance to the Soviet Union in its exploitation of the troubles due to Chinese penetration into Sinkiang and Mongolia, and to Chinese policies designed to further the interests of the settlers.

The situation in Tannu Tuva differed from that in the other border territories because of the Russian unwillingness from an early period to accept the Chinese contention that it was part of Outer Mongolia, and the tentative Russian claims to at least a condominium there with the Manchu Empire. Since 1921 it had been under Soviet control and in 1944 it was formally annexed, becoming the Tuvinian Autonomous Region of the RSFSR.[3]

---

[1] Beloff, i, Appendix E.   [2] ibid. Appendix D.   [3] ibid. p. 239.

Outer Mongolia had in the nineteen-twenties fallen within the Soviet orbit, and the close relations between the two countries were given formal shape by their defensive alliance of 12 March 1936. Nevertheless the Chinese Government continued to regard Outer Mongolia as part of China, and the subject remained one of those in dispute between the Soviet Union and the Chinese National Government.

This issue was settled in 1945 by the provision in the Yalta Agreement that 'the status quo in Outer Mongolia [the Mongolian People's Republic] shall be preserved.' The United States pressed the Chinese Government to accept the Russian view that this implied the total independence of the country.[1] It was therefore agreed between the Chinese and Soviet Governments in an exchange of notes at the time of the signing of the Soviet-Chinese treaty of 14 August 1945 that the Chinese Government would recognize 'the independence of Outer Mongolia in her existing boundaries', an important phrase in view of the wide distribution of the Mongol people, subject to a plebiscite.[2] This plebiscite was held on 20 October 1945. It bore a close resemblance to elections in other Communist-controlled countries and, despite the difficulties of transport in the large and sparsely populated country, 98·4 per cent. of the electorate were reported to have cast their votes, all of them voting in favour of independence. It may be pointed out, of course, that any form of voting which put the single question of independence from China would have been bound to produce an affirmative vote; the question of the nature of the Outer Mongolian régime was not put to the electorate. Chiang Kai-shek who, in a speech on 24 August, had even commended the Outer Mongolian example as a method of treating the problem of other 'frontier racial groups' accepted the verdict of the plebiscite, and on 5 January 1946 China accorded official recognition to the Mongolian People's Republic.[3]

In the pre-war period the Chinese Communists had taken the view that, after their eventual victory, Outer Mongolia would become part of a Chinese Communist Federation. At the time of the Soviet-Japanese neutrality pact of 13 April 1941,

[1] *Relations with China*, pp. 113–17.
[2] Texts of notes in Moore, *Soviet Far Eastern Policy*, p. 277.
[3] Gerard M. Friters, *Outer Mongolia* (London, Allen & Unwin, 1951), pp. 209–14.

the Communists had defended the declaration made about the territorial integrity of the Mongolian People's Republic and had referred to the ultimate winning back of the 'lost lands of China' as a sacred task of the Chinese People, without apparently including Outer Mongolia among them. One possible reason may have been that the incorporation in any form of Outer Mongolia in China might have raised the question of the future status of Inner Mongolia which the Chinese Communists, like all other Chinese parties, regarded as an integral part of China.[1] The demand for a union of Inner and Outer Mongolia had always been stronger in the former where Chinese penetration was much more marked, and 'pan-Mongolianism' had always been strongly deprecated by the Russians in both Tsarist and Soviet times. Whatever the underlying motive, the Chinese People's Government, when declaring the 1945 treaties invalid after the conclusion of those of 1950, specifically engaged itself to respect the independence of the Mongolian People's Republic.[2]

The validity of the existing Soviet-Mongol alliance was due to expire in March 1946, and on 27 February a new 'Treaty of Friendship and Mutual Assistance' was concluded. By this treaty, which was to run for ten years, there were to be military consultations between the two Powers in the event of an external threat, military and other aid in the event of an armed attack, and a provision for the withdrawal of troops sent into the territory of the other party as soon as the need for their presence was at an end.[3] An agreement on economic and cultural matters was signed at the same time.

Despite the provisions of the treaty there was no announcement that the Soviet troops stationed in Outer Mongolia since the emergence of the Japanese threat, which was now at an end, would withdraw. The numbers of this force have been variously estimated.[4] The border between Sinkiang and Outer Mongolia was not clearly defined despite the reference to existing boundaries in the Soviet-Chinese notes, and there were claims and counter-claims by peoples on either side of it, complicated by

---

[1] Friters, *Outer Mongolia*, pp. 207–8.
[2] *Vedomosti Verkhovnogo Soveta* (Supreme Soviet Gazette), 16 November 1950.
[3] Text in Appendix, below, p. 267.
[4] Friters, 'Where Russia and China meet', *Listener*, 23 March 1950.

the habits of the Kazak nomads. Reports of armed clashes were current in 1944. In 1947 a more important incident occurred involving Mongolian and Chinese troops. According to the Chinese version, Mongolian troops invaded the Peitashan district of Sinkiang in June and used aircraft and tanks of Soviet manufacture. The Chinese National Government lodged protests with both the Outer Mongolian and Soviet Governments. On 13 June Tass denied that Russian planes had participated in the fighting, and on 15 June Moscow Radio broadcast a statement alleging that it was the Chinese who had violated the Mongolian border and announcing that a protest and a demand for compensation had been lodged with the Chinese Government. On 17 June *Pravda* further alleged that the American Consul at Urumchi had been implicated in this incident, and on 25 June the Americans were accused of having provoked it in order to prove to the American taxpayer that China genuinely needed assistance against a Soviet threat.

The Chinese protests were rejected by the Soviet Union and the Mongolian People's Republic. In August the dispute was given as the reason for China's reversal of its previous support of the application of the Mongolian People's Republic for admission to the United Nations, and versions of the dispute were presented by both the Soviet and Chinese delegations.[1] The fighting petered out late in the summer but in the following spring the Russians reported a new invasion by the Chinese.[2]

No Western observers have been admitted to the Mongolian People's Republic and the extent and nature of Soviet control is not easy to judge.[3] It is admitted in all Soviet literature that the Mongol economy is closely linked with that of the Soviet Union: indeed the Mongolian People's Republic has no direct trade with any other country. In 1949 the link with the Soviet Union was made closer by the completion of a railway linking the Siberian system with Ulan Bator, the Outer Mongolian capital. Stalin was credited by Marshal Choibolsan with

[1] Friters, *Outer Mongolia*, p. 287.
[2] *Soviet Monitor*, 3 April 1948.
[3] One cannot attach overmuch importance to statements such as those made by two émigré Mongolian officers that in addition to the Russian troops in the country there were a million and a half Russian immigrants, a number greater than the native population (*NYT*, 12 and 22 March 1948).

having taken the initiative in the construction of this line.[1] In 1947 the Soviet press gave publicity to the adoption by the Mongolian People's Republic of a five-year plan of the Soviet type. Russian cultural influence has also increased. A revised Mongolian script was adopted based on the Russian alphabet. This move could be justified on the grounds that the old script was inadequate for a modern educational programme. Its adoption was declared by the Prime Minister, Marshal Choibolsan, in an article published in *Pravda* on 26 November 1949, to be of 'great assistance' in linking the Mongolian people to the 'advanced socialist culture of the Soviet Union.'[2]

References were made in the Soviet press on the appropriate occasions to the advantages of Soviet-Mongolian friendship and to the disinterested assistance given by the Soviet Union to the Mongolian people. In the article already referred to Marshal Choibolsan also spoke about his country's relations with the new China. 'The great historic victory of the Chinese people', he said, was a matter which closely concerned the peoples of the Mongolian People's Republic, since it opened a path for a free and happy life for all the other fraternal Mongolian tribes who had until recently been under the yoke of the 'Kuomintang clique'.

This reference to Inner Mongolia was somewhat guarded, which was not unnatural in view of the obscurity surrounding developments there in the post-war years. Inner Mongolia is usually held to include parts of the Chinese provinces of Jehol, Chahar, Suiyuan, and Ninghsia, where the Japanese had attempted to use the Mongolian autonomist movement as a weapon against the Chinese Government. There is also a majority of Mongols in parts of the western fringe of Manchuria: Barga and the old province of Liaoning.

At the end of the war in 1945, Russian troops were in occupation of most if not all of the Mongol-inhabited country previously under Japanese control and were said on their withdrawal at the end of the year to have taken with them most of the livestock

---

[1] *Pravda*, 9 November 1949.

[2] Choibolsan, or Choibalsang, had been the dominant figure in Outer Mongolian politics since the mid-nineteen-thirties. He ended his career in proper Communist fashion by dying in Moscow in February 1952. Much attention was paid in the Soviet press to his obsequies. He was succeeded by Tsedenbal, who paid a visit to Moscow in August 1952.

and other movable wealth as well as a few thousand Mongolians, some as hostages, others as future instruments of their policy. Some of these Mongolians were said to have returned a few months later and organized a local military force, and there were reports of the creation of an autonomous régime in northern Chahar where the Communists profited by the resentment due to the Chinese Government's discouraging all expressions of Mongol nationality.[1] The Russians were, however, believed by the Mongols to have done their best to discourage Mongol nationalism from going too far, in accordance with their previous attitude of keeping Mongolia partitioned between Russian and Chinese spheres of influence.

Subsequent Nationalist victories in China made the situation in Inner Mongolia still more obscure. It appears that in 1947 a Government working closely with the Chinese Communists was set up at Wangyehmia (in Eastern or Manchurian Mongolia) by a Tumet Mongol, Yun Tse (also known by his Mongol name Ulanhu, or U Lan-fu). Although he was Moscow-educated, U Lan-fu's chief links were with the Chinese Communist Party. In 1949 he headed the delegation which was sent from Inner Mongolia to the People's Political Consultative Conference. A local anti-Communist régime having capitulated, acceptance of Communist authority was enforced without great difficulty. Inner Mongolia was constituted an autonomous region of the Chinese People's Republic.[2]

There has been some disagreement abroad as to what this autonomy for Inner Mongolia in fact implied. It has already been noted that in his speech on 12 January 1950 the American Secretary of State, Acheson, referred to Inner Mongolia as a part of China in which the Soviet Union was seeking to obtain a dominant position for itself. But of Soviet penetration in Inner Mongolia to a greater extent than elsewhere in China there appears to be no reliable direct evidence. Some, however, feel that 'autonomy' could lead to 'independence' and point to the parallel with Outer Mongolia. In this connexion again it might be remarked that whereas the Russians in dealing with Outer Mongolia have emphasized the demarcation be-

[1] *NYT*, 8 and 12 February 1946; James Burke, 'China's Losing Game in Mongolia', *FES*, 7 July 1948.
[2] *NYT*, 13 June 1948, 30 September 1949; *The Times*, 5 July 1949.

tween Mongol-inhabited and Chinese territory, the Chinese Communists prefer in talking of Inner Mongolia to emphasize the harmony said to prevail between the two elements of its mixed population, and not to stress national differences.[1]

SINKIANG

In the nineteen-thirties the Soviet Government exercised a dominant influence in Sinkiang through the agency of the Chinese Governor of the province, Sheng Shih-tsai, who owed his position, indeed, partly to their support.[2] In 1942, with the Russian fortunes at a low ebb, Sheng switched his allegiance and renewed his ties with the Kuomintang. In the spring of 1943 the Russians withdrew their specialists from Sinkiang for more vital work elsewhere, as well as their troops at Ili and Hami, and abandoned their special position.

In 1944, as has been seen, some rather obscure military operations began on the frontier with Mongolia and these continued into 1945.[3] In August 1944 the Chinese Government removed Sheng from his position.

In November 1944 the latent opposition to Chinese rule among the Turki population of Sinkiang broke into open resistance in the Ili region which was the farthest from China and the most accessible to the Russians, and a 'Republic of East Turkestan' was set up. Despite reports that the rebels were receiving Soviet aid, or at least active encouragement, the Soviet Union confirmed in an exchange of notes at the time of the signing of the Soviet-Chinese treaty of 14 August 1945 that 'as to latest events in Sinkiang . . . it [had] no intention to interfere with China's internal affairs.'[4]

In the autumn of 1945 the Ili rebels attempted to extend their authority to the rest of the province, but were halted after considerable ground had been gained.

A local agreement between the Chinese authorities and the

---

[1] The most recent evidence suggests a steady consolidation of Peking's hold on Inner Mongolia. See the comments from the Hong Kong correspondent of *The Times* on U Lan-fu's appointment as Governor of Suiyuan (*The Times*, 23 July 1952).

[2] Beloff, i. Appendix D; cf. N. L. D. McLean, 'Sinkiang Today', *International Affairs*, vol. 24, no. 3, July 1948.

[3] *NYT*, 3 June 1946.

[4] Moore, *Soviet Far Eastern Policy*, p. 276.

Russians was apparently negotiated under the auspices of the Soviet Consul in January 1946.[1] By its terms the Turkis of the Ili region were granted a considerable degree of local autonomy and freedom of trade with other parts of China and with foreign countries. Trade with foreign countries was to be subject to the provisions of China's commercial treaties. It was also reported that two other unpublished agreements had been signed at the same time and that a new Deputy Governor had been appointed in the person of a Moscow-educated teacher, Akhmedan Kasimov. A further military agreement concluded in June provided for the garrisoning of the Ili region by six locally raised Turki regiments.[2] Elections were held for representatives in the provincial government. The Chinese, however, cleared the rebel forces from the region of the Pamirs which they had occupied in 1945 and reopened the routes to India.

Nationalist opposition to Chinese rule remained strong though divided between its pro-Soviet wing and another section of conservative Islamic tendencies which would have preferred local autonomy under nominal Chinese suzerainty.[3]

Early in 1947 there were reports that the agreements of 1946 were not being properly implemented on the Turki side, and that the north of the country, with its mineral riches, was in fact wholly detached from Chinese rule. In July 1947, after the appointment by the Chinese National Government of a new Governor, Masud Sabri, a strongly pro-Kuomintang Turki, there was a new revolt. Once again there were reports of Soviet propaganda emphasizing the ties between the rebel tribes and their fortunate kinsmen over the Soviet frontier, as well as the importance of their economic links with the Soviet Union, and urging them to resist the encroachment of the Chinese. Soviet control of the Sino-Soviet airline to China, across Sinkiang, also contributed to Soviet influence in the province.[4] It was hardly a coincidence that the fighting should also have flared up again on the border with Outer Mongolia. The Russians who, as has been seen, were accused of participat-

[1] NYT, 3 June 1946; cf. McLean, loc. cit.
[2] The Times, 16 March 1946; NYT, 22 July, 18 August 1946.
[3] McLean, International Affairs, July 1948.
[4] NYT, 12 and 23 September 1947, 1 February 1948; NYHT, 3 October 1947.

ing in the attack by the Chinese National Government, denied any share in the affair and talked of American 'provocation'. In order not to antagonize the Russians the Chinese refused an American military attaché permission to visit the province.[1] The situation seems to have eased in Sinkiang in the latter half of 1948, after an announcement of a programme of reform. In December the Chinese appointed a new Governor, and early in 1949 the rebels were reported to have dropped calling their separatist régime 'the East Turkestan Republic'.[2]

In March 1949 talks were held between Soviet and Chinese representatives at Urumchi, but they broke down after a fortnight apparently on account of claims put forward by the Russians concerning the north-west of Sinkiang. It was later made known that in May the Sino-Soviet airline agreement had been renewed for a further five years but that the Chinese National Government had refused to enter into any agreements for the joint economic development of Sinkiang.[3] Later on the Kuomintang's main representative, General Chang Chih-chung, abandoned the Nationalists and became a member of a coalition Government in Sinkiang headed by the Communists.

In September Chang together with Seyfuddin, an important leader of the Turki movement, attended the People's Consultative Conference at Peking, and the Sinkiang Provincial Government declared its adherence to the new Communist régime.[4] *69429*
After this date Sinkiang was rapidly sealed off from the non-Communist world. The United States Consulate was closed and evacuated in October 1949, and in the same month all communication with India and Pakistan was severed. Late in 1951 a group of 177 Kazak tribesmen were given sanctuary in India after crossing the frontier from Tibet. They were the remnants of a much larger expedition which had left Sinkiang after the entry of Communist forces in August 1949 and which had earlier included Chinese Nationalist troops, 'White Russian' cavalrymen and others. Their journey had been by a long roundabout route through China proper and Tibet, and had

[1] *NYT*, 26 and 27 August 1948.
[2] ibid. 30 March 1949.
[3] ibid. 31 May 1949; *The Times*, 5 October 1949.
[4] *NYT*, 25 September 1949; O. Lattimore, *Pivot of Asia* (Boston, Little Brown, 1950), p. 102.

involved them in fighting with Chinese Communist and Outer Mongolian forces. They reported that the Communists were in complete control of Sinkiang.[1]

It was widely held after 1949 that the Russians were themselves operating extensive mineral concessions in Sinkiang and that the north-west of the province was still in fact separately administered, with Russian influence dominant there.[2] As has been seen, Sinkiang was represented at the Sino-Soviet negotiations in Moscow at the beginning of 1950, and its delegation took part in concluding two economic agreements on 27 March. Two mixed companies were to be set up, one for oil and the other for non-ferrous metals. Capital, control, and profits were to be shared equally between the Russians and the Chinese. One side would provide the chairman of the board of each company and the other the general manager, with deputies from the other side. The positions were to alternate every three years but the first general managers were to be Russians. Judging by what has happened elsewhere in similar companies, the provision giving the Russians the nomination of the general manager would effectively secure their control, anyhow for the first three years: the agreements were of thirty years' duration.[3]

The Soviet press put forward the argument that despite the element of foreign participation this investment was a constructive and not an 'exploitative' one and that full respect for Chinese sovereignty had been maintained.[4] According to reports from China, the Peking Government regarded itself as fully in control of Sinkiang, and in March 1950 it actually announced a programme for the large-scale immigration of Chinese into the province.[5] It was announced that a coalition Government had been formed representing the various nationalities of Sinkiang, with the Chinese element in a minority.[6] The first conference of People's Representatives in the province took place in January 1951.[7]

A less favourable picture of developments in Sinkiang was given in reports from India which spoke of further large-scale

[1] *The Times*, 3 November 1951.
[2] Department of State release, *NYT*, 26 January 1950.
[3] *Soviet Monitor*, 29 March 1950; *The Times*, 30 March 1950.
[4] *New Times*, 26 April 1950.   [5] *Scotsman*, 22 March 1950.
[6] Chou En-lai quoted in *Izvestia*, 1 October 1950.
[7] *Pravda*, 20 January 1951.

fighting between the Chinese and Turki tribesmen and of increasing Soviet influence. The Russians admitted that there had been some trouble but attributed it to the intrigues of a former United States Vice-Consul.[1]

It did not appear that the essentials of the Sinkiang problem had been altered by the emergence of the Communist régime. Racial antagonisms in Sinkiang are still important, and the Russians having recovered their strength were able to reimpose the same influence that they exerted in the nineteen-thirties, modified only by the fact of their much closer relations with the central Chinese Government. Should the Chinese Government ever make difficulties over the extent to which the Russians were benefiting by their share in the exploitation of the country's mineral resources, the Soviet Union would be in a strong position to maintain its holdings and to influence through Sinkiang the 12 million Moslems of China proper. What is less clear is the extent to which the unity of the province had been restored under Communist rule, or whether, in other words, any trace of a separate régime still existed in the north-west.[2]

[1] *Pravda*, 14 July 1950.

[2] An article in *Pravda* on 28 January 1952 entitled 'In Sinkiang' gives a rosy picture of conditions in the country but makes no mention of any Russians being there. The possible relation between events in Sinkiang and Soviet policies in other Turki-speaking areas such as Persian Azerbaijan, Afghan Turkestan, and Turkish Kurdistan lie outside the scope of this book, but see McLean, *International Affairs*, July 1948.

VI

The Soviet Union and Japan

DURING most of the war against Germany, Soviet policy towards Japan was based on the neutrality pact concluded on 13 April 1941. The Soviet attitude was not cordial but remained correct. Operations in the Pacific and in China were reported from the Allied communiqués and Japanese communiqués were reprinted only when they referred to internal Japanese developments. On 30 March 1944 an agreement limiting Japan's fishing rights in Soviet waters and surrendering to the Soviet Union Japan's oil and coal concessions in North Sakhalin was signed in Moscow. The Japanese, it was made known, had undertaken to conclude such an agreement at the time of signing the neutrality pact.[1] From the middle of 1944 the Soviet press began to adopt an increasingly unfriendly attitude and to express the view that Japanese defeat was inevitable. A more definitely hostile note was struck by Stalin in his speech on 7 November, when he referred to Japan as an aggressor; but this was not followed by any increased hostility in the Soviet press.[2]

On 5 April 1945 Molotov handed the Japanese Ambassador a formal denunciation of the neutrality pact. The Soviet note stated that this pact had been concluded before the outbreak of the war between the Soviet Union's allies and the Japanese. During the war Japan had taken various unfriendly steps with regard to the Soviet Union, and it had been prevented from joining in the war only by the determined resistance that the

---

[1] Moore, *Soviet Far Eastern Policy*, pp. 136–42, 257–9.

[2] The remark by Stalin seems to have come as something of a shock to the Japanese who had unsuccessfully proposed to the Russians in September 1943 and April 1944 that they mediate between them and the Germans, and who had, on 16 September 1944, suggested for the third time the dispatch of a special envoy to Moscow. See the book by the former member of the Japanese Foreign Office Toshikazu Kase, published under the title *Journey to the Missouri* (New Haven, Yale University Press, 1950) and in England under the title *Eclipse of the Rising Sun* (London, Cape, 1951), pp. 96, 162–5.

Russians had put up against the Germans. Since Japan was aiding Germany, the enemy of the Soviet Union, and fighting the Soviet Union's allies, the neutrality pact had lost all meaning and could not continue in force.

Molotov assured the Ambassador that the pact would remain valid for the remaining year of its duration, but the wording of the Soviet note suggested that the Soviet Union regarded it as already obsolete. A rather hostile reference to Japan was included in Stalin's May Day speech. On the whole, however, the Soviet press concentrated on European developments, and there was little to indicate a preparation of the Russian public for the idea of a Far Eastern campaign.[1] Apparently it was only the visit of envoys from China and Outer Mongolia to Moscow in July 1945 that aroused Japanese suspicions.[2] The Japanese on 13 July suggested a drastic readjustment of their relations with the Soviet Union, proposing the evacuation and neutralization of Manchuria, together with a simultaneous withdrawal of Soviet troops from the border area. They also offered to forgo some of their fishing rights in exchange for increased Soviet oil supplies. Finally, they requested the Soviet Union to act as a mediator between themselves and the Western Allies. The Emperor proposed sending Prince Konoye to Moscow, but the Russians delayed replying until the 16th, and then asked for a clarification of the purpose of this mission. The Japanese Government sent their Ambassador Sato new instructions on 21 July to the effect that Konoye would bring the Japanese conditions for peace together with a request for Soviet mediation.[3]

Further approaches by Sato on 30 July and 2 August brought no result. Stalin had gone to Potsdam. He there informed the other Allied leaders of the Japanese proposals, and an unconditional surrender formula for Japan was agreed upon.

[1] Kase, *Eclipse of the Rising Sun*, pp. 154–5.

[2] There is an exception in the form of a travel article on Shanghai and Manchuria, in *New Times*, 1 June 1945, in which the author refers to Port Arthur as a Russian city.

[3] Byrnes, *Speaking Frankly*, p. 211. During May and June there had been informal approaches to Malik, the Soviet Ambassador in Tokyo, with a view to a new non-aggression pact and possible mediation by Russia between Japan and the Western Powers. (Kase, *Eclipse of the Rising Sun*, pp. 170–1, 187–8.)

[4] M. Kato, *The Lost War* (New York, Knopf, 1946), pp. 232–3; Kase, *Eclipse of the Rising Sun*, pp. 193–4, 205, 219, 222; cf. *The Forrestal Diaries*, pp. 74–75.

Judging by articles in the Soviet press in the summer of 1945, the Russians shared what later proved to be the exaggerated opinion held by the Western Powers of Japan's ability to continue hostilities after the end of the war in Europe.[1] Were the war in the Far East to end without their participation, however, they feared that their interests would be neglected in the final settlement. And the possibility of this happening suddenly became apparent during the Potsdam Conference with the successful explosion of the first atomic bomb in New Mexico.

The Americans were still uncertain that they could dispense with Russian aid and were unwilling to incur the responsibility of breaking the Yalta Agreement. The Russians were not only anxious to take part in the military operations as soon as possible but also wished for an adequate excuse to disregard the fact that the neutrality pact was still theoretically in force. Stalin therefore requested the Allies to make a formal demand that the Soviet Union should enter the war. A formula was invented for the purpose by invoking the Moscow Declaration and articles 103 and 106 of the proposed United Nations Charter, so that Soviet co-operation with the Powers at war with Japan would be entered into 'with a view to joint action on behalf of the community of nations to maintain peace and security.'[2]

The basis for the post-war settlement in Japan was contained in the Anglo-American 'Proclamation to the Japanese People' issued from Potsdam on 26 July 1945, and signed by Truman, Churchill, and Chiang Kai-shek. (This document is usually referred to as the Potsdam Declaration.) Molotov endeavoured to have its publication postponed when the draft was sent to the Russians, and was disturbed to find that he was too late to prevent its release. It was explained to him that the Soviet Union had not been consulted because the Allies did not wish to embarrass the Soviet Government by presenting it with a document concerning a country with which it was not yet at war. In addition to the call for unconditional surrender, the Proclamation set out certain provisions governing an ultimate settlement.[3] The terms of the Cairo Declaration were to be

---

[1] See e.g. E. Zhukov in *Izvestia*, 2 June 1945. The issue of Russian aid in the final defeat of Japan as it presented itself to the United States Government is discussed in Welles, *Seven Major Decisions*, pp. 146–67.

[2] Byrnes, *Speaking Frankly*, pp. 207–9; cf. p. 21 n. above.

[3] Text in RIIA, *United Nations Documents*, 1941–5, pp. 206–7.

carried out and Japanese sovereignty limited 'to the islands of Honshu, Hokkaido, Kyushu, Shikoku, and such minor islands' as the Allies should determine. Members of the Japanese forces were to be allowed to return to their homes when they had been totally disarmed. The Japanese were not to be 'enslaved as a race' but there was to be 'stern justice' for war criminals.

The Japanese Government shall remove all obstacles to the revival and strengthening of democratic tendencies among the Japanese people. Freedom of speech, of religion, and of thought as well as respect for fundamental human rights shall be established. Japan shall be permitted to maintain such industries as will sustain her economy and allow the exaction of just reparations in kind but not those industries which will enable her to rearm for war.

Japan was to be allowed 'access to, as distinct from control of' raw materials. Eventually she was to be allowed to participate in world trade. There was to be a military occupation of Japan which was to continue until the Allied objectives had been accomplished and until there had been established in accordance with the freely expressed will of the Japanese people a 'peacefully inclined and responsible Government'.

On 6 August the first atomic bomb was dropped on Hiroshima. On 8 August the Soviet Union declared war on Japan, and on 9 August the second atomic bomb was dropped on Nagasaki.

The Soviet declaration of war ignored the neutrality pact altogether, and was based on the refusal of Japan to shorten the war by capitulating.[1] The reasons for the Soviet entry into the war were represented as being the security of Russia's Far Eastern borders and the lessening of the sufferings of the Allied nations and the broad masses of the Japanese people themselves by shortening the war.[2] The Russians paid very little attention then or later to the importance of the atomic bomb in the conclusion of the Japanese war, attributing the Japanese collapse exclusively to their own victories in Manchuria. Apologists for subsequent Soviet policies have argued that the Russians looked upon the dropping of the atomic bombs as a deliberate attempt to prevent their achieving a direct victory and securing the position previously assured to them by the inter-Allied

[1] *Izvestia*, 9 August 1945.
[2] See e.g. Avarin in *MKiMP*, no. 8, 1945.

agreements, and that it was in fact the first move in the cold war.[1] In noting this argument it should be pointed out that the Russians could not have invaded Japan themselves by sea unless ferried over in American ships. Therefore the war could not have been won by them directly, since total defeat in Manchuria would not itself have sufficed to destroy the Japanese will to resist. In fact, the threat of invasion from the sea had already caused the Japanese to withdraw some of their best troops from Manchuria, thus weakening the front against the Russians.[2]

On 10 August the Japanese Foreign Minister handed Malik a copy of a message sent that morning, through Switzerland, in which Japan announced her willingness to accept the conditions of the Potsdam Declaration. The Japanese Government made it clear, however, that it understood the Declaration as not implying any demands that would diminish the prerogatives of the Emperor as an independent sovereign and requested a formal assurance on this point.[3]

Immediately on receiving this message, Molotov summoned the American and British Ambassadors in order to inquire as to the attitudes of their Governments towards the Japanese request. His own view was that the reservations concerning the Emperor were not in accordance with the formula of unconditional surrender. The American reply, to which Soviet adherence was requested, informed the Japanese that the surrender would be unconditional. But it specifically referred to the Emperor as the authority responsible for seeing that the Japanese Government carried out the terms of the Potsdam Declaration. From the moment of the surrender the Emperor was to be subject to the Allied Supreme Commander, and the Japanese were ultimately to choose freely their form of government.[4]

Molotov tried to postpone a reply as to whether the Soviet

[1] P. M. S. Blackett, *Military and Political Consequences of Atomic Energy* (London, Turnstile Press, 1948), Ch. 10. Professor Blackett's thesis was commended by Soviet historians. See *Mezhdunarodnye Otnosheniya*, p. 607.

[2] According to Japanese sources, Russia had begun to strengthen her Far Eastern forces from about March 1945. (Kase, *Eclipse of the Rising Sun*, pp. 165-6.)

[3] ibid. pp. 238-9.

[4] W. Macmahon Ball, *Japan: Enemy or Ally* (New York, Day, 1949), p. 45; Byrnes, *Speaking Frankly*, pp. 209-10.

Government accepted this formulation of the terms to be put to Japan, but finally agreed to the note which was sent on 11 August. He put forward the additional point that in case the Japanese agreed to surrender on this basis, the Allies should 'reach an agreement on the candidacy or candidacies of the Allied High Command to which the Japanese Emperor and the Japanese Government were to be subordinated'.[1] The American Ambassador, Harriman, was apparently amazed at this demand and asked Molotov at once whether General MacArthur would be acceptable. Molotov replied that he himself thought so but would have to consult his Government, adding that it was conceivable that there might be two Supreme Commanders, General MacArthur and Marshal Vasilevski. Harriman was extremely angry at this, and declared that since the United States had carried the main burden of war for four years, while the Soviet Union had been engaged for only two days, it was unthinkable that the Supreme Commander should be anyone but an American. After consultation with Stalin, Molotov rapidly climbed down on this point, explaining the clash as a mistake by the interpreter. MacArthur was formally nominated by President Truman, with the concurrence of Stalin, who appointed Lieutenant-General Kuzma Derevyanko to represent the Soviet Union at the surrender ceremony. The Americans also rejected the Soviet suggestion that the surrender of the Japanese on Hokkaido should be taken by the Red Army, saying that the American forces had the right to accept the surrender on all the main Japanese islands. There was also a misunderstanding on the part of General Deane, who passed on to the Soviet High Command General MacArthur's directions for the cessation of hostilities without adding that it was for information only. His apologies were accepted and, as has been seen, the Russian offensive against the Japanese continued. It is possible that the Russians regarded this incident as an attempt to interfere with their further advance. False reports of Russian landings on Hokkaido and of American landings on the Kuriles also led to misunderstandings, as did also the amendment of MacArthur's General Order No. 1 to provide for the surrender of the Japanese forces in the Kuriles to the Russians. Still another cause for Russian suspicion was the delay (due to weather con-

[1] Deane, *Strange Alliance*, p. 278.

ditions) of the plane sent to bring General Derevyanko to Manila for the surrender ceremony, which was taken as an intentional effort to exclude Soviet participation. The only thing that went quite smoothly was the rapid release to the Americans of General Wainwright and other American prisoners found by the Russians in Japanese hands.[1] But this may well have been due to a desire to get rid of American observers in Manchuria.

Whatever may be thought of the rights and wrongs of these incidents, it is clear that Soviet-American co-operation in relation to Japan started very badly. And the Russians seemed in no hurry to improve matters. Stalin's victory speech on 2 September treated the war almost exclusively as one between Japan and the Soviet Union, and actually included a cold reminder that in 1918 Japan had taken advantage of the hostile attitudes of Great Britain, France, and the United States towards Russia to attack her.[2]

In the negotiations with the United States over the future of Japan, the main Soviet effort was directed towards obtaining a share in the effective control of the country.[3] At his meeting with Hopkins on 29 May 1945 Stalin had said that he expected that the Soviet Union would share in the actual occupation, and that he would like an agreement with the United States and Great Britain.

But the idea of Soviet troops stationed in a part of Japan did not appeal to the Americans, and for his part Stalin would not send Russian troops to serve under an American commander.[4] The first American proposals were made on 21 August; a Far Eastern Advisory Commission was to be set up, to consist of the representatives of all the Powers which had participated in the war against Japan. This Commission was to have advisory powers only and was to have its headquarters in Washington though it could meet in other places as the occasion required.[5]

The Soviet Union and China accepted these proposals, but

[1] Deane, *Strange Alliance*, pp. 279–84.
[2] *The Times*, 3 September 1945.
[3] The negotiations on this point are described in detail by George H. Blakeslee in Dennett and Johnson, eds., *Negotiating with the Russians*, Ch. 5.
[4] *The Forrestal Diaries*, pp. 105–6.
[5] On the insistence of Bevin, the Commission was later authorized to meet in Tokyo as well (US Department of State, *Occupation of Japan, Policy and Progress* (USGPO, 1947), pp. 67–68).

owing to a demand by the countries of the Commonwealth for a more active share in the control of Japan the establishment of the Far Eastern Advisory Commission was postponed. A United States Government document entitled 'The United States Initial Post-Surrender Policy for Japan' published on 6 September stated:

Although every effort will be made, by consultation and by constitution of appropriate advisory bodies, to establish policies for the conduct of the occupation and the control of Japan which will satisfy the principal Allied Powers, in the event of any differences of opinion among them, the policies of the United States will govern.[1]

When the Council of Foreign Ministers met in London in September, Molotov announced a reversal of the Soviet attitude towards the proposed Advisory Commission. Although the Council had been convened in order to discuss European affairs, and although Byrnes refused to include Japan on the agenda, Molotov complained that the Japanese terms of surrender were not being carried out. He argued that the repatriation of Japanese soldiers was dangerous and that the Americans would do better to follow the Russian example and put the prisoners to work. Byrnes replied that repatriation was expressly provided for in the Potsdam Declaration and assured Molotov that all those suspected of war crimes would be held.

On 24 September Molotov read a prepared statement proposing the establishment of a Control Council for Japan, representing the United States, Great Britain, the Soviet Union and China, with an American Chairman, with much wider powers than those of the Advisory Commission. The Americans replied that they were not prepared to discuss the issue at a meeting which was intended to deal with other matters. This drew from Molotov the remark that the policies being pursued by General MacArthur made him wonder whether it was 'useful for the Soviet Government to continue having a representative in Tokyo'.[2] He asked whether the press reports concerning a great treasure, said to have been discovered in Tokyo bay, had anything to do with the American refusal to discuss the Japanese situation.

[1] *Occupation of Japan*, p. 75.
[2] Byrnes, *Speaking Frankly*, p. 214.

The London Conference ended in a complete deadlock and the Soviet press, discussing the disagreement between the Allies, accused the Americans of endangering peace in Asia and inter-Allied relations. It was pointed out that some Americans were talking of Japan becoming a useful buffer-State to aid in controlling Russian activities in the Far East, that this would mean the preservation of the existing political, social, and economic system in Japan, and so the revival of Japanese militarism.[1]

After British agreement to the establishment of the proposed Advisory Commission had been secured, Byrnes informed Molotov of the fact and said that its first meeting would be on 30 October and that he hoped the Soviet Union would be represented. In his reply on 1 October Molotov said that so long as the Japanese had not been disarmed there had been justification for the concentration of authority in the Allied Commander-in-Chief, but now there should be some Allied organ through which 'the four Powers who played the decisive rôle in the defeat of Japan would put into effect in relation to Japan an agreed policy and assume joint responsibility.' Therefore the Soviet Government could not agree to the setting up of the Advisory Commission until the four Powers had created a Control Council.[2]

President Truman attempted to find a way round the impasse in Soviet-American relations by sending a cordial personal letter, which was delivered by Harriman to Stalin at his holiday resort at Gagri on 25 October. This letter made important concessions to the Russians on certain European questions, but did not mention Japan. Stalin immediately seized on this point, apparently much to Harriman's surprise, which suggests that the Americans did not appreciate the importance that the Japanese issue had assumed. Stalin repeated Molotov's point that the Soviet Union was unwilling to join the Advisory Commission because the situation had changed since the Soviet Government had agreed to the idea in August. The Soviet representative in Tokyo, General Derevyanko, had not been kept informed of what was going on and had not been consulted, in fact he had been treated like 'a piece of furniture'.

---

[1] See e.g. D. Petrov, 'Eliminating Seats of Aggression or Preserving Them?', *New Times*, 1 October 1945.

[2] Byrnes, *Speaking Frankly*, p. 215; *Negotiating with the Russians*, pp. 122-3.

Stalin had therefore recalled him, rather than take responsibility for General MacArthur's actions. He further complained that the Japanese press and radio had been allowed to vilify the Soviet Union. Major steps in policy had been taken by General MacArthur without anyone informing the Soviet Union. Agreement between the Soviet Union and the United States would not be achieved in the Advisory Commission, but required direct negotiations between them. He recalled that the Soviet Union had kept thirty to forty divisions on the Manchurian border throughout the war, and had offered to participate in the occupation of Japan.

The question of Russian participation in the occupation seems to have been raised formally once more in this period, but the Americans were prepared to go no farther than having a number of Soviet troops under MacArthur's command, as an integral part of the Eighth Army—a position similar to that occupied by the Commonwealth forces. The Russians were not prepared to accept anything less than a separate zone, as in Germany and Austria.[1]

On 27 October the United States Government put forward further proposals which contained the germ of the subsequent compromise. These were for two bodies: a Far Eastern Commission and an Allied Military Council. According to the proposed terms of reference, the former body would take broad policy decisions, to which the United States Government would give effect by directives, reserving the right to issue interim directives on urgent matters not covered by policy decisions of the Commission. The Allied Military Council meeting in Tokyo under the chairmanship of the Supreme Commander would have the function of 'consulting with and advising the Supreme Commander in regard to the implementation of the terms of surrender and occupation of Japan and of directives supplementary thereto.' But the Supreme Commander's 'decision upon all matters' was to be 'controlling'.[2]

Pending a Soviet reply to these suggestions, the Advisory Commission met on 30 October with no Soviet representative present. On 1 November a Tass message made it clear that the

[1] Byrnes, *Speaking Frankly*, pp. 216–17; *Occupation of Japan*, p. 141; *NYHT*, 21 December 1945.
[2] Dennett and Johnson, eds., *Negotiating with the Russians*, p. 124.

Russians were sticking to their demand for a Control Council.[1]
In a speech on 6 November 1945 Molotov declared: 'the Soviet
Union attaches great importance to the negotiations among the
Allies on the establishment of a proper control by the main
Allied Powers over the terms of capitulation of Japan. The
difficulties which arise from this issue have not yet been
removed.'[2]

Negotiations on the American proposals went on in Moscow
throughout November. The Soviet Government wished to
secure a veto in the proposed Far Eastern Commission and to
prevent the issue of interim directives by the United States
which would be a way of circumventing it. It also objected to
the suggested membership of India, which was a member of
the existing Far Eastern Advisory Commission. At the same
time the Russians tried to change the proposed Allied Military
Council into an Allied Control Council or Control Commission
and to give it 'control over the execution of the terms of surrender of Japan'. The Supreme Commander would be obliged
to refer back to the Governments or to the Far Eastern Commission matters upon which the Council disagreed.

As has been made clear by an American participant in the
American-Soviet exchanges over these rival conceptions of the
proper form for the control machinery to take, the differences
between the American and Soviet viewpoints were fundamental.
The Americans wished for machinery that would embody the
primary responsibility of the United States for the control of
Japan, the Russians wished for a genuine share in this responsibility.

In the exchanges of view the Soviets gave the impression that
they were suspicious that United States policies might lead to the
development of a Japan which would be antagonistic and a threat
to the Soviet Union. They pointed out that Japan for two generations had been a constant menace to Russian security in the Far
East and that they wished now to be free from this menace.[3]

During these exchanges certain concessions were made to the
Soviet viewpoint, including an acceptance of the principle of

[1] *Soviet News*, 2 November 1945.
[2] *NYT*, 7 November 1945.
[3] George H. Blakeslee in Dennett and Johnson, eds., *Negotiating with the Russians*,
p. 127.

unanimity of the Great Powers (i.e. of the veto) in the Far Eastern Commission, provided that the right of the United States to issue interim directives remained unimpaired.

Further negotiations took place during the Moscow Conference of Foreign Ministers in December 1945; and on 19 December agreement was reached. The Eleven-Power Far Eastern Commission (on which India was to have a seat despite previous Soviet objection) was to replace the Far Eastern Advisory Commission and to meet in Washington. It was to have no power to instruct the occupation authorities directly, and the Great Powers were each to retain a veto. The interim directives which the United States was empowered to issue were not to deal with fundamental changes in the Japanese constitutional structure, or in the régime of control, or 'with a change in the Japanese Government as a whole', and they were to be submitted to the Commission for review. But since they were to remain in force until the Commission decided otherwise, and since the United States had the power of veto, this left the ultimate control with the Americans.

The second body set up was an Allied Council for Japan with its headquarters at Tokyo. This was to have four members representing the United States, the Soviet Union, the British Commonwealth, and China. The Russians failed in an attempt to have the Council called a 'Control Council' and its authority was severely limited. The Supreme Commander was to issue all orders for the implementation of the surrender terms and the occupation and control of Japan, and was merely to consult with and advise the Council in advance on matters of substance. If a member of the Council disagreed with the Supreme Commander on the implementation of a major policy decision of the Far Eastern Commission, he was to withhold action until agreement had been reached in the Commission where again the American veto could prevail.[1]

At the Moscow Conference Molotov also secured the allocation to the Soviet Union of a quarter of the surviving smaller surface vessels of the Japanese navy, which the Americans had intended to scuttle. To a Soviet inquiry about the Japanese merchant navy, Byrnes replied that it was being used for

[1] US Department of State, *Occupation of Japan*, p. 69; Byrnes, *Speaking Frankly*, p. 218; Macmahon Ball, *Japan: Enemy or Ally*, p. 20.

repatriation and that it would ultimately be considered in the reparations settlement. It seems likely that the Russians wished to claim a share of the Japanese fishing fleet, but Bevin remarked that this was essential for the feeding of the Japanese people.[1]

Finally, Molotov returned to the question of the disposal of the Japanese mandated islands. The United States wished to be entrusted with the administration of these as strategic areas, under a United Nations trusteeship agreement. The United Nations General Assembly was in session during the meeting of the Council of Foreign Ministers in New York and some of the pending trusteeship agreements were up for consideration, in the hope that the United Nations Trusteeship Council could now be established. The American representative Dulles had taken the view that the definition of 'States directly concerned' which had to be consulted before trusteeship agreements were submitted for particular territories should only be decided upon after the Trusteeship Council had been set up. But he had been strongly opposed by the Soviet representative who contended that all the five permanent members of the Security Council had to be included. At the Council of Foreign Ministers Molotov asked Byrnes to support the Soviet viewpoint. But Byrnes contended that interpretations of the United Nations Charter could not be made subject to bilateral agreements between the USSR and the United States. He pointed out also that the Soviet attitude would have to be taken into account in considering the question of the ultimate disposition of the Kurile Islands and of South Sakhalin. He recalled that President Roosevelt had repeatedly declared at Yalta that territorial cessions could only be made at a peace conference. He added that the United States Government would presumably stand by Roosevelt's promise to support the Soviet claim at the peace conference, but would want to know by then what the Soviet attitude would be towards the proposal of the United States that the Japanese mandated islands should be placed under United States trusteeship. Molotov quickly grasped the implication of this reminder, and when the United States proposal was later voted on in the Security Council it received the support of the Soviet representative.[2]

---

[1] Byrnes, *Speaking Frankly*, p. 219.
[2] ibid. pp. 219–21.

On 2 January 1946 the Soviet Government nominated representatives to the Far Eastern Commission and Allied Council.[1] The Russian representative took his seat when the Far Eastern Commission first assembled at Washington on 26 February 1946. The Soviet delegation to the Allied Council, headed by General Derevyanko, who was accompanied by a large military mission, arrived in Tokyo early in the same month. The Far Eastern Commission deliberated at Washington behind closed doors and its final reports did not divulge the discussions and controversies that took place. An open breach between the American and Soviet viewpoints was actually avoided until January 1948, when the Soviet representative insisted on a vote on the question of the Japanese police, and blocked the admission of Pakistan to membership of the Commission, possibly in order to obtain a bargaining position for pressing the claims of the Mongolian People's Republic.[2]

One subject which came within the purview of the Commission was that of reparations. The Soviet Union demanded 14 per cent. of the total reparations, claiming that this was very modest in view of its outstanding role in the crushing of Japan.[3] It also took the view that the property removed from Manchuria as 'war booty' should not be taken into account. As a result of this dispute it appears that the Soviet Union was not given a share in the interim allocations, decided upon by the Far Eastern Commission during 1946. In May 1947 the Commission approved a formula to govern the division of the amount to be received from Japan by way of reparations. The shares of particular countries were to be determined on

a broad political basis taking into due account the scope of material and human destruction and damage suffered by each claimant country as a result of the preparations and execution of Japanese aggression, and taking also into due account each country's contribution to the cause of the defeat of Japan, including the extent and duration of its resistance to Japanese aggression.[4]

[1] The existing Far Eastern Advisory Commission undertook in December 1945 a trip to Japan, whence it returned in February 1946, but despite the view of its Chairman that the new Far Eastern Commission would simply be a continuation of the Advisory Commission, the Russians refused to be represented on the latter.

[2] *Daily Telegraph*, 29 January 1948.

[3] *Pravda*, 14 September 1946.

[4] US Department of State, *Activities of the Far Eastern Commission* (USGPO, 1947), p. 20.

Since the Soviet Union had suffered no damage, and since her claims to have taken an important share in defeating Japan were generally rejected, this wording was unfavourable from her point of view. Furthermore, there was a general tendency to scale down the total of reparations in view of the decision to raise the permitted level of Japanese industry. Since the United States was bearing the responsibility and expenses of the occupation she was naturally more concerned with Japan's general economic recovery than with reparations.[1]

The Russian press deprecated the whittling down of reparations and accused the United States of collusion with Japanese capitalists. The reports already mentioned of a find of treasure in Tokyo Bay were possibly given publicity as a counterweight to the American protests about the Manchurian removals. The occupation authorities were also accused of confiscating and sending to the United States various Japanese valuables, works of art, and so on.[2] But the dispute over 'war booty' was not mentioned in the Soviet press until 7 February 1947.

Byrnes's contention that Roosevelt had made it clear at Yalta that definitive transfers of territory could only be made at a peace conference, and that the Yalta Agreement meant no more than that the United States would support, at such a conference, the Russian claim to South Sakhalin and the Kuriles, was confirmed by the Under-Secretary of State Acheson at a press conference on 22 January 1946. His view was promptly disputed by Tass which declared that the transfer was final.[3] The Soviet press also protested strongly when in June 1947 the Japanese Foreign Minister Yoshida declared that Japan would like to obtain in a peace settlement the return of some of the islands, including the Kuriles.[4]

In fact both South Sakhalin and the Kuriles were fully incorporated into the Soviet Union, taking part in the 1946 elections to the Supreme Soviet.[5] There were reports that considerable numbers of Russians had settled in South Sakhalin. Not much information was available about the Kuriles, which lack Sakhalin's mineral riches. In 1949 the waters around the

[1] Macmahon Ball, *Japan: Enemy or Ally*, pp. 96–100.
[2] *Pravda*, 8 April; *Soviet News*, 29 April 1946; M. Markov, 'Reparations from Japan', *New Times*, 10 September 1947.
[3] *Soviet News*, 28 January 1946.
[4] *Izvestia*, 14 June 1947.   [5] *The Times*, 20 February 1946.

islands were heavily patrolled and Japanese fishing boats pene-
trating into them were intercepted.[1] By 1951 nine out of ten
such boats were being detained along with their crews instead
of being allowed to return home as previously.[2]

By 1947 the American Government had decided against
trying to negotiate a peace treaty for Japan within the framework of the Council of Foreign Ministers, a procedure that had
proved so unsuccessful in relation to Germany and Austria and
which would give the Soviet Union a veto, while denying any
share in drawing up the treaty to countries like Australia which
had been at war with Japan ever since December 1941.[3]

It was proposed instead that the Far Eastern Commission
should prepare a draft treaty for consideration at a peace
conference; this suggestion was made known to the Soviet
Government on 11 July 1947 when 19 August was suggested as
the date upon which such a conference should be called. On 22
July the Soviet Government rejected this suggestion in a note
stating that the Americans had put it forward on their own
without consulting the Soviet Union, China, and Great Britain,
and that they had ignored their obligation under the war-time
agreements and the Moscow Agreement to bring the Soviet
Union into full consultation. The note suggested instead that
there should be a preliminary discussion by the Council of
Foreign Ministers.[4]

In a further American note of 13 August it was argued that
the Moscow Agreement to set up a Far Eastern Commission
had constituted a recognition of the fact that its members were
those States with a primary interest in policy towards Japan,
and that they were therefore competent to handle the matter of
a peace settlement.[5] A Soviet reply on 29 August repeated the
previous Soviet argument that the Council of Foreign Ministers
was the only body competent to prepare a treaty.[6] The Soviet
Government made an effort to induce the Chinese National
Government not to support the American proposal. Soviet
comment asserted that China's interests would not be safeguarded under the system of voting by a two-thirds majority.

[1] *NYT*, 8 October 1949.
[2] R. Guillain in *Manchester Guardian*, 4 September 1951.
[3] Byrnes, *Speaking Frankly*, p. 224.
[4] *Soviet Monitor*, 23 July 1947.
[5] *NYT*, 16 August 1947.   [6] *Soviet News*, 2 September 1947.

But the Russians rejected the Chinese proposal that voting at the conference should be governed by the same rules as that in the Security Council. They suggested that if the Chinese so wished the Council of Foreign Ministers could meet in China itself in January 1948.[1] There was a rumour that the Soviet Government had decided to prevent the other Powers from arranging a peace conference without its participation, by warning China that its taking part in such a conference would be a violation of the Sino-Soviet treaty of August 1945 by which each country was pledged not to make peace without the other.[2] At any rate, by the end of 1947 there was a complete deadlock between the Soviet Union and the other Powers concerned over the method by which a Japanese peace treaty should be negotiated.

OCCUPATION POLICIES, 1946–8

The opening meeting of the Allied Council in Tokyo did not take place until 5 April 1946. The atmosphere for its deliberations was inauspicious, since it was known that General Mac-Arthur had strongly opposed its establishment. By this time, too, the activities of the Soviet Military Mission were making themselves felt and the position of General Derevyanko (as both head of the Mission and Soviet representative on the Council) was obviously a difficult one.[3] MacArthur's speech at the opening meeting, the only one he ever attended, made it clear that in his view he should not be subject to any control in handling the problem of the occupation. He did not mention the existence of the Far Eastern Commission at all. As regards the Council, he stated:

As the functions of the Council will be advisory and consultative, it will not divide the heavy administrative responsibility of the Supreme Commander as the sole executive authority for the Allied Powers in Japan, but it will make available to him the several view-points of its members on questions of policy and action. I hope it will prove to be a valuable factor in the future solution of many problems.[4]

[1] *Soviet News*, 12 August and 29 November 1947.
[2] *NCDN*, 25 November 1947.
[3] Macmahon Ball, *Japan: Enemy or Ally*, p. 23.
[4] SCAP, Government Section, *Political Reorientation of Japan, September 1945 to September 1948* (Washington, USGPO, 1949), Appendices, p. 746.

He stated that he had given directions to the authorities that the Council should be furnished with copies of all directives together with the requisite background information, and such other material as it might specifically ask for. Matters of substance would normally be laid before it, before action was taken upon them. General MacArthur reviewed his past policies and issued a warning against 'sharp and ill-conceived criticism' of the occupation policies which would play into the hands of the evil forces of the world.

The American Chairmen of the Council did nothing to encourage it to extend the scope of its activities. Its meetings were held fortnightly, the minimum provided for in the Moscow Agreement, and were largely taken up with the reading of long reports from the Supreme Headquarters (SCAP).[1] After April 1946 SCAP normally controlled the work of the Japanese Government without the issue of formal directives. Its officers claimed that all important matters had already been covered by previous directives and argued that it was important to avoid giving the impression that the Japanese Government and Diet were the mere instruments of the occupation authorities. It was therefore wiser for General MacArthur to convey his wishes to the Government informally. But the result of this was that there were no directives for the Council to consider and even when it did make recommendations it had difficulty in ascertaining whether they had been carried into effect. For it was made clear that the Supreme Commander did not consider himself obliged to explain to the Council why he had or had not taken their advice.[2] The Soviet delegate used the Council chiefly for the purpose of asking for specific information. And since there was no likelihood of his point of view being adopted on any major issues, the object must have been to reinforce Soviet propaganda. The opportunity for this was given by the fact that the meetings of the Council were held in public. It could thus be used as a platform for expressing the general Soviet attitude towards Japanese questions which was simultaneously inspiring the propaganda emanating from the Soviet Military Mission in Tokyo and from the Japanese Communists.

[1] Immanuel C. Y. Hsu, 'Allied Council for Japan', *Far Eastern Quarterly*, February 1951; Mark Gayn, *Japan Diary* (New York, Sloane, 1948), pp. 180–2.
[2] Macmahon Ball, *Japan: Enemy or Ally*, pp. 28–32.

After 7 August 1947 the scope of the Council was still further curtailed since it was informed that the Supreme Commander would no longer furnish it with data on request. The Chairman declared that 'it had been abundantly clear that it has been a misuse of the Council to employ it as an information agency'. The freedom of members to propose topics for discussion was now severely limited and the number of items on the Council's agenda showed a sharp decline.[1] As a result, General Derevyanko was temporarily recalled to Moscow, his place being taken by his deputy, Major-General Kislenko.[2]

An attempt was made to prevent the Russians making direct propaganda use of the disputes on the Council. On 7 August 1946 the Council adopted, in the face of Soviet opposition, a ruling prohibiting its members from issuing press releases between the submission of items for the agenda and their discussion in the Council; but the Russians continued to hold press conferences and to express at them criticism of the occupation authorities.[3]

It was indeed impossible to limit the propaganda activities of the Russians, so long as the Soviet Military Mission existed. It was considerably larger than any other mission, numbering about 500 persons as against 150, for instance, in the British mission. And although it did not get itself accredited to the headquarters of the Supreme Commander, its expenses were paid by the Japanese Treasury on orders from SCAP. The sums demanded rose repeatedly, and in July 1946 SCAP deferred payment until it had received accounts for the sums spent, which the Russians refused to give. Subsequently the mission was reduced in size; but early in 1947 it still numbered 312 persons against the 334 persons of the other 16 foreign missions combined.[4]

It maintained two liaison officers with the Japanese press, but also no doubt helped to support the large number of pro-Soviet societies and propaganda magazines which rapidly appeared on the Japanese scene. SCAP maintained control to some extent over foreign propaganda, for instance by licensing

[1] Hsu, *Far Eastern Quarterly*, February 1951.
[2] *NYT*, 4 September 1947.
[3] ibid. 9 August 1946; *CSM*, 4 September 1946.
[4] Gayn, *Japan Diary*, pp. 299–300.

films; and from December 1946 it prohibited the importation of unauthorized printed matter. But the presence of the Soviet mission made this prohibition a fiction as far as Communist literature was concerned. Much use was made of cultural propaganda in the familiar Soviet manner.[1] Furthermore, Soviet radio propaganda was easily heard in Japan since it was relayed by powerful transmitters established in the Soviet Far East. SCAP, which was for its own purposes assisting in the widespread distribution of radio receivers among the Japanese people, thus became an unwilling accomplice of the Russians in this respect.

The nature of the issues upon which the Russians were going to clash with the occupation authorities became clear at a very early stage in the proceedings of the Council. After criticizing as too restricted the directive issued by General MacArthur on 4 January 1946 for a political 'purge', the Russians attacked the occupation authorities for failing even to fulfil this limited task. On 13 November Derevyanko raised the subject in a speech in which he declared that between 80 and 100 members of the Diet were unsuitable persons. The American representative brushed aside his charges and turned the Council's attention to other topics.[2]

In considering Soviet criticism of the occupation authorities as expressed both at the Council and in the Soviet press, it is necessary to keep in mind the fact that it sprung from fundamental differences of approach and of purpose. In this the Far Eastern scene reflected the same kind of problems as were leading in Europe to the rapid estrangement of the Soviet Union from its recent allies. Both the Russians and the Americans talked of democracy. But whereas the Americans naturally meant parliamentary democracy of the Western kind with an economy based primarily on private enterprise, the Russians thought of democracy as that state of affairs which should most rapidly assist the Communists to seize power. This meant that any real exchange of views between the Russians and the Americans was out of the question. It was not immediately apparent that this was so, because the Russians for general political reasons showed a reluctance to admit officially the

---

[1] Dallin, *Soviet Russia and the Far East*, p. 269.
[2] *The Times*, 14 November 1946.

existence of a serious rift between themselves and the Americans, and were content to let criticism of the occupation authorities be voiced largely by the British Commonwealth representative on the Council, the Australian Macmahon Ball.

The Soviet press was not inhibited by these diplomatic considerations, and from an early stage claimed that the 'democratization' of Japan was not proceeding properly. It commended the programme which the Communist Party of Japan was advocating:

abolition of the Emperor's power; careful fulfilment of the conditions of the Potsdam Declaration; work, food, and shelter for the people; land for the peasants; liberation of the small business from pressure of monopoly capital; punishment of war criminals; confiscation of all revenues received by concerns during the war; and the establishment of a single, national democratic front.[1]

But when in October 1946 Stalin was asked by an American journalist what his opinion was of the Japanese occupation, he replied: 'There are some successes; but better successes could be obtained.'[2]

The Russians maintained their objection to the retention of the Emperor, whom they considered to be a war criminal. The Russian delegate to the Far Eastern Commission at Washington raised the question of the Emperor having been allowed to go free by the occupation authorities, but without any result. And subsequently the Russians let the Japanese Communists do most of the attacking.[3]

There were other respects also in which the new Japanese Constitution did not meet with Soviet approval. They did not accept as sincere the clauses renouncing war. And they criticized the electoral law as undemocratic.[4]

The Russians were even more concerned over the position of the great economic combines—the Zaibatsu. Their leaders were not indicted as war criminals, and although the dissolution

[1] *Red Fleet*, 3 April 1946, quoted in *CSM*, 4 April 1946.
[2] *Moscow News*, 30 October 1946.
[3] *Soviet News*, 16 April; *NYHT*, 30 May and 9 June; *Red Star*, 17 April 1946.
[4] I. D. Levin, 'On the Project of the Japanese Constitution and the New Electoral Law', *Sovetskoe Gosudarstvo i Pravo*, 7 July 1946. The text of the Japanese Constitution, promulgated by the Emperor on 3 November 1946 and effective from 3 May 1947, is in J. C. Adams and others, *Foreign Governments and Their Backgrounds* (New York, Harper, 1950), pp. 849-65.

of these concerns was ordered in November 1945, the liquidation commission was only set up in August 1946, and by the end of the following month the industrial shares confiscated were estimated by the Russians to represent only a fraction of the total capital.[1]

With regard to land reform, the Russians advocated the immediate expropriation of large estates without compensation. The Americans considered that expropriation 'did not accord with democratic principles' and were supported in this stand by other members of the Allied Council. Eventually a compromise scheme worked out by Macmahon Ball was endorsed by Derevyanko and adopted by the Council. This provided for the compulsory sale to the Government of holdings exceeding a small maximum size and their resale on easy terms to the tenants. The Japanese Government was reluctant to implement the land reform and it passed the appropriate legislation apparently only under pressure from the occupation headquarters. Implementation of the law was very slow, as was pointed out by Derevyanko in the Allied Council on 23 July 1947.[2]

There were certain contradictions in the Russian criticisms of the occupation authorities. While they complained about the difficult economic situation and its effects upon the population, they refused to agree to the Japanese increasing their food supply by extending their fishing areas.

One relatively minor matter which illustrated the tendency of all issues to be caught up in the fundamental Soviet-American rivalry was that of the affairs of the Greek Orthodox Church in Japan. After the death of the Metropolitan, Allied headquarters refused to admit a Soviet nominee for the position of bishop, and sent for a bishop from the United States.[3]

Much more important was the question of the treatment of war criminals. As has been seen, the Russians objected to the immunity of the Emperor and leading members of the Zaibatsu. It was complained that by leaving the arrests of those accused to the Japanese police, some were enabled to commit suicide and

---

[1] M. Lukianova, 'Japanese Monopolies during the War and Post-war Periods', *MKiMP*, October–November 1946.
[2] *Soviet Monitor*, 25 July 1947; cf. Macmahon Ball, *Japan: Enemy or Ally*, Ch. 5.
[3] *Soviet News*, 19 June 1947.

all of them to destroy incriminating documents.[1] The trial of
the major criminals proceeded very slowly owing to the application of Anglo-Saxon rules of procedure for which the Russians
could find no justification. There were clashes between the
Russian prosecutor and the defence counsel who maintained
that the Russians brought undue pressure to bear on the
witnesses.[2]

In 1947 Soviet criticism of the occupation authorities grew
much sharper. At a meeting of the Council in May, Derevyanko charged the occupation authorities with total failure in
their task and with having done nothing to rehabilitate the
country's economy or to improve the lot of the peasants.
Moscow radio accused MacArthur of failing to implement the
Potsdam Declaration, of obstructing the decisions of the Far
Eastern Commission, and of handling the reparations problem
in such a way as to make sure that Japan's future would be that
of a strategic base for the United States.[3] There were further
Soviet reports about alleged plans for rebuilding the Japanese
army, and about the alleged construction of airfields in Japan.
It was asserted that Japanese pilots were being recruited into
the American Army Air Force.

The Soviet press contrasted the alleged disregard by the
Americans of the recommendations of the Allied Council, and
their refusal to submit the question of a Japanese peace treaty
to the Council of Foreign Ministers, with Soviet Far Eastern
policy which was represented as a consistent struggle for peace
and security, as demonstrated by the conclusion of the treaty
with China and the withdrawal of Soviet troops from Manchuria.[4]

Comment on the economic policies of the occupation authorities followed similar lines, the Americans being accused of
attempting to convert the country into a 'colony'. The permission given to the Japanese in August 1947 to resume foreign
trade was discussed in this context. The Russians also continued to complain that the Japanese Government was not

[1] M. Markov, 'The Approaching Trial of Major Japanese War Criminals', *New
Times*, 15 April 1946.
[2] *Red Star*, 17 September 1946; *Soviet News*, 25 July 1947; A. Trainin, 'From
Nuremberg to Tokyo', *New Times*, 17 March 1948.
[3] *CSM*, 14 May; *Soviet News*, 20 May 1947.
[4] *Soviet News*, 3 September 1947.

fulfilling its obligations to democratize and demilitarize the country, and that its measures had left unchanged the dominating position of the old ruling class. The dissolution of the Japanese military institutions was alleged to be merely a formal one; and Derevyanko alleged that the two demobilization bureaus that had been set up were in fact largely devoted to anti-Soviet intelligence work.[1] In following the course of these Soviet attacks upon the occupation authorities and the Japanese Government, the question arises how much of what the Russians said was really believed by the Soviet Government, and how much of it was propaganda in the narrowest sense. It is not a question that admits of an easy answer, but the later attractiveness to some American circles of the idea of a Japanese barrier to further Soviet expansion no doubt derived some stimulus from the doubts cast by the Russians upon American sincerity from the very beginning of the occupation régime.

The direct activities and propaganda of the Soviet Government and its representatives form the background to the career in this period of the Japanese Communist Party. The party, which had long been illegal in Japan, was allowed to emerge once more into the open. A SCAP directive of 4 October 1945 provided the basis for the release from imprisonment of a number of its leaders which actually took place on 10 October 1945. In his first report on non-military activities in Japan and Korea, General MacArthur wrote:

The (Japanese) Communist Party has not yet formally reconstituted itself although it has carried on a vigorous programme of activity and its presence has been keenly felt on the political scene. Published statements by party leaders indicate that they will carry on a 'Popular Front' programme approaching that of the Socialist Party in many respects. They have stated that the Japanese people are not ready for socialism.

The main objective of the Party will be to break the hold of the 'financial oligarchy'. They seek to establish a 'democratic Japan' in accordance with the Potsdam Declaration. They have announced that they would leave medium and small industries in the hands of the capitalists.

The Communists have been the only group to call for the total abolition of the imperial institution, but there are some indications

---

[1] *Soviet News*, 9 October 1946 and 14 June 1947; *Izvestia*, 14 June 1947; Gayn, *Japan Diary*, pp. 152–7.

that this stand may be modified with the arrival of the Japanese Communist group at present staying at Yenan, the headquarters of the Chinese Communist Party. This group, according to newspaper reports, does not regard the Emperor question as a burning issue and is willing to compromise on the point to provide a basis for unity with other labour factions.[1]

The leaders of the Japanese Communist Party at this juncture included many people with substantial experience in the Soviet Union. The Secretary-General, Kuyichi Tokuda, had been responsible for years for the selection of students for training in Moscow. Sanzo Nosaka had spent the years 1931–40 in Moscow, being for a time a member of the Presidium of the Comintern. Later he resided with a group of Japanese Communists at Yenan. Shojiro Kasuga, the specialist on underground activity, was a graduate of the Moscow Communist University for the Toilers of the East.[2] But on its revival the party strenuously asserted that it did not maintain any links with Moscow and did not wish to establish any ties with it in future. The policy of national independence was stressed by a prominent party leader, Yoshio Shiga, in October 1945, and repeated by Tokuda at the first post-war Congress of the party in December, and again in a foreign policy statement of 4 April 1946. This attitude was clearly intended to win popular support among the Japanese masses. Nosaka's slogan was 'towards a lovable Communist Party', and his proclaimed goal was the expansion of the membership to a million. For this purpose he was prepared to modify the radical opposition of the party to the Emperor. On this point, indeed, there seem to have been divisions in the party.[3] The Socialists, however, rejected several Communist approaches to them to form a 'United Front'.

These tactics were at first quite successful, and the Communist Party's influence on the radical elements in Japan developed rapidly. The circulation of its newspaper *Akahata* (*Red Flag*) became considerable. When the occupation authorities decided, however, to hold a general election on 10 April

[1] *NYT*, 3 January 1946; cf. Evelyn S. Colbert, *The Left Wing in Japanese Politics* (New York, IPR, 1952), pp. 95 ff.

[2] Paul Langer and Rodger Swearingen, 'The Japanese Communist Party, the Soviet Union and Korea', *Pacific Affairs*, December 1950, pp. 339–55.

[3] *The Times*, 13 November 1946; *NYT*, 14–16 January 1947; Rodger Swearingen, 'Nosaka and the Cominform', *FES*, May 1950.

1946, Derevyanko strongly argued against it, maintaining that it was necessary to postpone the election until the 'liberal' forces could build up their strength. The election did not indeed bring the Communist Party its expected successes. It obtained 2 million votes, but this secured to it only five seats. The Soviet press attributed this to the undemocratic nature of the electoral law and to the police pressure exercised on the voters.[1]

The disappointment of the Communists was increased in July, when the Social Democratic Party decided to form a democratic political front without the Communists. Meanwhile the occupation authorities and the Japanese Government had taken action to restrict Communist activities in general. At a meeting of the Allied Council on 15 May Derevyanko asked for information about charges brought against the Japanese Government by the Communist Party in their May Day message. The American Chairman, Atcheson, declared that the allegations were not based on fact and were derived from an unsigned document, which bore signs of having been translated into Japanese from a foreign language [i.e. Russian]. He cautioned members of the Council against giving public support to any political party in Japan, but stated that the United States Government did not favour Communism in Japan any more than in the United States. This forthright statement was endorsed by the American State Department.[2] Steps were also taken to limit Communist loquacity in the Japanese Parliament. On 2 December 1946 Nosaka criticized MacArthur for his reactionary policy and for restricting the activities of the Communist Party, but maintained that the party was nevertheless making progress.[3]

In characteristic fashion the Communist Party, when checked on the political front, began to concentrate more on the activities of the labour movement. The Japanese labour movement had been set free from legal restrictions by a law of 21 December 1945. There rapidly emerged a Congress of Industrial Unions under Communist influence, together with two similar groupings, one of them connected with the Social Democrats and one of them independent.[4]

[1] *Izvestia*, 1 April; *NYT*, 17 April; *New Times*, 1 May 1946.
[2] *NYT*, 16–17 May 1946.   [3] *NYHT*, 3 December 1946.
[4] B. Gribov, 'The Japanese Trade Unions', *New Times*, 16–18 April 1947; Martin, *Allied Occupation of Japan*, pp. 84–85; M. S. Farley, *Aspects of Japan's Labor*

In the autumn of 1946 there were a number of strikes; but they were mainly on straightforward economic issues, and the trade union leaders refrained, for the most part, from using political slogans, although they did not disguise their dislike of the Yoshida Government. The Government passed a new Labour Relations Adjustment Act on 20 September, which restricted the right to strike. Nevertheless the strike movement continued to grow and assumed a clearly political character. It was decided to call a general strike on 1 February 1947, to which the Communist Congress of Industrial Unions offered support. On 31 January, however, General MacArthur banned the strike and the Japanese Minister of Home Affairs interpreted the order to mean that the strikes of individual unions could also be banned, as a part of an attempted general strike.[1] The strike movement collapsed almost immediately and the unions found themselves much weakened. A movement to combat Communism in the trade unions had been organized, before the end of 1946, with strong support from Allied headquarters, and this now began to make headway.

New elections were held in April 1947. These marked a setback for the party, which this time secured only just over one million votes and only four seats. The return of war prisoners from the Soviet Union did not, it seems, strengthen the Communist position as much as had been expected.[2] When the party celebrated its twenty-fifth anniversary in Tokyo in July 1947, it was said to number about 70,000 members, predominantly workers, with some intellectuals and ex-servicemen. Its endeavours to gain peasant support had not been successful.[3]

Labour unrest died down for a time under the new Social Democratic Government of Katayama, formed after the April 1947 elections. But the rising cost of living soon brought about a renewal, and by the end of the year Communist influence in the labour movement, although weaker than previously, was still strong. The occupation authorities did their best to isolate the Japanese trade union movement from the international Communist-inspired labour movement; but a delegation from the

Problems (New York, Day, for Institute of Pacific Relations, 1950), pp. 70 ff.; Colbert, Left Wing in Japanese Politics, pp. 132 ff.

[1] Farley, Japan's Labor Problems, pp. 152 ff.
[2] NYT, 7 and 13 June 1947.
[3] NYHT, 18 June and 20 July 1947.

World Federation of Trade Unions was admitted to the country for a short period.[1]

On 4 October 1947 Nosaka published an article on new tactics for the Japanese Communist Party.[2] These took into account the failure of the strikes and demonstrations of the early part of the year, and the article inaugurated a period of more peaceful penetration and propaganda. The question of the Japanese prisoners of war gave rise to American accusations against the Russians. The Russians claimed that they had captured 594,000 prisoners during the Manchurian campaign. They had also interned a large number of Japanese civilians in Manchuria, South Sakhalin, and the Kuriles. Molotov stated in September 1945 that the prisoners were held by the Red Army and were being set to work. In December 1946 the Soviet press mentioned that they were being employed in the Soviet Union itself. About 800,000 Japanese were said to be working at the construction of the new Siberian railway, and the two highways which were being built parallel to it. Others were employed on different projects such as gold mining. Repatriated prisoners gave the information that prisoners were distributed in 754 different camps, the principal one being near Khabarovsk. They also stated that some 2,000 officers were said to be employed in engineering factories in Leningrad and were enjoying preferential treatment.[3]

The economic value of this labour to the Russians was reduced by the malnutrition and sickness prevalent among the prisoners. The prisoners, however, offered a valuable audience for Soviet propaganda and were subjected to intensive indoctrination. Their sole source of information was a newspaper edited by Japanese Communists and published in Khabarovsk. Political meetings were conducted in the camps, and before they were repatriated prisoners were asked to sign letters of appreciation addressed to Stalin and expressing support for a policy of friendship with the Soviet Union and for the establishment of Communism in Japan. Despite the denials of the Japanese Communist Party it would appear that it had direct

---

[1] *New Times*, 30 May 1947; *Trud*, 29 May 1947; Farley, *Japan's Labor Problems*, pp. 172–82.

[2] *NTT*, 4 October 1947.

[3] ibid. 17 December 1946; 18 October 1947; 15 May 1948.

contacts with the Soviet repatriation agency.[1] On the other hand, one of the American correspondents who interviewed groups of repatriates in the summer of 1947 said that they showed no traces of Communist indoctrination.[2]

Repatriation of the prisoners did not begin for a long time after the end of the war; as late as 26 June 1946 when the subject was broached by the American member of the Allied Council, the Soviet member refused to discuss it.[3] This refusal was repeated on subsequent occasions.[4] In October 1946 the Soviet Government decided to begin the repatriation of prisoners of war and of civilian internees. By February 1947 145,000 had returned to Japan and repatriation was proceeding at the rate of about 50,000 a month.[5] In March 1947, at the Moscow Conference, Marshall expressed concern about the large numbers still remaining in Russia.[6]

In October 1947 the American Chairman of the Allied Council referred to the petitions that had been received asking for the return of the remaining prisoners and offered to provide shipping to enable repatriation to be completed within five months. He declared that there were rumours of heavy mortality amongst the prisoners and of intensive efforts to indoctrinate selected ones with anti-American views. He also claimed that it was the degree of response to such indoctrination which was believed to govern priorities in repatriation.[7] The Soviet representative Kislenko asserted that the matter was not one for the Council to deal with. The Soviet Union was faithfully fulfilling its undertaking to repatriate 50,000 prisoners a month and the item had only been placed on the agenda in order to incite anti-Soviet feelings among the Japanese.

Another difference arose over the Japanese settlers in South Sakhalin. The Russians wished to retain their services and asked the authorities for permission for their families to join them. This permission was refused since the Russians would

---

[1] Paul Langer and Rodger Swearingen, 'The Japanese Communist Party, the Soviet Union and Korea', *Pacific Affairs*, December 1950.
[2] *NCDN*, 16 May 1947; *NYT*, 13 June 1947; *NYHT*, 18 June 1947.
[3] *NYT*, 13 and 26 June 1946.
[4] *NYHT*, 19 September 1946; *NYT*, 30 October 1946.
[5] *Soviet News*, 6 March 1947; Macmahon Ball, *Japan: Enemy or Ally*, p. 95.
[6] See above, p. 56.
[7] *NYT*, 30 October 1947.

give no assurance that the families and the settlers would be permitted to return to Japan if they so wished.[1]

OCCUPATION POLICIES, 1948–51

At the end of 1948 the economic situation in Japan was very unsatisfactory. Mining and industrial production was only about 45 per cent. of the 1930–4 average, and extensive imports of food were causing heavy expenditure.[2] The occupation authorities could not be directly blamed for this situation since they had been given no direct responsibility for ensuring Japan's economic welfare. On the other hand, in so far as they had in fact purged the Japanese administration, or interfered to break up the great economic combines, they had made it more difficult for the Japanese to tackle their own problems by their habitual methods. And the uncertainties of the future were not conducive to any great initiative on the part of the Japanese, who could also blame the costs of the occupation for part of their difficulties.

In the light of these circumstances the particular policies for which the Soviet representatives on the Council had been pressing, and the advanced labour and trade union legislation in which they had taken particular interest took on a double aspect. Though such policies were justified in the name of 'democratization', their more immediate effects were to increase Japan's economic difficulties and thus to provide a fertile field for Communist agitation. Soviet opposition was certain to be aroused by any attempt to revise this programme in a more realistic direction, both because such a revision would tend inevitably to restore some of the features of the old Japan, and because, if successful from the economic point of view, it would remove some of the circumstances in which Communism was likely to thrive.

Nevertheless the decision to strike out on a new path was reached and the first official indication of the change in the American attitude was given in a statement on 8 January 1948 by the Under-Secretary of the Army, K. C. Royal. He said that the new conditions in the world had produced 'an inevit-

---

[1] ibid. 7 September 1946; cf. Dallin, *Soviet Russia and the Far East*, p. 276.
[2] R. A. Fearey, *Occupation of Japan: Second Phase, 1948–50* (New York, Macmillan for IPR, 1950), p. 123.

able area of conflict between the original concept of broad demilitarization and the new purpose of building a self-supporting nation'. There would be no further deconcentration of industry and some of the purged elements would have to be restored to spheres of activity. A new plan for the economic stabilization of Japan was now prepared.[1]

This important change in the policy of the occupation authorities was less reflected in the proceedings of the Far Eastern Commission than might have been expected. This body had been called on to make increasingly few decisions of consequence and the Soviet delegate to it had not hitherto been particularly intransigent. As late as February 1948 the Soviet delegate, while announcing his disapproval of the measures proposed concerning Japanese disarmament, announced that he would abstain from voting on the resolutions and merely press for amendments. No agreement was reached, however, on the problem of reparations or on the level of industry to be permitted to Japan.

The proceedings of the Allied Council in Tokyo continued to be of not much greater importance. Derevyanko, who had been recalled to Moscow in August 1947, did, it is true, return to his post on 1 September 1948. But the procedure of the Council gave the Soviet representative, whoever he might be, very little opportunity for expressing his views, and he often preferred to address himself to the Supreme Commander by letter. The position got still more difficult when the Americans once more raised the question of the Japanese prisoners of war on 15 December 1949. The Soviet delegates walked out in protest against the discussion of this matter, and did the same on every subsequent occasion when the question was raised. When on 19 June 1950 the Chinese People's Government demanded representation on the Council, the Soviet representative sent a letter indicating his support for this demand.

The refusal of the Far Eastern Commission to expel the Kuomintang representative caused the Soviet representative to boycott this body also. But on 19 October 1950 the boycott ended and the Soviet representative Payekin resumed his seat.

[1] J. B. Cohen, 'Japan: Reform versus Recovery', FES, 23 June 1948; Fearey, Occupation of Japan, pp. 124 ff.; Macmahon Ball, Japan: Enemy or Ally, pp. 129–30, 167–9.

On 8 November 1950 Kislenko attended a meeting of the Allied Council in Tokyo and raised the matter of Chinese representation on it, but was ruled out of order. Presumably in the altered circumstances brought about by the Korean war, the propaganda value of both bodies was too great for the Soviet Government to indulge its resentment at their proceedings by the boycott. The Council had become simply a platform from which both the Russians and the Americans could direct their rival appeals to Japanese opinion.

The Soviet mission in Tokyo was reorganized at the end of May 1950 when fifty-three of its members, including both Derevyanko and Kislenko, left for Russia and thirty-seven new members arrived. On 30 August Kislenko returned to Tokyo as the definitive successor to Derevyanko.

A new view about the proper level of Japan's future economy was closely connected with the question of reparations. It was illogical to remove further industrial equipment from the country while at the same time a great deal of money was being spent to secure its economic recovery. The Americans were opposed to reparations from current production, because Japan obtained most of her raw materials from abroad. On 12 May 1949 the American representative at the Far Eastern Commission announced that the United States intended to stop reparations deliveries and in effect recommended that no further reparations should be collected.[1] The reparations actually obtained up to that date consisted mainly of Japan's overseas assets, and some industrial equipment removed under the advance transfer programme. The former was valued at about $3,000 million and the latter at $35 million, with another $5 million in preparation for delivery. The Soviet Union did not receive any of this, and therefore got no reparations besides the 'war booty' in Manchuria. The occupation authorities had seized about $130 million worth of gold and other precious metals, which were reserved for distribution by the Far Eastern Commission after occupation costs had been met. But it was obvious that the whole sum would, in fact, be taken up in this way.[2] Nevertheless, the Soviet Union did not develop this into a major grievance, and accusations about the American breaches

[1] *FES*, 29 June 1949.
[2] Fearey, *Occupation of Japan*, p. 145.

of the Potsdam Declaration did not include the subject of reparations, presumably in order to avoid unpopularity in Japan.

This desire to win popularity must be taken as a partial explanation of why the Russians represented themselves as the champions of a complete and unrestricted revival of all Japan's industries other than those devoted to armaments. On 23 September 1948 the Soviet member made a statement at the Far Eastern Commission advocating this policy, and arguing that only in this way would the needs of the Japanese people be satisfied, legitimate claims for reparations be met, and Japan cease to be so dependent upon 'external factors . . . alien to her interests'. The peoples of Asia would also benefit by a revival of Japanese exports. Appropriate international control could prevent this removal of restrictions ending in a development of war industries.[1] A similar stand was taken by the Soviet delegate to the Conference of the United Nations Economic Commission for Asia and the Far East, which was held at Lapstone in Australia in November to December 1948.

This programme proved less valuable to Soviet propaganda than might have been expected because of the considerable measure of economic recovery which actually took place in Japan in 1949. It was aided by a programme on the part of SCAP based on an interim directive of 10 December 1948. This authorized the Supreme Commander to apply and carry out jointly with the Japanese Government a series of measures involving important aspects of the country's economy, such as the balancing of the budget, alterations in taxation and credit policy, the stabilizing of wages, and the introduction of measures for the control of prices and of dealings in foreign currencies. The Russians argued that these measures would bring about fundamental changes in the control régime and should therefore have been submitted to the Far Eastern Commission. They added that the directive actually violated previous decisions of the Commission, for example, by failing to stipulate that only those forms of economic activity should be encouraged which would strengthen 'democratic' forces and prevent the restoration of Japanese economic strength from contributing to the rebuilding of her war industry.[2]

[1] *Information Bulletin* of the Soviet Embassy at Washington, 6 October 1948.
[2] *Soviet News*, 3 and 21 February 1949; *Pravda*, 6 March 1949.

The Japanese economic recovery slowed down by the beginning of 1950 owing to the shrinkage of both the domestic and the foreign markets.[1] The outbreak of the Korean war in June 1950 gave Japanese industry a stimulus in quite a new direction.

Soviet criticism of the stabilization programme was mainly concentrated on the wage stop. The Soviet press also stressed the subjugation of Japan to American monopoly interests, declaring that the stabilization programme completely tied Japan's economy to that of the United States. The United States, it was pointed out, now supplied 62 per cent. of Japan's imports against a pre-war average of 25 per cent. Some effort was made to secure the support of other countries for the Soviet protests by emphasizing that Japan was being encouraged by the Americans to compete in Asia with exports from Europe, and in particular from Great Britain.[2]

On the whole, however, the Soviet interest in the economic position of Japan was increasingly overshadowed by fears that Japan was being rearmed. In January 1948 Kislenko asked the Allied Council for information about ten separate items relating to the alleged remilitarization of Japan, but was refused the information.[3] In February, as has been seen, the Soviet representative on the Far Eastern Commission dissented from its views on Japan's disarmament, particularly as regards arms permitted to the civil police and delays in the destruction of war materials. References to alleged American plans for rebuilding a Japanese army appeared at frequent intervals in the Soviet press; and much was made of remarks of General MacArthur to the effect that the American occupation forces were not there to hold down the Japanese, which was unnecessary, but to transform the country into an outpost for the defence of Anglo-Saxon interests, and that although he did not intend to use Japan as an ally, it would not be difficult to form a Japanese army to co-operate in the country's defence.[4] According to the SCAP information bureau these remarks were published

---

[1] Farley, *Japan's Labor Problems*, pp. 218–19.
[2] *Pravda*, 3 March and 15 September 1949; N. Pyatinsky, 'Japanese Textile Industry in 1948', *Vneshnaya Torgovlya*, April 1949; H. Eidus, 'American Policy of Militarization and Fascization of Japan', *Voprosy Ekonomiki*, 8 August 1950.
[3] *Soviet News*, 9 and 14 January 1948.
[4] *Pravda*, 9 March 1949.

in violation of confidence, but their contents were not officially denied. On 3 May 1950 Derevyanko sent a letter to Mac-Arthur asking for information as to the veracity of press reports concerning the restoration and modernization of Japan's air and naval bases. After the outbreak of the Korean war, Soviet reports and comments on the alleged remilitarization of the country miltiplied still further. There were reports that the Japanese army was being revived under the guise of a police corps, and there was a Soviet protest at the Far Eastern Commission about the reported preparations to use Japanese forces in Korea.[1] The alleged utilization of Japanese industry for the purpose of producing arms for the Korean war was loudly condemned, and a variety of reports on the subject were published, including one about the production of parts for atom bombs.[2]

Despite these strained relations with the occupation authorities there was some development of trade between the Soviet Union and Japan. Such trade had been negligible in the pre-war period, but since the Soviet Union had acquired territories previously owned or controlled by Japan, and trading predominantly with her, it had become mutually advantageous. In October 1947 a barter agreement was concluded providing for the exchange of Sakhalin coal for Japanese rolling-stock and fishing trawlers. Trade increased in volume during 1948. Its subsequent development can be seen in the following table:

	Exports to Japan	Imports from Japan
	(in $000)	
Second half of 1948	2,538	1,985
First half of 1949	..	4,493
Second half of 1949	1,933	2,787
First half of 1950	..	723
Second half of 1950	738	..

(Source: SCAP, *Bulletin*, no. 52, p. 37)

These statistics indicate that although the flow of goods from Japan was fairly even, the Soviet Union did not supply any goods for long periods. The reason for this, according to press reports, was that the Russian prices were too high.[3] As a result

[1] *Pravda*, 2 December 1950; *Soviet Monitor*, 7 December 1950.
[2] On the last point see *Pravda*, 3 November 1950.
[3] *SCMP*, 4 June and 1 December 1949.

the Japanese accumulated a favourable balance which they could not spend, and exports to the Soviet Union were stopped for this reason in April 1950; although they were resumed on a modest scale later in the year after the beginning of the Korean war.

The Japanese Communist Party continued in 1948 its bid to enlist mass support by a programme intended to appeal to the widest possible circles and maintained its efforts to establish a 'united democratic power'. Every opportunity was used to foment industrial strife, and by the middle of the year Communist penetration of the trade unions of Government workers, a particularly poorly paid section of the community, had proceeded a long way. On 22 July General MacArthur addressed a letter to the Prime Minister, Ashida, proposing a revision of the Civil Service Act, to the effect that civil servants should have no right to strike or use other delaying tactics or to employ collective bargaining. An appropriate ordinance to this effect was issued by the Japanese Cabinet on 31 July.[1] This action was severely criticized by the Soviet representatives in the Allied Council and the Far Eastern Commission, and it was violently attacked by the Communist Party.[2] It was explained by the occupation headquarters that their action had been taken in order to prevent a paralysing strike planned for 7 August.

Nevertheless, the rise in the cost of living and a rise in unemployment produced favourable circumstances for Communist propaganda. In the elections of January 1949 the Communist Party polled about 3 million votes (9·6 per cent. of the total) and secured 35 seats in the House of Representatives, compared with their previous 4. The conservative 'Democratic Liberals' also gained at the expense of the Social Democrats and moderates. Soviet comment on the results declared that the successes had been won despite an oppressive electoral law and the pressure exerted by the Government and the occupation authorities.[3]

In its propaganda the Communist Party stressed its complete independence from the Soviet Union. It tried to secure support

[1] Farley, *Japan's Labor Problems*, pp. 189–90.
[2] Colbert, *Left Wing in Japanese Politics*, pp. 270 ff.
[3] *Izvestia*, 26 January; *Pravda*, 1 February 1949. For a short account of Japanese parties and politics in this period see Adams and others, *Foreign Governments and Their Backgrounds*, Ch. 50.

from farmers and among the intelligentsia and even in business circles, declaring that business men would come to oppose the new Yoshida Government, which was destroying the chances of Japanese trade with Communist China.[1] In contrast to contemporary pronouncements by Communist leaders in France and Italy, Tokuda did not declare that the Japanese workers would welcome liberation by Soviet troops. He stated that the situation in Japan was quite different, and that the Japanese workers would resist any foreign invaders, though he insisted that it was quite clear that the Soviet Union had no intention of invading Japan.[2] In interviews with American and British correspondents, Nosaka declared that despite its previous relations with the Comintern the Japanese Communist Party had now become fully independent. He hoped that the recent victories of the Chinese Communists would be of assistance to it. It had adopted their methods of organization and hoped to co-operate with them. The Japanese Communists hoped that the Chinese People's Government would soon be represented on the Allied Council. The Japanese Communists also envisaged co-operation with the Soviet Union on terms of equality, and they had shown their independence by their plan of appealing to the Allied Council to speed up the repatriation of the 400,000 prisoners of war still in the Soviet Union.[3] This appeal was never made.

Despite their electoral successes in January 1949, the Communist representation in the Diet was still too small to prevent the passage of a 'stabilization and austerity budget' which involved a considerable retrenchment of staff in Government services and private industry.[4] The party resorted to a campaign of demonstrations aiming at the overthrow of the Yoshida Government, and the discrediting of the occupation authorities.[5]

The Communists were handicapped to some extent by the

[1] Statement by Nosaka in an interview, CSM, 18 March 1949. Yoshida had replaced Ashida as Prime Minister in October 1948.
[2] NYHT, 1 March 1949.
[3] CSM, 18 March 1949.
[4] Fearey, Occupation of Japan, p. 112.
[5] The actual figures of unemployment in Japan at this time are difficult to ascertain. The Russians claimed that unemployment reached 10 million in March (Farley, Japan's Labor Problems, pp. 225-6; Pravda, 4 and 5 March 1949).

divisions within the Japanese labour movement. The Congress of Industrial Unions became fully Communist controlled in 1949 and joined the World Federation of Trade Unions. But large numbers of anti-Communists left it and its total membership fell from the 1½ million in 1946 to 500,000 in 1949. Other Japanese unions joined the new anti-Communist International Confederation of Free Trade Unions.[1]

The main opportunity given to the Communists was that afforded by the dismissal of numerous railway workers— 100,000 by mid-July 1949 according to Soviet sources. There were many cases of obstruction and sabotage of the railways despite the fact that strikes were practically banned by the occupation authorities during this period. The tension on the railways culminated in the murder of Shimoyama, the president of the National Railway Corporation who had been in charge of the programme of dismissals. The Soviet press declared that he had in fact committed suicide and that the story that it was a murder had only been invented in order to give an excuse for suppressing working-class organizations.[2]

These events coincided with general reports of a growth of Communist influence, particularly in the Yamagachi prefecture and on the island of Hokkaido, close to the Soviet outposts on the Kuriles. As a result there were demands in Japanese political circles that the party should be suppressed, and the Diet set up a committee to examine 'un-Japanese activities'. But the occupation authorities did not agree to ban the party.

The widespread outbreaks of violence in 1949 could not be directly traced to the Communist Party. But the party was, in fact, at this period almost openly advocating a resort to force, and a statement by MacArthur on 4 July 1949 assailing Communism 'as national and international outlawry' suggested that the Supreme Commander would now support the Japanese Government in measures of suppression. Increased police action followed and proved successful by the autumn. Raids on the offices of the Communist newspaper *Akahata* and on certain party headquarters showed that the party did not command enough support for successful resistance and was being driven

---

[1] Farley, *Japan's Labor Problems*, pp. 222–3.
[2] Fearey, *Occupation of Japan*, pp. 112–13; *Izvestia*, 8 August 1949; *Pravda*, 17 August 1949.

back on to the defensive, particularly since economic conditions were improving.[1]

These failures led to a serious crisis in the Japanese Communist Party, which began in January 1950 with a violent attack on Nosaka in the Cominform Journal, branding him as anti-democratic, anti-Socialist, and anti-Japanese.[2] The party leaders in Japan do not seem to have expected this attack, and refused to accept the first reports of the article as authentic. After it had been confirmed by a Moscow dispatch, the party took some time to adjust itself to the new situation and began by backing Nosaka, expelling Ko Nakanishi, who was known to support the attack.[3]

On 12 January a spokesman of the party gave an interview to the press and read a prepared statement, agreeing that there were some defects in Nosaka's arguments, but saying that these could be remedied in practice, and extolling him as a courageous, patriotic lover of the masses, who had the confidence of the people.[4] This did not satisfy the Soviet critics. On 21 January *Pravda* reproduced an article from the Japanese Communist Party paper which had been published on the 17th. This accused Nosaka of having advocated a purely parliamentary campaign instead of more direct action and called for a confession of his errors. Subsequently he made a full recantation, and the party's Politburo accepted the criticisms of the Cominform.[5] However, Nosaka remained the leading figure in the party, in contrast to the fate of persons similarly attacked by the Cominform in the European countries. The course of this crisis suggests that the Japanese Communist leaders had not been altogether misrepresenting the facts when they stated that the party was not directly controlled from Moscow. It looks as though it had been left to draw its own conclusions from the Soviet and international Communist press and radio. Even after this incident it was possible to make mistakes; for another

[1] Fearey, *Occupation of Japan*, pp. 116–18.

[2] *For a Lasting Peace*, 6 January 1950; cf. Colbert, *Left Wing in Japanese Politics*, pp. 285–92.

[3] *CSM* and *NYHT*, 11 January 1950. Some weeks later Nakanishi was himself condemned by the Soviet press, apparently for having advocated 'social revolution' as early as the autumn of 1949, ahead of the party line (*Pravda* and *Izvestia*, 3 February 1950).

[4] *CSM*, 12 January 1950; *The Times*, 13 January 1950.

[5] 'Nosaka and the Cominform', *FES*, 17 May 1950.

important member of the Politburo, Yoshio Shiga, was attacked in April by *Akahata* (*Red Flag*), apparently for having gone too far in attacking the party's previous line.[1]

A new programme for the party was elaborated by Tokuda in his report to the Central Committee in January 1950, and this seems to have received Soviet approval since it was reproduced in *Pravda* on 15 April. It demanded the fulfilment of the Potsdam Declaration and took a strong stand against a separate peace between Japan and the Western Powers, an issue that was now coming to the fore. The object of the party was still to create a 'united front of workers, peasants, fishermen, and other strata of the nation'. It was therefore important to take heed of the demands of the masses in order to attract them to the party and secure an electoral victory; but it was also necessary to organize local struggles especially amongst the unemployed, which could later be merged into the general national struggle. A new wave of strikes in February 1950 did in fact create the most critical situation in Japan since February 1947.[2] The Communists were assisted at this time by the fact that the non-Communist labour movement and the Social Democrats were also opposed to the Government on the issues of a separate peace and rearmament, as well as on its deflationary policy.

Rumours at this time, that the Russians had announced semi-officially that they would return the Kuriles to Japan if a suitable régime came into being, were presumably another device to secure support for the Communist Party. On 1 May a new party document was published with the title: 'On the fundamental duties of the Japanese Communist Party in the coming Revolution.'[3] On the following day, in a statement concerning the third anniversary of the Japanese Constitution, MacArthur said that consideration should be given to the question of whether the Communist movement should any longer be given 'the validity, sanction and protection of the law'.[4]

A new series of clashes followed between the Communists and the authorities. On 30 May there took place in Tokyo the

[1] *NYT*, 16 April 1950; cf. Colbert, *Left Wing in Japanese Politics*, pp. 295-9.
[2] Farley, *Japan's Labor Problems*, pp. 237-9.
[3] *The Times*, 2 May 1950.
[4] Fearey, *Occupation of Japan*, pp. 205-6; *NYT*, 3 May 1950.

first direct clash between Communists and American soldiers.[1]
At the beginning of June MacArthur ordered the exclusion
from public office of twenty-three members of the party's Central Committee, including six members of the Diet, and during
the following days similar steps were taken with regard to other
members of the party. MacArthur rejected in the strongest
terms the protest made against these measures on 24 June by
the Soviet member of the Council.[2] In the by-elections in this
month to the Upper House of the Diet the Communist representation was reduced.

Further developments in Japan were closely connected with
the outbreak of the Korean war in June 1950. The 'liberation'
of Korea was one of the major items in the programme of the
Japanese Communist Party, which had maintained close contacts with the Communist movement in that country and which
had organized a 'Korean league' among Koreans resident in
Japan. This organization had been dissolved in September
1949.[3]

When the war broke out, the Japanese Communist press followed the Soviet line and, on orders from the Supreme Commander, the Japanese Government suspended the publication
of *Akahata* and other Communist papers.

The Central Committee of the party was unable to carry out
its functions after the purge in June and soon afterwards it was
announced that a new 'provisional central leading authority'
had been set up to act in place of the different party organs
until the next party Congress. The new authority was under
the chairmanship of Etsuro Shiino and did not include either
Nosaka or Tokuda;[4] the arrest of these two men and other leading figures was ordered by the Government for failing to answer a summons to an interrogation by the Attorney-General.[5]
One must presume that the party leadership was largely an

[1] *NYHT*, 31 May 1950.

[2] ibid. 7 and 17 June 1950; *Soviet News*, 28 June 1950.

[3] According to some reports the Japanese Communists had known for at least
ten weeks about the planned attack on South Korea since the leaders of the various
organizations under their control had had a secret meeting early in April in order to
prepare for the expected developments (Langer and Swearingen, *Pacific Affairs*,
December 1950, pp. 351–3). On the 'Korean league' see Colbert, *Left Wing in
Japanese Politics*, p. 110.

[4] *Soviet Monitor*, 9 and 16 June 1950.

[5] *SCMP*, 17 July 1950; *Pravda*, 12 October 1950.

underground one after this time, but the party was not banned as such and still had six members in the Diet; some of its legal activities could thus continue. The publicly revealed membership of the party was halved between its peak in February 1950 and the summer of 1951. During 1951 interference by the Government with Communist activity continued on an increasing scale.

The controversy over the fate of the Japanese prisoners of war continued. A Soviet communiqué issued in May 1949 stated that 418,166 prisoners had been repatriated since 1 December 1946. This meant that the repatriation rate had been much lower than the 50,000 a month which had been agreed upon. The communiqué also mentioned for the first time that the Russians reckoned that 70,800 prisoners had been set free in 1945 in the actual area of hostilities. It admitted that 95,000 prisoners were still being held and declared that all these would be repatriated by November apart from a certain group who were suspected as war criminals.[1] This communiqué took no account of the many thousands of Japanese civilians who had been repatriated on a voluntary basis according to the statements made by the Russians in 1946, and it was generally held on the basis of reports by repatriated prisoners that the Russians had understated both the total number of prisoners taken and the number of casualties among them.[2]

In 1949 94,973 men were repatriated and this accounted for all the prisoners mentioned in the May communiqué. Nevertheless early in 1950 the Russians repatriated three further groups of prisoners, totalling 8,700. The last of these groups included many senior officers.[3] In April 1950 the Soviet Government announced that repatriation was complete apart from 1,487 war criminals, and 971 more who had committed serious crimes against the Chinese people and were to be handed over to the Chinese Central People's Government.[4]

On 12 June 1950 the United States Government sent a note to the Soviet Union in which it alleged that the Soviet Government was still holding a considerable number of Japanese prisoners. The charge was repeated at a meeting of the Allied

---

[1] *Soviet News*, 25 May 1949.   [2] *SCMP* and *Daily Telegraph*, 25 May 1949.
[3] *NYT*, 10 January, 9 February, 18 April 1950.
[4] *Soviet News*, 24 April 1950.

Council in August when the number was given as 370,000. The Soviet Government strenuously denied these accusations.[1] As counter-propaganda against the reports of harsh treatment, Tass circulated a communiqué about the thousands of letters of thanks, said to have been addressed to Stalin by the returning prisoners, expressing friendship with the Soviet people and gratitude for the treatment they had received.[2]

The trial of war criminals by the International Military Tribunal in Tokyo went on for over two and a half years. Its decision was made public in November 1948. Despite their criticisms of the procedure, Soviet commentators were satisfied with the verdict, which included an unqualified recognition of the fact of Japanese aggression against the Soviet Union.[3]

In December 1949 a Soviet Military Tribunal held a trial at Khabarovsk of twelve senior Japanese officers accused of taking an active part in the preparation and employment of bacteriological weapons, and sentenced them to corrective labour camps for periods of from three to twenty-five years. It was said that the germs had been used since 1940 against the Chinese and Mongolians, and had been prepared for use against the Soviet Union and the United States.[4] On 1 February the Soviet Government sent notes to the United States, Great Britain, and China asking that an international court should be appointed by the Supreme Commander in Japan to try the Emperor and four generals as responsible for the general direction of bacteriological research and production. Further notes making the same demands were sent on 30 May 1950 and 30 December 1950, but no reply was made. The Soviet press insinuated that the United States Government was protecting the guilty for interested motives. On 11 May 1950 a Soviet note also protested against MacArthur's order releasing certain war criminals

[1] *Pravda*, 25 August 1950.

[2] *Soviet Monitor*, 6 May 1950. In 1951 it was believed that 60,000 prisoners were being held on Sakhalin as a potential 'army of liberation' (R. Guillain, *Manchester Guardian*, 4 September 1951).

[3] A. M. Vasilev, 'On Rapid Trial and Punishment of War Criminals', *Sovetskoe Gosudarstvo i Pravo*, 3 March 1949. By 1950, however, the Russians were arguing that the Tokyo trials, like the Nuremberg trials, showed attempts by international reaction to save the imperialist leaders (M. Raginsky and S. Rosenblut, *The International Trial of the Major Japanese War Criminals*, Moscow-Leningrad, Academy of Sciences, 1950).

[4] *New Times*, 1 and 8 January 1950.

who had served part of their prison sentences. Similar protests were made in August 1950 and February 1951.

THE NEGOTIATIONS FOR A JAPANESE PEACE TREATY

In the second half of 1948 the Soviet Union began to press for the speedy conclusion of a peace treaty with Japan; the refusal of the United States to discuss the question at the Council of Foreign Ministers was ascribed to the American wish to build up Japan as a military base against the Soviet Union. At the Paris session of the Council of Foreign Ministers in May–June 1949 the Soviet representative, Vyshinsky, suggested that Ministers should be giving thought to this subject and said that his Government wished to know when a meeting of the Council could be held with the participation of China to prepare a draft treaty as laid down in the Potsdam Agreement. On objections being raised, the matter was for the moment allowed to drop.[1] The Soviet wish for an early peace treaty was restated by Derevyanko at a 'Soviet-Japanese friendship meeting' on 10 November 1949.[2]

In a speech at Berkeley on 16 March 1950, Acheson explained the United States point of view by saying that the Soviet leaders should recognize the interest which nations other than those represented in the Council of Foreign Ministers had in the question of a peace treaty with Japan and should refrain from taking up positions or insisting on procedures which would block progress towards such a treaty.[3] The Soviet attitude was illustrated again by an article in *Pravda* by Viktorov in which he stated that the Soviet Union insisted on a procedure for preparing the treaty which should provide for the participation of all interested countries similar to what had actually been the case in relation to the treaties with Bulgaria, Hungary, Rumania, and Finland.[4] This comment suggested the possibility that the Soviet Union might be prepared to waive its right of veto in the drafting of the treaty.

In Japan itself the Communists took the lead in opposing suggestions that if there were no general agreement Japan might do well to conclude a peace treaty with the non-Communist

[1] *The Times*, 24 May 1949.
[2] *Akahata* (*Red Flag*), quoted *SCMP*, 13 November 1949.
[3] *NYHT*, 17 March 1950.   [4] *Pravda*, 19 March 1950.

Powers alone.[1] On 1 June 1950 the Japanese Government indicated that in view of the differences between the Soviet Union and the United States and the consequent obstacles to a general peace, it would be prepared to sign a treaty with any of the Allied nations that would recognize Japanese independence.[2] On 14 September 1950 President Truman authorized the State Department to initiate informal discussions with regard to a peace treaty with the other Governments represented on the Far Eastern Commission.[3]

The principles proposed by the United States as a basis for such a treaty were circulated to the interested Governments early in October through their delegations to the United Nations General Assembly. On 6 October John Foster Dulles, who was in charge of these approaches, had an unofficial discussion on the subject with the Soviet delegate Malik. The report ran that Malik had been unable to disclose the Soviet attitude to the United States list of principles, but that he had jestingly suggested that the United States did not really desire a treaty at all since this would mean withdrawing United States forces from Japan.[4] But on 20 October Malik indicated that the Soviet Union was prepared to enter informal talks.[5]

The prospects for an agreement were not promising since in a speech at the United Nations on 23 October Vyshinsky charged the United States with intending to rearm Japan and to use Japanese troops in Asia.[6] There had been previous charges by the North Koreans that Japanese troops were actually being used in the Korean fighting.

On 26 October Dulles had a private talk with Malik and gave him a memorandum on the peace treaty; the press reported that Malik had raised no objections to the proposed procedure and had agreed to refer the memorandum to Moscow.[7] This was denied by the State Department and the report was described as totally unfounded by the Soviet delegation to the United Nations.[8] On 20 November, however, Malik handed a document to Dulles, which asked for an explanation of some of the points in the memorandum. Despite the private character of

[1] *CSM*, 16 May; *Pravda*, 28 May 1950.
[2] *NYT*, 2 June 1950.
[3] ibid. 15 September 1950.
[4] ibid. 10 October 1950.
[5] ibid. 21 October 1950.
[6] *Pravda*, 25 October 1950.
[7] *NYT*, 31 October 1950.
[8] ibid. 3 November 1950.

the discussions, the Soviet Government published the contents of the whole exchange and the State Department followed suit by publishing the American proposals and the Soviet reply. The Soviet attitude was not intransigent on points of procedure. The Russians did not insist that the Council of Foreign Ministers must be the body to draft the treaty, though they raised the point whether a treaty with only some of the Powers that had fought Japan could be considered in view of the fact that it would violate the United Nations declaration of 1 January 1942.[1]

The main Soviet objections were to the proposed territorial and security provisions, which may be summarized as follows: Japan would (a) recognize the independence of Korea; (b) agree to a United Nations trusteeship with the United States as the administering authority of the Ryukyu and Bonin islands; (c) accept the future decisions of the United Kingdom, the Soviet Union, China, and the United States, on the status of Formosa, the Pescadores, South Sakhalin, and the Kuriles. In the event of no decisions being taken within a year after the treaty came into effect, the United Nations Assembly would decide on the status of these territories. Special rights and interests in China would be renounced. The Russians objected to a new decision being taken on Formosa, the Pescadores, South Sakhalin, and the Kuriles, which had in their view been finally disposed of by the Cairo and Yalta Agreements. They also argued that the proposed United Nations trusteeship had not previously been envisaged and was contrary to the declaration that the Allied Powers had no designs whatever of territorial expansion.

The American proposals stated that

the treaty would contemplate that pending satisfactory alternative security arrangements such as the United Nations assumption of effective responsibility, there would be continuing co-operative responsibility between Japanese organs and the United States and perhaps other forces for the maintenance of international peace and security in the Japan area.[2]

On this point the Russians questioned whether any occupation

---

[1] *Soviet News*, 24 November 1950; *NYT*, 25 November 1950.
[2] *NYT*, 25 November 1950.

troops would remain in Japan after the conclusion of the treaty and whether the reference to 'Japanese organs' meant that Japanese armed forces would be created. They also questioned the plans for Japan's future economy but did not comment on the American proposal that further reparations should be re-nounced. On 4 December 1950 the Chinese Central People's Government put forward an emphatic demand to be allowed to participate in the negotiations and raised objections to the American proposals similar to those advanced by the Soviet Union.[1]

The United States replied to the Soviet Government on 28 December rejecting the Soviet criticisms of its proposals and refusing to deal with the Chinese Communists.[2] Information released at this time suggested that the United States was discussing with other members of the Far Eastern Commission the terms of proposed separate bilateral treaties with Japan, and that these would impose no restrictions on Japan's rearma-ment. It was made clear that, in the American view, there was no hope that the Soviet Union would agree to the peace terms that the United States wished for, and that if the Soviet Govern-ment were permitted a veto on these terms there would be no prospect of any treaty in the foreseeable future.[3]

On 10 January 1951 Truman approved the proposal that a Presidential mission headed by John Foster Dulles should be sent to Japan to explore Japanese views, especially regarding future arrangements for collective security. Dulles saw Malik in New York to acquaint him with the purpose of his journey. It was made clear that his mission was a purely exploratory one and that it was intended to be preliminary to future talks in which the Soviet Union would be asked to take part.[4] After his visit to Japan, Dulles returned to Washington by way of Manila, Canberra, Wellington, London, and Paris.[5]

The Dulles mission was violently attacked in the Soviet press, which declared that his real object was to create in the Pacific an aggressive grouping directed against the Soviet Union and China.[6] At a press conference after his return Dulles, who had

---

[1] *Soviet Monitor*, 6 December 1950.   [2] *NYT*, 29 December 1950.
[3] ibid. 1 January 1951.   [4] ibid. 11 and 16 January 1951.
[5] US Department of State, *Japanese Peace Conference San Francisco, September 1951* (USGPO, 1951).
[6] *Izvestia*, 11 February 1951; *Pravda*, 20 February 1951.

earlier stated that he was going to see Molotov, expressed the hope that the Soviet Union would participate in further negotiations and hinted that unless the Soviet Union signed the proposed treaty its right to continue in occupation of the Habomai islands near the Japanese coast and of the Kuriles might be challenged.[1]

Dulles had several conversations with Malik and three documents were exchanged between the two Governments.[2] But on 3 March Malik issued a statement denying that he was conducting negotiations with Dulles and intimating that he had no intention of doing so.[3]

In the course of March, a United States draft treaty was worked out and circulated to a large number of countries. It was sent to the Russians on 29 March and their reply was received on 7 May. This document declared that the United States proposals were incompatible with existing agreements; that the treaty should be negotiated by the Council of Foreign Ministers, including for this purpose a representative of the Peking Government; and that the Council should draw into consultation all the members of the Far Eastern Commission.[4] A further United States memorandum on 19 May stated that the differences between the United States and Soviet Governments were insufficient to prevent the conclusion of a treaty, but asked the Soviet Government to clarify its attitude to the zones of interest that it had acquired in Manchuria and to explain its alleged retention of approximately 200,000 Japanese prisoners.

A Soviet reply on 10 June returned to the complaint that the American draft had not provided for Japanese disarmament, the withdrawal of foreign troops from Japan, or the prohibition to Japan of participation in a coalition directed against any of the signatory Governments. The draft, it was claimed, ignored the fact that Japan's economy had been placed in an 'enslaving dependence' on the United States, disregarded the question of democratic rights for the Japanese people and the territorial provisions of the Cairo and Yalta Agreements. There should be no separate peace treaties, and the Council of Foreign Mini-

---

[1] *NYHT*, 1 March 1951.
[2] US Department of State, *Japanese Peace Conference*, p. 6.
[3] *NYT*, 4 and 6 March 1951.   [4] *Soviet News*, 25 May 1951.

sters was the only appropriate body for dealing with the whole matter. Nevertheless the Russians did not ask that the Council should be convened and proposed instead the calling of a peace conference in July or August. This conference should include representatives of all the States whose forces had taken part in the war against Japan and should examine the existing drafts for a treaty.[1]

At the beginning of July the Soviet press, which had not paid much attention to the negotiations about a peace treaty, began to refer to the alleged American intention of concluding a special treaty with Japan by which that country would be turned into an armed base.

Meanwhile in June the United States draft treaty was combined with a separate British draft into a single text which was circulated to the other Powers, giving them until 13 August to propose changes in it. It was published on 12 July and severely criticized in the Soviet press.

The Soviet note of 10 June was answered by the United States on 14 July. The reply pointed out that the Soviet Government had not really objected to any provisions of the draft but was protesting because the treaty would not restrict Japan with regard to the right of individual or collective self-defence, a right recognized in the United Nations Charter as 'inherent'. The procedure proposed by the Soviet Government would exclude from the negotiation of the Treaty France and 'many Pacific and Asiatic countries which bore a far heavier burden in the Japanese war than did the Soviet Union'. In conclusion, the Russians were invited to send a delegation to the signing of the treaty which would take place at San Francisco early in September.[2] A formal invitation to do so was sent to the Soviet Union along with all the other States on 20 July.

It was thus clear that the Soviet Union was being asked to attend the Peace Conference merely to affix its signature to the text of a treaty which would be based on the Anglo-American draft, modified in some respects to meet the criticisms of other Governments to which it had been circulated. In view of the strong criticism of this document in the Soviet press, it was generally assumed that the Soviet Union would not send a dele-

[1] *Soviet Monitor*, 11 June 1951.
[2] *NYT*, 15 July 1951.

gation to San Francisco. But on 12 August the Soviet Government informed the United States Government that it intended to send a delegation, and that this delegation would submit the Soviet proposals concerning a Japanese peace treaty.[1] An American reply on 16 August noted this intention but recalled that the purpose of the Conference was the signature and conclusion of 'the final text of the peace treaty' previously circulated.[2]

Neither the Soviet decision to attend the Conference nor the American reply to the announcement of the Soviet Government's intentions was commented on in the Soviet press. Soviet comment on the draft treaty continued to emphasize the claim that it involved the restoration of Japanese militarism. The Russians used their familiar tactics of not publishing comments of their own on the impending Conference but reproducing foreign ones, especially from Communist China. This had the additional advantage of emphasizing the solidarity on this issue of the Soviet and Chinese Governments. On 3 September *Pravda* quoted a Shanghai newspaper to the effect that the expectations of the American imperialists that they could dominate the San Francisco Conference had been thwarted by the Soviet decision to attend it, and by the refusal of India and Burma to participate. Even if the 'bandits' were to succeed in getting their draft of a peace treaty with Japan through the Conference, it would be nothing but a fiction. What significance could it have when the peoples of Asia and of the whole world were opposed to this criminal document? The Tass dispatch from San Francisco itself on the formal opening of the Conference on the evening of 4 September said much the same thing and added that the draft treaty was a violation of the international agreements of Cairo, Yalta, and Potsdam. It stressed President Truman's admission that the United States intended to include Japan in a 'Pacific defensive system' and to permit its rearmament.

Gromyko's behaviour at the Conference was milder than might have been expected from the previous tone of the Soviet press. He first proposed that the Central People's Government of China should be invited to take part in the Conference—a

---

[1] *Soviet Monitor*, 17 August 1951.
[2] *NYT*, 17 August 1951.

proposal that was ruled out of order—and also objected to the proposed rules of procedure which imposed severe limitations on the time available for speeches. He used the one hour to which he was entitled to make a speech on 5 September in enumerating the principles upon which a treaty with Japan should be based, according to the Soviet view. He demanded that the agreements of Cairo, Yalta, and Potsdam should be adhered to, that Japan should be demilitarized and the occupation troops withdrawn, that democratic tendencies among the Japanese people should be strengthened and territorial questions settled. Japan should not be allowed to contract any alliances against a State with which it had been at war, and should be prohibited any war industries. On the other hand she should be allowed to develop a peaceful economy which would permit her to satisfy legitimate claims for reparations. 'It would', he said, 'be much easier for Japan to do this than to pay for the damage by using directly the labour of the Japanese population, as is provided for by the American-British draft.'[1]

Gromyko also criticized the proposal to withdraw various islands from Japanese sovereignty and to place them under American administration in the guise of a United Nations trusteeship. He made the familiar criticisms of the procedure that had been followed in preparing the draft treaty. Finally he proposed the following series of concrete additions and amendments to it:

1. Chinese sovereignty over Manchuria, Formosa, the Pescadores, and the Pratas and Paracel islands and the islands of Nanshatsyuntao, including Spratly Island, was to be acknowledged, and Japanese sovereignty over the islands which had been part of Japan until 7 December 1941, with the exception of those specified as going to China.

2. All foreign troops were to be withdrawn within ninety days of the treaty entering into force.

---

[1] This remark referred to the following clause in the draft: 'Japan will promptly enter into negotiations with Allied Powers so desiring, whose present territories were occupied by Japanese forces and damaged by Japan, with a view to assisting to compensate those countries for the cost of repairing the damage done, by making available the service of the Japanese people in production, salvaging and other work for the Allied Powers in question' (US Department of State, *Draft Treaty of Peace with Japan with Draft Declarations by the Government of Japan* (Washington, USGPO, 1951), p. 16).

3. Reparations were to be the subject of a conference of the States concerned.

4. The treaty was to be ratified by its signatories, Japan included, and to become effective for all States that ratified it when the ratification instruments had been deposited by Japan and a majority of a list of States, which included the Chinese People's Republic and the Mongolian People's Republic.

5. Japan was to undertake 'to remove all obstacles on the way to the regeneration and consolidation of democratic tendencies among the Japanese people'.

6. Japan was to undertake not to allow 'the revival of Fascist and militarist organisations' and 'not to enter into any coalitions or military alliances' directed against any Power which had taken part in the war against her.

7. Japan's army was to be limited to 150,000 men with not more than 200 medium and heavy tanks, her navy to 25,000 men with a total tonnage of 75,000, her air force to 20,000 men with 350 planes, none of them bombers. Japan was to conduct no military training other than that required for the permitted forces.

8. Japan was not to possess, produce, or experiment with atomic weapons, self-propelled projectiles, guns capable of firing at a range of more than 30 kilometres, sea-mines and certain types of torpedoes.

9. Japan's peaceful industry, trade, and merchant shipping were to be unrestricted.

A final proposal more specifically related to the Soviet Union's own security requirements was that the straits around the Japanese islands should be demilitarized. These straits, it was proposed, should be open to the passage only of those naval vessels belonging to Powers adjacent to the Sea of Japan.[1]

Acheson refused to regard the Soviet proposals as being officially submitted or as open to discussion by the Conference, and proposed a motion, which was accepted, curtailing further discussion.

Gromyko made another statement on 7 September protesting against the procedure that had been adopted at the Conference, and warning those who signed the treaty that they would have

[1] *A. A. Gromyko on the Japanese Peace Treaty* (pamphlet published by *Soviet News*, London, 1951).

to take the responsibility for whatever might be the consequences in the Far East. He alleged that the treaty was an
instrument of aggression since it was to be followed by a bilateral agreement for the stationing of American troops in Japan.
Together with Poland and Czechoslovakia, the Soviet Union
withheld its signature from the treaty. At a press conference on
the day on which the treaty was signed by the remaining countries present, 8 September, Gromyko again voiced the Soviet
objections to its provisions but refused to comment on reports
that the Soviet Union might conclude a separate peace with
Japan.

In retrospect it appeared that the Soviet Union's attitude to
Japan had not been defined at the time of the San Francisco
Conference. The main appeal of the Soviet proposals was to
China and other Asian countries rather than to Japan. And the
provisions for limiting rearmament were likely to be welcome
to sections of opinion in other countries which felt that the
United States was too eager to take at their face value the
peaceful and democratic protestations of the new Japan. The
proposal that the Japanese should get back the Ryukyu and
Bonin islands was obviously anti-American rather than pro-
Japanese in inspiration. It could hardly counteract the certain
Japanese hostility to the demands for reparations, for the final
cession of South Sakhalin and the Kuriles, and for the neutralization of the straits around Japan.[1]

It was clear that the Soviet statements at the Conference
were made simply for the record, and the appearance of the
Soviet delegation seemed unlikely to mark an important stage
in Soviet policy. For the time being the Americans were still
firmly in control, and there was obviously but little that the
Russians could do to alter this situation in their favour.

[1] 'Communist Policy in Japan', *The Times*, 21 February 1952.

VII

The Soviet Union and Korea

THE DIVISION OF KOREA

THE Cairo Declaration of 30 November 1943 stated that the three signatory Powers, the United States, Great Britain, and China, were 'determined that in due course' Korea should become free and independent. Although this implied the expulsion of the Japanese from that country, there appears to have been no agreement as to whether Korea should be granted independence immediately, or only after a period of international tutelage. President Roosevelt himself favoured the idea of an international trusteeship for Korea and discussed it with Eden in March 1943.[1]

During the Yalta conversations, Korea received little attention. There seems to have been a suggestion that Korea might fall within one of the categories of trusteeships envisaged in the proposed charter of the United Nations. The United States presented the view that if such a trusteeship were created for Korea, it should be a multi-Power trusteeship, and the Russians apparently concurred.[2] Stalin asked Roosevelt whether any foreign troops would be stationed in Korea and expressed approval when Roosevelt replied that this would not be necessary; but there was no formal arrangement.[3] During his talks with Hopkins in Moscow in May 1945 Stalin agreed that there should be a trusteeship for Korea under the United States, Great Britain, China, and the Soviet Union, but Hopkins's notes on the talks do not mention the question of military occupation.[4]

At the plenary session of the Potsdam Conference on 22 July at which trusteeships were discussed, it appeared that the Soviet

[1] Hull, *Memoirs*, ii. 1596; A. L. Grey, jun., 'The 38th Parallel', *Foreign Affairs*, April 1951.
[2] G. M. McCune, *Korea Today* (London, Allen & Unwin for IPR, 1950), p. 43. According to Harriman, Stalin's first reaction when trusteeship was proposed was to ask why this was necessary if the Koreans could produce a satisfactory Government (*Forrestal Diaries*, p. 56).
[3] Sherwood, *White House Papers*, ii. 857.
[4] ibid. ii. 892.

Government wished 'to exchange views on a possible trusteeship over Korea'.[1] At a discussion on the future campaigns against Japan on 24 July, the Russians asked the Americans about the possibility of their invading Korea but were told that this would not be practicable until after a landing in the main islands.[2] The Korean theatre thus fell wholly within the sphere of operations allotted to the Soviet forces. By announcing on 8 August its adherence to the Potsdam Declaration the Soviet Union endorsed the Cairo Declaration and was thus committed to the principle of a four-Power trusteeship for Korea and to the view that the country should ultimately recover its independence.

The Soviet military operations against the Japanese in Korea began on 12 August with landings at points a little over 100 miles from Vladivostok. These were followed by a landing at Wonsan farther to the south.

The question of the problem of allotting zones of occupation to the American and Russian forces had been considered by the United States Government before the Soviet landings took place. This was in connexion with the drafting of General Order No. 1 which the Supreme Commander, General Mac-Arthur, was to cause the Japanese Government to issue in order to direct the surrender of the Japanese armies. In paragraph 1 of this document it was provided that Japanese forces north of 38° north latitude were to surrender to the Soviet Commander, while those to the south of this line were to surrender to the American Commander. The choice of the 38th parallel as the line of division between the Soviet and the American forces was thus taken on purely military grounds with no thought of possible political consequences. It may even have been made at a relatively subordinate level in the American administration.[3] The draft of General Order No. 1 was submitted to Stalin, who

[1] Leahy, *I Was There*, p. 476.

[2] ibid. p. 484. US House of Representatives, Committee on Foreign Affairs, *Background Information on Korea* (Washington, USGPO, 1950), p. 3.

[3] *Background Information on Korea*, pp. 2–3; Grey, loc. cit. pp. 481–5; Welles, *Seven Major Decisions*, p. 164. Grey's suggestion that the line had been chosen because it was south of the Russian landing at Wonsan is difficult to accept because the document was drafted before the landings began. The 38th parallel had been proposed as a political demarcation line between Russian and Japanese interests in 1896 and again in 1904. But it is uncertain if this historical precedent was known in the US War Department where the General Order was drawn up.

requested and obtained some minor amendments, but the Russians, who were still meeting stiff resistance from the Japanese in Manchuria, made no reference to those provisions of the order relating to the 38th parallel. The conclusion of hostilities thus found Russian and American troops facing each other across a line which virtually divided Korea into a northern and a southern half.

The two parts of the country, which in ancient times had been separate political units, are somewhat dissimilar. The north is a dry-field area which in 1945 had larger agricultural units than the south, and a greater proportion of owner-farmers. It was also more industrialized, but the population was only about 8 million against something like 20 million in the south. The south is predominantly an area of rice culture in irrigated fields, and its economy was basically one of small tenant-farms. Northerners and Southerners were traditionally different in character, rather like the contrast between Northerners and Southerners in China.[1]

Nevertheless a division, even of a temporary kind, was obviously contrary to the wishes of the Koreans, who demanded immediate unity and independence. But local leadership was almost wholly lacking and all the Koreans with any political experience were in exile. One strongly conservative group had formed a so-called 'Provisional Government' at Chungking, which kept a representative, Syngman Rhee, in the United States and was tolerated, though not officially recognized, by the United States and China. On the other hand, the large number of Koreans in the Soviet Union had been strongly organized by the Communists. During the war their leaders were transferred to Yenan, in Communist-held China, where they formed a Korean Emancipation League with a reputed membership of nearly 2,000.[2] Even before the end of the war the Soviet press was denouncing the 'Provisional Government', and particularly Rhee. It was clear that the Russians would support the more radical elements in Korea, and would insist on such policies as drastic land reform and a close linking up of the Korean economy with the country's continental neigh-

[1] McCune, *Korea Today*, pp. 58–60.
[2] Dallin, *Soviet Russia and the Far East*, pp. 255–8; McCune, *Korea Today*, pp. 27–29.

bours, China and the Soviet Union, rather than with overseas Powers.[1]

The Russians did not receive any co-operation from the Japanese in North Korea, who sabotaged mines and factories before retreating to the south. The breakdown of the civil administration enabled local 'People's Committees' to take over the Government in the whole area occupied by the Russians, who gave them their full support. These Committees were the product of an underground movement which had been organized, according to some observers, by Soviet-trained Koreans, who had infiltrated into the country during the war.[2] Other Communist émigrés probably returned in the wake of the Red Army. Most important of all, perhaps, the leading members of the Korean Communist Party which had dissolved itself in 1928 were released from prison. These included their leader, Pak Heun Yong, who took the lead in reforming the party. Soviet sources stress the spontaneous nature of these political developments.[3] But there is no doubt as to their tendency, and it seems probable that the People's Committees were mainly under Communist influence from the beginning.[4]

Immediately after the Japanese capitulation a preparatory commission was formed in Seoul for the purpose of organizing a more permanent political structure. Under its auspices, more than 1,000 delegates from the People's Committees met at Seoul on 6 September and elected a 'Central People's Committee of the Korean Republic'.[5] The chairman of this body was Lyuh Woon Heung, seemingly not a Communist but with a record of opposition to the Japanese. Elections were ordered for 31 March 1946. Meanwhile, a programme for taking over the property of the Japanese and of 'traitors to the Korean people', and for fairly widespread socialization and other radical reforms was drawn up.

[1] B. Yavorov, 'Korea, Past and Present', *New Times*, 15 August 1945.
[2] E. Grant Meade, *American Military Government in Korea* (New York, Columbia University Press, 1945), p. 42.
[3] For a Soviet account of events in Korea, 1945–8, see the chapter by F. I. Shabshina, 'Korea after the Second World War', in *Krisis Kolonialni Sistema*.
[4] Meade suggests that this was not always the case (*American Military Government in Korea*, p. 56), but the levers of control were clearly in Soviet hands from the start.
[5] This is Shabshina's terminology (in *Krisis Kolonialni Sistema*). Dallin talks of the 'Provisional Commission' of the Korean People's Republic (*Soviet Russia and the Far East*, p. 252).

The American Commander of the occupation forces refused to have dealings with this Committee, and its authority was limited to the area under Soviet occupation. In South Korea the Americans worked through the existing administrative machine. There was thus from the very beginning a complete difference between the arrangements made for the administration of the two halves of the country, and no provision had been made for liaison between the two occupation forces. General Hodge indeed had full authority to settle local problems with the Soviet Commander, but the latter seemed to have no corresponding powers. American inquiries were not replied to, and the Russians sealed off North Korea along the parallel with a cordon of troops and tanks. This situation was particularly disadvantageous from the economic point of view since Korea under the Japanese had been a single economic unit. The northern half of the country had supplied coal, electric power, and some heavy industrial products while being dependent on the South for foodstuffs. When, early in the occupation period, the Americans sent some trains to the North, expecting that the Russians would allow the railway system to be run as a unit, the rolling stock was retained in the North. Requests for coal were not complied with, and although electric power was not cut off, its supply was not based on any formal agreement and was hence regarded as precarious.

The Korean problem was discussed on American initiative at the Moscow Conference of the Council of Foreign Ministers in December 1945, and was dealt with in part three of the agreement concluded on 27 December. The agreement provided that a Joint Commission, representing the United States and Soviet occupation commands, should be set up in order to assist in the formation of a Provisional Government. For this purpose it was 'to consult with the Korean democratic parties and social organizations' and to submit recommendations to the Governments of the Soviet Union, China, Great Britain, and the United States. Following upon consultations with the Provisional Korean Government, the Commission was to submit to the four Powers proposals 'for the working out of an agreement, concerning a four-Power trusteeship of Korea for a period up to five years'. A conference representing the two occupation commands was to be convened within two weeks for the consideration of urgent problems and for the elaboration of measures for permanent co-ordination in administrative and economic matters.[1]

The Soviet press fully endorsed the proposals for a trusteeship. *Moscow News* wrote:

This will be the first practical experiment in joint trusteeship on the part of the principal Allied Powers, and, if successful—and if properly effected it cannot fail to be successful—it may be applied later to the solution of a number of similar questions concerning the future of one or another mandatory or colonial territory.[2]

An article in *Izvestia* expressed confidence that the trusteeship would result in the co-ordination of Soviet and American policies, in a swift economic recovery and a return to political stability in Korea.[3]

The conference between representatives of the two commands met on 16 January in Seoul, the Soviet delegation of seventy-three persons having arrived there on the previous day. The Americans wished to put the question of restoring the economic unity of the country before the question of establishing a Provisional Government. They therefore proposed a unified operation of railways and other communications and of electric power, as well as uniform policies on matters of banking, currency, and commerce, the establishment of the free movement of goods and of certain categories of persons between the two zones, and the setting up of joint control bases along the 38th parallel, which should remain unfortified. The Soviet delegation wished to discuss only specific subjects, such as the supply of power, the exchange of certain commodities and equipment, and the re-establishment of traffic by rail and road between the two zones. It refused to consider a unified operation of utilities, which would impinge on absolute Soviet control in North Korea. When the American delegation disclosed that, as a result of poor yields due to war-time shortages of fertilizer and the great influx of refugees from the North, South Korea was not in a position to supply rice, the Soviet delegation ruled out commercial exchanges from the consideration of the conference. After three weeks of discussion, a limited agreement was

---

[1] McCune, *Korea Today*, pp. 275–6.
[2] Quoted in the *Manchester Guardian*, 31 December 1945.
[3] *Izvestia*, 12 January 1946.

reached on communications and on liaison between the two commands, but subsequent attempts by the Americans to implement even this limited agreement were largely unsuccessful. The conference resulted only in intermittent exchanges of mail and of small military liaison teams.[1] An agreement was reached on the admission of weekly American convoys to travel twenty-five miles across Soviet-occupied territory in order to reach the Onjin peninsula, which juts out into the sea from a point on the west coast of Korea north of the 38th parallel, but which extends south of it, and was consequently occupied by an isolated American garrison.[2] The movement of Koreans across the parallel was not permitted. American journalists were not allowed to enter the Soviet zone and in retaliation Soviet correspondents were excluded from the South.[3] In consequence of this, subsequent developments in North Korea must largely be gathered or deduced from Soviet sources.

North Korea was mainly being run, as has been seen, by local elements selected for their pro-Soviet leanings. It was thus quite easy for the Russians to secure public expressions of approval for the policy of trusteeship. But in the South, the nationalist elements indulged in many demonstrations in favour of complete and total independence. In order to counteract the consequent unpopularity of the Americans, the State Department let it be known that the Moscow Agreement had been primarily based on a Soviet draft proposal.[4] On 23 January Tass replied by accusing the United States Command in Korea of permitting anti-Soviet propaganda to be carried on and of having itself inspired the protests against the Moscow Agreement. On the following day it issued a further statement denying the United States allegation that it was the Soviet Union that had insisted on the establishment of a trusteeship. According to the Soviet version, the Americans had presented proposals to the conference providing for a unified administration with Korean advisory organs, the whole to be under a multi-Power trusteeship for a period of from five to ten years. The Soviet delegation had then presented its own proposals, which were more favourable to the cause of Korean indepen-

---

[1] US Department of State, *Korea's Independence* (Washington, USGPO, 1947), pp. 3–4.   [2] *NYT*, 10 March 1946; Gayn, *Japan Diary*, pp. 378–84.
[3] *NYT*, 22 February and 10 March 1946.   [4] *CSM*, 21 January 1946.

dence since they provided for the establishment of a Provisional Government instead of merely advisory organs. The Russians had also proposed that five years should be the extreme limit for the duration of the proposed trusteeship. The American delegation had then withdrawn its draft in favour of the Soviet proposals, to which minor amendments were suggested, and it was thus the Soviet draft that had been the basis of the decisions adopted at Moscow.[1]

The Seoul conference had not dealt with the question of setting up a Provisional Korean Government and had decided to set up for this purpose a Joint Soviet-American Commission of ten members. In preparation for the meeting of this body, the head of the United States delegation to it, General Hodge, issued a statement on 11 March setting out the United States viewpoint on the problem. He said that the American occupation forces had endeavoured to establish in their zone freedom of speech, of assembly, of religion, and of the press. He considered that an early unification of the country both economically and politically was an absolute prerequisite for the accomplishment of the Commission's tasks. The United States delegation, he said, did not favour any particular Korean party or group.[2]

The Soviet attitude to the idea of the political unification of Korea seemed unfavourable. The Soviet press particularly attacked Syngman Rhee and accused him of having promised mining concessions to American politicians and business men in return for promises of support.[3] The well-known North Korean figure Cho Man Sik, who was believed to be the only Northern politician acceptable to Rhee, disappeared after rumours that he had been placed under house arrest by the Soviet authorities.[4]

When the Joint Commission met at Seoul on 20 March, General T. F. Shtykov, the leader of the Soviet delegation, declared that the Soviet Union hoped that Korea would

[1] USSR, Ministry of Foreign Affairs, *The Soviet Union and the Korean Question* (Moscow, 1948), pp. 7–10. Later Soviet writings laid even greater stress on the alleged American plans for the 'enslavement' of the Korean people. See e.g. in addition to the chapter by Shabshina already referred to, M. Markov, 'The Soviet Union and the Korean Question', *New Times*, 15 December 1948; G. Tavrov, 'The Korean Problem after the Second World War', *Sovetskoe Gosudarstvo i Pravo*, no. 7, 1950.

[2] McCune, *Korea Today*, pp. 276–8.

[3] *Pravda*, 13 March 1946.   [4] *NYT*, 14 March 1946.

become 'a true democratic and independent country, friendly
to the Soviet Union, so that in future it will not become a base
for an attack on the Soviet Union'. He condemned without
naming them 'certain anti-democratic groups' opposed to
Korea's unification, and expressed the conviction that the Provisional Government should be established on the basis of a
wide unification of all 'democratic parties and organizations,
supporting the decisions of the Moscow Conference'.[1] The
Russian view prevailed that the establishment of the Government should be discussed first, before the question of unification
of the country's economy and administration.[2] From the outset
the Russians clashed with the Americans decisively over the
propaganda against trusteeship being carried on by numerous
political groups in South Korea. For the Americans to accept
Shtykov's view that only those Koreans supporting the trusteeship decision should be consulted on the formation of the
Provisional Government would mean excluding a very large
proportion of the political parties in South Korea. The Russians even insisted on excluding groups which had in the past
expressed their opposition to trusteeship. A complete deadlock
was reached, and the Russians refused to proceed to the discussion of economic or administrative questions. The Commission adjourned *sine die* on 8 May, Shtykov having received
orders to return to North Korea.[3] During the period of the
Commission's deliberations tension had been increasing, and
there were reports that considerable numbers of Soviet troops
evacuated from Manchuria had been moved into North Korea.[4]
There were also clashes between American and Russian troops
along the 38th parallel.[5]

The Russian version of the reason for the breakdown in the
talks was given in an article in *Izvestia* on 15 May 1946. This
asserted that the American list of organizations to be consulted
in South Korea excluded many important democratic elements.
It defended the Soviet refusal to discuss the economic unification of the country on the grounds that this was a matter for the
Koreans themselves, and should hence be left to the Provisional
Government when it had been formed.[6]

[1] McCune, *Korea Today*, pp. 279–81.   [2] *CSM*, 23 March 1946.
[3] US Department of State, *Korea's Independence*, pp. 4–5.
[4] *The Times*, 6 April; *Scotsman* 27 April; *Chicago Daily News*, 19 June 1946.
[5] *NYT*, 15 April 1946.   [6] cf. *Pravda*, 3 June 1946.

The breakdown of the talks was the final step in the separation of North and South Korea. In the North the People's
Committees were organized at the provincial, district, and
local levels, and with Soviet support administered the whole
country. In October and November 1945 there had been
elections to the local committees on the basis of universal
suffrage. A 'people's militia' was also set up armed with
Japanese rifles and working in close contact with the Red
Army to eradicate 'subversive elements'.[1]

Various parties and organizations, all of them pro-Communist
in outlook, were organized at this time no doubt with official
encouragement: the People's Party, the Workers' Confederation of Labour, the Women's Union, the Communist Youth
League, and the Peasant Union. In February 1946 a provisional
People's Committee of Northern Korea was set up as a central
organ of authority. The President of the Committee was Kim
Il Sung (also known as Kim Ir Sen) who had been a leader of
the partisan detachments operating against the Japanese in
Manchuria and Northern Korea and who had been a member
of the Communist Party since 1930.[2]

This Committee began to set in motion a series of revolutionary changes in the economic and social structure of Northern
Korea. The first and most important of these was the land
reform set out in a decree of 5 March 1946. This provided for
the confiscation not only of land belonging to the Japanese and
to 'traitors to the Korean people' but also of land belonging to
other owners if exceeding a maximum of five cho (about 12¼
acres) or if permanently rented out irrespective of acreage.
This land was to be distributed in small plots free of charge to
agricultural labourers and small-holders, and the newly created
small peasantry was to hold the land in perpetual ownership.
According to Soviet sources the carrying out of this reform
involved the distribution of land to 725,000 labourers and small-

[1] On events in North Korea see the articles by J. N. Washburn in *Pacific Affairs*,
June 1947 and March 1950. An American correspondent, who was allowed to
visit the country briefly in July 1947, confirmed the existence of a strong police
and other armed forces. Co-operation with the Soviet occupation troops was
facilitated by the fact that the majority of them spoke the language, which suggests,
if true, that they were composed of Korean residents in the Soviet Union (*CSM*,
26 July 1947).

[2] See Shabshina in *Krisis Kolonialni Sistema*, pp. 258 ff., and the accounts by
Washburn and McCune for this and the succeeding paragraphs.

holders; a large class of persons was thus given a vested interest in the stability of the new régime. On the other hand, the problem of the North Korean food supply was met by a tax in kind of about one-quarter of the crops produced.

A measure was also passed on 10 August 1946 nationalizing without compensation all enterprises belonging to the Japanese or to those described as traitors to the Korean people. The nationalization law made it clear that the Koreans were indebted for this achievement to the Soviet army, for it stated that

the Soviet army having entered the territory of Korea with the object of destroying the Japanese army, liberated Northern Korea from Japanese slavery, assured democratic freedoms for the Korean people, took under its protection the private and public property of the Koreans, preserved national property and created the opportunity for the most rapid economic and cultural rebirth of the Korean State.[1]

The extent of direct Soviet participation in the country's economic life was obscure. Some scope in the economy was left to private initiative at this stage, very much as in the Communist areas in China. Labour legislation was passed in June 1946 and trade unionism was actively encouraged. By the end of 1947, 380,000 out of a total of 430,000 workers belonged to trade unions.[2]

On the cultural side the usual efforts were made to establish links with the Soviet Union and the strictly controlled North Korean press followed the Soviet line on all international matters, and contrasted favourably the activities of the Soviet occupation authorities with those of the Americans in the South.

In the middle of 1946 a new 'Single Democratic National Front of North Korea' was formed for the political organization of all pro-Soviet elements. In August the Communist Party was amalgamated with the People's Party and was henceforth styled the Workers' Party; as such it provided the nucleus and motive force of the Democratic Front. Elections to the provincial, town, and district people's committees were held in

---

[1] Shabshina in *Krisis Kolonialni Sistema*, pp. 264–5.
[2] McCune, *Korea Today*, pp. 209–12. The picture of prosperity given by the North Korean press was offset by the fact that large numbers of refugees crossed over into South Korea (Meade, *American Military Government in Korea*, p. 95).

November 1946, and to village and regional committees early in 1947. These elections were conducted on the Soviet pattern, that is to say with a single list of candidates representing the Democratic National Front, who received 99·6 per cent. of the votes cast. The composition of the committees subsequent to the election showed the use in North Korea of the device familiar in both Communist China and the Soviet Union, of filling a large proportion of the places with so-called 'non-party' figures.[1] This had already been proved elsewhere to be no bar to absolute Communist control.

A Congress of delegates from the committees met at Pyongyang from 17 to 20 February 1947. It unanimously approved all the legislation passed by the Provisional People's Committee and also adopted a national economic plan. It further elected a permanent body, the People's Assembly of North Korea, consisting of 237 members. This met on 21 and 22 February and elected a Presidium, a Supreme Court, and a new People's Committee of North Korea, which became in effect an executive Cabinet. Although the Labour Party had only 88 members in the Assembly, it supplied 16 of the 22 members of the Cabinet, which was headed by Kim Il Sung. The organs of the Government in North Korea now dropped the adjectives 'provisional' or 'interim', thus suggesting that the structure was intended to be permanent.[2]

After the breakdown of the Joint Commission in May 1946, the Americans made repeated efforts to resume negotiations, but their proposals were all rejected.[3] They were thus forced to contemplate the setting up of a more independent form of Government in the other zone; and from the end of September various sections of both the central and provincial administrations were handed over to the Koreans, although the Americans remained in an advisory capacity. An ordinance published on 24 August 1946 had set out details of a Provisional Legislative Assembly of 90 members, half of whom were to be indirectly elected, and half nominated by the American Governor. This

---

[1] The actual figures were: the Labour Party, 1,102 members; the Democratic Party, 351; the Chondo-kya Friends Party, 253; non-Party, 1,753 members (*Soviet Monitor*, 16 November 1946; McCune, *Korea Today*, p. 174).

[2] McCune, *Korea Today*, pp. 175–7. Tass denied on 6 March that the new North Korean Government had introduced military conscription.

[3] US Department of State, *Korea's Independence*, p. 5.

decision precipitated a struggle for power between the right-wing groups, which began to agitate for an independent South Korea, and left-wing groups, which were opposed to this policy and to the elections which were held to be a step towards it. It was announced that the Communist Party, continuing its previous policy of non-cooperation with the Military Government, would not participate in the Assembly; but its activities in South Korea were somewhat checked by the law of 20 February 1946, requiring the registration of all political parties and of their members. Further measures, limiting the Communists' freedom of action, were put into force in the second half of the year, after a wave of strikes and riots. There were many imprisonments and prosecutions.

The South Korean elections proceeded as arranged, though many irregularities were reported.[1] Extreme conservatives secured an overwhelming majority, but the nominated members included many more progressively inclined persons, though no members of the Communist Party.[2] The Soviet press commented on the low poll, and declared that the indirect system of voting adopted was undemocratic.

The Provisional Assembly was inaugurated on 12 December 1946, and Syngman Rhee left for the United States to secure support for the setting up of an independent South Korea; though early in the following year General Hodge issued an official communiqué denying that it was the intention of the United States to support the permanent separation of the two halves of the country.[3] He was still facing considerable economic difficulties, which added, no doubt, to political discontent. There were further disorders and riots in February and March 1947, and a struggle between two opposing labour organizations. This resulted in the suppression of the Communist-backed Congress of Trade Unions. Soviet comment naturally made use of every report of trouble in the South to contrast it with the peace and progress prevailing under its own rule in the North.[4] The visit of a delegation from the WFTU in April also provided material for anti-American propaganda.

[1] Gayn, *Japan Diary*, pp. 395–9.
[2] McCune, *Korea Today*, pp. 78–80.   [3] ibid. p. 81.
[4] See e.g. E. Pigulevskaya, 'Korea after Liberation', *MKiMP*, no. 6, 1946, and *New Times*, 1 May 1947.

Once the Russians had established their North Korean Government they completely reversed their tactics concerning the Joint Commission. They themselves began to press for its work to be resumed, and endeavoured to blame the Americans for the obstacles put in its way. But a note on 26 October 1946 made it clear that they still stood by the exclusion from the consultations of all groups who would not accept the Moscow decision. An American proposal on 24 December, attempting to meet the Soviet point, led to no result.

On 3 April 1947 the Soviet Commander Colonel-General I. M. Chistiakov was replaced by Lieutenant-General G. P. Korotkov. On 8 April the Korean question was taken up again on the diplomatic level. In a letter addressed to Molotov, General Marshall reviewed the events leading to the stalemate in Korea and asked Molotov to agree that the Commanders should be instructed to reconvene the Joint Commission as soon as possible, 'on a basis of respect for the democratic right of freedom of opinion', and to fix a date upon which the two Governments should review the progress made. On 19 April Molotov suggested that the Joint Commission be reconvened on 20 May, but did not make clear upon what basis. After another inquiry from General Marshall on 2 May, he agreed on the 7th to accept as a basis for reconvening the Commission the American proposals of 24 December 1946, which had previously been rejected. The Joint Commission eventually met at Seoul on 21 May.[1] After lengthy discussions it was agreed on 12 June 1947 that the Commission would consult all Korean groups 'truly democratic in their aims and methods' who would sign a document supporting the Moscow decision on trusteeship and the work of the Commission.[2] This agreement followed the American formula of 24 December 1946. The Commission

---

[1] US Department of State, *Korea's Independence*, pp. 5–7 and Appendix 8. The position of the American members of the Joint Commission was now very awkward since, although the Americans repeatedly demanded the resumption of the negotiations, the right-wing elements in South Korea organized in the South Korean Anti-Trusteeship Committee were engaged in steady propaganda against the whole idea upon which the activities of the Commission were based. The Americans had either, therefore, to suppress the largest anti-Communist group available to them in South Korea or wreck the fulfilment of the Commission's purpose (McCune, *Korea Today*, p. 66).

[2] US Department of State, *Korea's Independence*, pp. 8–10; McCune, *Korea Today*, pp. 64–68.

invited the political groups to send in written expressions of their views on the projected Provisional Government and to submit applications to be heard at separate consultations to be held at Seoul and Pyongyang at the end of June. But disputes arose out of Soviet objections to the inclusion of certain groups in the proposed consultation and there were other disputes over the imprisonment of leading political figures on both sides of the 38th parallel. After vain attempts to reach an agreement, the Americans proposed on 12 August that the oral consultations be abandoned and that the Joint Commission proceed at once to set up a Provisional Government on the basis of the written material received. The Soviet reply turned down the idea of a freely elected national legislature and proposed instead a Provisional Assembly composed of equal numbers of delegates from North and South, representing those parties only that 'fully supported' the Moscow Agreement. The Americans refused to accept this suggestion partly on the grounds of the disparity in population between the two zones.

On 23 August Molotov accepted a suggestion made to him in a note from Marshall on the 11th, that the Joint Commission should be asked to report on the progress of its deliberations. But he again declared that the Soviet Union would not agree to consultations being held with groups affiliated to the Anti-Trusteeship Committee, and protested with vigour against the measures taken against left-wing elements in the South. The Commission was unable to reach a unanimous agreement and the Russians would not even agree that two separate reports should be made with a covering letter explaining that no agreement had been possible.[1]

THE ORIGINS OF THE KOREAN WAR

A new American proposal was contained in a note from the Acting Secretary of State Robert Lovett on 26 August 1947. This suggested a four-Power meeting on 8 September to consider how the Moscow Agreement might be speedily carried out. Elections should be held in the two zones to establish zonal legislatures, representatives of which would set up a National Provisional Legislature charged with the formation of a

[1] US Department of State, *Korea's Independence*, pp. 8–10; McCune, *Korea Today*, pp. 64–68.

Provisional Government for a United Korea. This proposal was accepted by Great Britain and China but was rejected by the Soviet Union, which argued that recommendations should not come from the four Powers but from the Joint Commission, and accused the United States of obstructing the Commission's work. Molotov in his note of 4 September repeated the suggestion already made by General Shtykov on 26 August for the establishment of a National Assembly made up of the representatives of the 'democratic parties and social organizations of all Korea' with equal representation of the two zones. The American Acting Secretary of State replied on 17 September stating that since agreement seemed impossible the matter would be referred to the General Assembly of the United Nations.[1]

Speaking in the General Assembly on 23 September, Vyshinsky opposed the inclusion of the Korean problem on the agenda. The blame for the deadlock lay entirely on the American side and the problem should be solved on the basis of the Moscow Agreement.

The Russians meanwhile were concentrating on a campaign in Korea, aimed at convincing the Koreans that the Soviet Union was genuinely in favour of the country's independence. On 26 September, at a meeting of the Joint Commission, General Shtykov declared abruptly that if the Americans agreed that all foreign troops should be withdrawn at the beginning of 1948, the Soviet Union would agree also.[2] This statement, while welcomed by left-wing organizations in South Korea, caused apprehension in conservative circles, where it was feared that the Americans might leave before the Russians, exposing the South to an attack from the North.[3] The American occupation authorities shared these apprehensions and also feared that an invasion from the North might be provoked by an attempt of the right-wing elements in South Korea to establish a forcible domination over the whole country.[4] They therefore described the Soviet proposal for withdrawal as a propaganda move and pointed to the disparity between the 200,000 troops stated to

[1] Korea's Independence, pp. 10–11 and Appendix 12.
[2] USSR, The Soviet Union and the Korean Question, pp. 42–46.
[3] NYT, 28 September 1947.
[4] CSM, 29 September and 1 October 1947.

exist in North Korea and the mere 50,000 police in the South.[1]

On 9 October Molotov sent Marshall a complaint that the Soviet Government had not yet received a reply to its proposal for the joint withdrawal of the occupying troops. He stated that this was the only solution now open since the United States had blocked the formation of a Provisional All-Korean Government.[2] On 18 October the Joint Commission met for the last time. The United States delegation refused to discuss the Soviet proposal for the simultaneous withdrawal of the occupying forces, and suggested that the Commission should adjourn pending the discussion of the Korean problem at the United Nations, whose General Assembly had agreed by a large majority on 23 September to include the question on its agenda. The Soviet Union now announced its withdrawal from the Joint Commission, and its delegates left Seoul on 21 October.[3]

During the discussions in the General Assembly the Soviet Union did its best to avoid all action by the United Nations in regard to Korea and renewed its own proposal for a simultaneous withdrawal of foreign troops. On 14 November the Assembly adopted by 43 votes to nil (with the Soviet bloc abstaining) a resolution which represented in an amended form the substance of the proposals put forward by the United States. This resolution proposed the holding in each zone of elections not later than 31 March 1948, as the first step towards the creation of a national assembly and subsequently of a national government for Korea. After such a government was set up it should create security forces of its own and arrange with the occupying Powers for the withdrawal of their troops. These measures were to be supervised by a United Nations Temporary Commission working on the spot with powers to recommend further steps to the Assembly.[4]

The nine nations named to provide members for the Temporary Commission included the Ukraine; but the Ukraine refused the assignment since the Soviet view was still that the matter was outside the competence of the United Nations.

[1] United States Information Service, *Bulletin*, 1 October 1947.
[2] USSR, *The Soviet Union and the Korean Question*, pp. 47–48.
[3] *NYT*, 21 October 1947.
[4] US Department of State, *Korea 1945 to 1948: a Report on Political Developments and Economic Resources with Selected Documents* (Washington, USGPO, 1948; reprinted 1950), pp. 48–49, 66–67.

The Temporary Commission met for the first time at Seoul
on 29 January 1948. The Soviet Union continued to maintain
a negative attitude towards its activities, with the result that
the Commission was unable to gain access to North Korea.
In consequence, it limited its functions to observing the elections held in South Korea and attempting to secure that they
should be as free and representative as possible.[1] But the Soviet
press and radio took the line that the United Nations Commission was merely a convenient screen behind which the
elections could be falsified, and that the decision to hold
separate elections showed that the Unites States intended to set
up a puppet Government which would permit them to use
South Korea as a base for their expansion in the Pacific.[2]

The North Koreans took the same line and did their best to
appeal to the strong sentiment for unity which undoubtedly
existed in South Korea as well. They succeeded in getting a
number of South Korean leaders to come to a Conference on 22
and 23 April. This Conference endorsed the Soviet viewpoint
and protested against separate elections being held in the
South.[3]

Meanwhile the North Korean People's Assembly had proceeded with the preparation of a draft Constitution, which was
adopted on 1 May. They claimed that this Constitution would
be valid throughout Korea, and declared Seoul to be the capital
and Pyongyang the temporary seat of Government.[4] The Constitution was clearly on the Soviet model.

The Soviet command in North Korea made public on 7 May
its reiterated support for the unification of Korea, and its
readiness to withdraw the Soviet troops at once, provided that
the American troops were simultaneously withdrawn.[5] On the
following day a reduction in the Soviet Army of occupation
was announced, and the replacement of General Korotkov by
General Merkulov.[6]

The South Korean elections took place on 10 May, not
without a great deal of disorder. It nevertheless seemed pos-

[1] McCune, *Korea Today*, pp. 223–7; *FES*, 15 May 1948.
[2] *Soviet Monitor*, 3, 17, 18 March; 11 April 1948.
[3] *NYHT*, 25 April; *Soviet Monitor*, 27 April; *Soviet News*, 29 April 1948; McCune, *Korea Today*, pp. 263–4.
[4] *Soviet Monitor*, 2 March; *Soviet News*, 5 May; *NYHT*, 1 May 1948.
[5] *Soviet News*, 10 May 1948.   [6] *NYT*, 9 May 1948.

sible to the United Nations Commission to regard them as a valid expression of the free will of the electorate in the part of Korea accessible to it and to accept an invitation to the first meeting of the National Assembly on 30 June.[1] The Commission did not divulge its attitude towards the claims of the Assembly to represent not only South Korea but also North Korea, for which 100 seats were reserved.

Some further unsuccessful efforts at unification by agreement were made in the late summer by North and South Koreans, but without success.[2] On the economic side also the links between the two halves of the country were being finally broken. The electricity supply from the North was cut off on 14 May, after the American authorities had refused to agree that South Korea should send representatives to the North to discuss terms for payment, on the grounds that this might be interpreted as a *de facto* recognition of the North Korean Government. Further fruitless negotiations on the question of electric power were carried on both locally and through diplomatic channels.[3] It also proved impossible to re-establish trade between the two parts of Korea. Some direct barter had been permitted by the South Korean authorities from December 1947, and there was a good deal of smuggling. The South Korean Department of Commerce acceded to the demand of the public for the legalization of all forms of trade with the North on 2 August 1948, but after full authority was transferred to the Government of the Republic of Korea the border was again closed. Trade on a restricted basis was resumed about a month later but terminated again by the South Korean Government on 23 April 1949.[4]

The transfer of governmental authority from the American Military Government to the Republic had been completed on 15 August, three days after the recognition of the Korean Republic by the Chinese National Government.[5] Meanwhile steps towards the creation of a 'Korean Democratic People's Republic' were continuing to be made in the North. On 12 July it was announced that general elections would be held on 25 August.[6]

[1] *United Nations Bulletin*, vol. 4, nos. 11 and 12, vol. 5, no. 3.
[2] McCune, *Korea Today*, p. 264.   [3] ibid. pp. 147–50.
[4] ibid. p. 261.   [5] ibid. pp. 230–1.   [6] *NYT*, 12 July 1948.

In the Supreme People's Assembly of 572 members which was to be chosen, 360 seats were reserved for representatives of South Korea. The Pyongyang radio subsequently claimed that elections had in fact been held in South Korea to choose these representatives and that a very high percentage of the electorate had voted. Other evidence suggests that this did not in fact happen. What did occur was a convention of delegates purporting to represent the South Koreans who met at Haeju just north of the 38th parallel on 22–24 August and selected 360 from among their number to sit in the Assembly.[1]

The report of the Temporary Commission was presented in October to the Paris session of the United Nations General Assembly. The Soviet bloc again unsuccessfully attempted to prevent the United Nations handling the question. On 12 December a resolution was passed by 48 votes to 6 with one abstention. The first of its three main points ran:

there has been established a lawful government (the Government of the Republic of Korea), having effective control and jurisdiction over that part of Korea where the Temporary Commission was able to observe and consult and where the great majority of the people of all Korea reside; that this Government is based on elections which were a valid expression of the free will of the electorate of that part of Korea and which were observed by the Temporary Commission; and that this is the only such Government in Korea.

Member States and other nations were recommended to take these facts into consideration in establishing their relations with Korea.

The second point was a recommendation that the occupying Powers should withdraw their forces from Korea 'as early as practicable'. The third point was the establishment of a new seven-Power Commission to continue the work of the Temporary Commission. It was to lend its good offices in unifying Korea and integrating all Korean security forces, and in facilitating the removal of barriers caused by the division of the country. It was to be available for observation and consultation in the further development of representative government in Korea and to observe the actual withdrawal of the occupation forces.[2]

---

[1] McCune, *Korea Today*, pp. 246–7.
[2] *Department of State Bulletin*, 19 December 1948.

The United States Government, which had on 24 August made an interim agreement with the Republic, providing that the Korean Government should be given jurisdiction over all security forces as soon as possible, and that meanwhile the United States should assist in training and equipping a Korean constabulary and coastguard, gave formal recognition to the new Government on 1 January 1949.[1]

Considerable political unrest in the South followed the establishment of the Republic of Korea.[2] On 1 December its Government promulgated a National Security Law, under which the Labour Party was outlawed. The party itself went underground while its affiliated organizations maintained a precarious existence. In the trade union movement only the right-wing organizations were recognized by the authorities, and these remained under strict control.[3] Despite these political troubles there was in 1948 a degree of economic recovery in South Korea, and progress was made with the distribution of land under a new land reform. Unlike the agrarian legislation in the North, this law enabled the purchasers to acquire full title of ownership. However, there was a continuing influx of refugees from the North which put an additional burden on the Republic's economy.[4] Soviet comment on South Korea stressed the completeness of the military and economic control which the United States had, in the Soviet view, established over the country. The agreement of 10 December 1948 by which the Republic of Korea was given a grant of $300 million under the Economic Co-operation Administration came under particularly heavy fire.[5]

In North Korea the Supreme People's Assembly met at Pyongyang on 2 September and continued in session until the 10th. On 3 September it unanimously ratified the draft Constitution with certain amendments. It reaffirmed the previous measures of nationalization but guaranteed the right of free development to small and medium industry and commerce.

---

[1] US Department of State, *Korea 1945–1948*, pp. 103–4; *Department of State Bulletin*, 9 January 1949.
[2] McCune, *Korea Today*, pp. 241–2; M. Markov, 'The Soviet Union and the Korean Question', *New Times*, 15 December 1948.
[3] McCune, *Korea Today*, p. 163.
[4] John Morris, 'The Two Koreas', *Listener*, 9 December 1948.
[5] See Shabshina in *Krisis Kolonialni Sistema*, p. 278.

It also continued in being the existing local, provincial, and central organs of Government. On 9 September the Assembly approved of the new Cabinet formed by Kim Il Sung. The North Korean radio stated that the twelve Ministers in the Cabinet included eight South Koreans; but some of them must have been working with the North Koreans previously, since at least seven of the new Ministers had held their positions in the old Government. On 10 September Kim Il Sung read to the Assembly the Government's programme, which put the unification and independence of the country as the primary objects to be sought. On 12 October the Soviet Union recognized the North Korean Government,[1] and on 18 October Shtykov, the previous Soviet representative on the Joint Commission, was appointed as first Soviet Ambassador, being awarded the Order of Lenin on 3 December. He arrived at Pyongyang on 11 January 1949. On 27 January the Korean Ambassador, Dyu Yen Ha (sometimes spelt Yo Wen Han), arrived in Moscow. At the second session of the National Assembly, on 2 February 1949, the Foreign Minister of the North Korean Government stressed the importance of the establishment of diplomatic relations with the Soviet Union.[2] Indeed the intimacy of the Soviet and North Korean Governments and the large share of the former in making possible the very existence of the latter were openly admitted on both sides.

On 10 September 1948 the North Korean People's Assembly had addressed a message to the Soviet and United States Governments requesting them to withdraw their troops from Korea. On 18 September the American Embassy in Moscow was informed that the Soviet Government would accede to this request and withdraw its troops by the end of the year.[3] A statement from the Soviet Government on 20 September announced that the evacuation of the remaining Soviet troops would begin in the second half of October and be completed

[1] Exchange of letters between Kim Il Sung and Stalin, *Pravda*, 12 October 1948.

[2] *New Times*, 20 October 1948; *NYT*, 4 December 1948; *Pravda*, 12, 16, and 30 January and 2, 5, and 10 February 1949. The North Korean People's Democratic Republic which, as has been seen, had already been recognized by Communist China, was soon recognized by the other countries closely associated with the Soviet Union: the Mongolian People's Republic, Poland, Czechoslovakia, Rumania, Hungary, Bulgaria, Albania, and Eastern Germany (G. Tavrov, 'The Korean Problem after the Second World War', *Sovetskoe Gosudarstvo i Pravo*, no. 7, 1950).

[3] US Department of State, *Korea 1945–1948*, pp. 114–15.

before the New Year.[1] This programme was carried out with much pomp and ceremony.[2] While the American reaction to the Soviet announcement had been sceptical, the Government of the Korean Republic had become alarmed lest the Americans might follow the Soviet example and thus precipitate a North Korean attack. Relations between the two halves of the country were very strained and there were a number of rumours in South Korea that risings or even an actual invasion had begun. On the other hand, the North Koreans also printed reports of hostile activities by South Korean troops and terrorists.[3]

Both Korean Governments applied in February 1949 for admission to the United Nations; and after the usual criticisms of the two sides had been made, it became apparent that no agreement could be secured for the acceptance of either.

A strong delegation from the North Korean Government, headed by Kim Il Sung and by the Vice-Premier and Minister of Foreign Affairs, the South Korean Communist Pak Heun Yong, arrived in Moscow early in March and concluded an agreement on economic and cultural co-operation, signed there on the 17th.[4] The treaty, of ten years' duration, while providing for the promotion of trade relations and for co-operation in the fields of culture, science, and the arts, was couched in rather general terms. It was accompanied by an unpublished agreement on trade turnover and payments providing for considerably increased trade in 1949 and 1950, an agreement for the grant to Korea of credits to pay for goods supplied in excess of the trade turnover agreement, and finally an agreement on the grant of Soviet technical assistance.[5]

In contrast to the agreements concluded by the Soviet Union with other friendly States, including Communist China, there appears to have been no general treaty of friendship and mutual assistance with North Korea, although Soviet press comment referred to the all-round assistance that the Koreans could expect from the Soviet Union.[6] Possibly the Soviet Union was

---

[1] USSR, *The Soviet Union and the Korean Question*, pp. 68–79.
[2] *Izvestia*, 31 December 1948; *Pravda*, 16 January 1949.
[3] McCune, *Korea Today*, pp. 242–3; *New Times*, 29 September 1948; *Pravda*, 26 January and 4 February 1949.
[4] Text in D. G. Tewksbury, ed., *Source Materials on Korean Politics and Ideologies* (New York, IPR, 1950; mimeo.), pp. 127–8, and in Appendix, below, p. 270.
[5] *Soviet Monitor*, 21 March 1949.   [6] *New Times*, 23 March 1949.

already considering the likely repercussions of a conflict over the unification of Korea, and wished to avoid public commitments, which would directly oblige her to go to the assistance of the North Koreans. The published treaty was duly ratified, and instruments of ratification were exchanged in July. The Government of North Korea persisted in treating itself as the Government of the whole country and drafted in May 1949 a rival land reform act for the southern part of Korea. This was manifestly for propaganda purposes only.[1] During May the Soviet press gave publicity to support in both North and South Korea for a plan for the formation of a United Korean Patriotic (or Fatherland) Front. (This was abbreviated as UPFF, or UDFF.) A Constituent Assembly of this organization opened at Pyongyang on 25 June and was attended by representatives of eighty parties and public organizations of North and South Korea. It adopted a programme calling for the unification of Korea, the immediate withdrawal of American troops, and the extension of the Northern régime to the South.[2] Soviet reports also dwelt upon the economic and industrial recovery of North Korea.[3]

Despite the opposition of the South Korean Government the United States had finally decided to withdraw its forces. They were gradually reduced in the latter half of 1948 and the first half of 1949. The last combat troops were withdrawn by 29 June. But in response to a request of the South Korean Government, the United States agreed to leave a large military mission of 500 men to assist in organizing the country's own defence forces. And American economic aid also continued.[4] All these measures met with the familiar denunciations in the Soviet press. Actually during 1949 the food position in South Korea improved and the mining of tungsten supplied a valuable export; but the lack of power supplies from the North meant the cutting of industrial output and severe unemployment.[5] In consequence there was still a great deal of unrest which the

---

[1] *Soviet Monitor*, 15 May 1949.   [2] *Izvestia*, 29 June and 1 July 1949.
[3] Tavrov in *Sovetskoe Gosudarstvo i Pravo*, no. 7, 1950; cf. A. Roth, *Manchester Guardian*, 6 October 1949; *Pravda*, 6 and 28 January 1950.
[4] McCune, 'Korea' in L. K. Rosinger, ed., *The State of Asia* (New York, Knopf for IPR, 1951).
[5] Joint report of Combined State Department and ECA Mission, *NYT*, 12–14, September 1949.

Soviet press could regard as evidence of political disaffection. And there were reports of actual guerrilla warfare by units of Communist partisans. These were on a sufficient scale to call for the attention of the South Korean army. Reports from the North Korean side gave no direct evidence of the methods of contact between these partisan units and the North Korean Republic, but it is fairly clear from the detailed knowledge of their activities, which the North Korean authorities showed, that they were in fact working in concert with them.[1] Near the 38th parallel and especially on the Onjin peninsula there were clashes in which the North Korean forces took part. But it is not improbable that many of the reports of activity on both sides of the border were considerably exaggerated. Certainly there was no confirmation of South Korean claims that the Russians were participating in the capacity of commanders or advisers.[2]

From the military point of view the North Korean régime was undoubtedly stronger than the Korean Republic, despite the much larger population of South Korea. In 1949 it was estimated that the North Korean army was about 150,000 strong, well equipped, trained, and organized by the Russians. In South Korea, however, the armed police, which was the nucleus of the army, was reported to number only 26,000 when the Republic took over in August 1948; but it grew rapidly since there were several semi-military youth organizations which could be drawn upon, and later estimates gave a figure of 1¼ million. On the other hand its equipment probably remained inferior.[3] The South Korean Government made much of the border clashes as a reason for seeking more American aid. But apart from equipment transferred to the South Korean Government when the occupation troops left, no direct aid reached South Korea until after June 1950, despite the appropriations made under the Mutual Defence Assistance Programme in October 1949 and an agreement under it with the South Korean Government signed on 26

---

[1] *For a Lasting Peace*, 24 March 1950.

[2] *NYT*, 5, 7, and 21 May; 7 July 1949.

[3] McCune, *Korea Today*, pp. 266–7. It has been stated that 20,000 Koreans trained in Manchuria by the Communists were sent to join the North Korean army when the Chinese civil war was ended (Schlesinger and Rovere, *The General and the President*, p. 99).

January 1950.[1] The weakness of the South Koreans did not prevent rather blustering language on the part of their leaders, Syngman Rhee giving the impression that it was only American pressure and fear of precipitating a world war that prevented him from calling on his troops to overrun North Korea.[2]

Soviet policy towards the further development of the Korean situation must be considered in the light of the impression given by the United States that Korea was not a country in the defence of which particular American interests were felt to be involved. In a speech on 12 January, the Secretary of State Dean Acheson had said that the Republic of Korea would have to depend for its defence upon its own efforts backed 'by the commitments of the entire civilized world under the Charter of the United Nations'.[3]

Syngman Rhee showed considerable suspicion of the new United Nations Commission when this body arrived at Seoul at the end of January 1949. This was because it announced its intention of trying to negotiate with the North Koreans, whereas for the South Koreans these were merely Russian puppets and any negotiations could be effective only if conducted directly with the Soviet Union.[4] Indeed after five and a half months of totally futile activities the Commission duly reported that the unification of Korea could not be achieved without an agreement between the United States and the Soviet Union. The Soviet press continued to show hostility to the very existence of the Commission.[5] When its report was discussed in the Ad Hoc Political Committee of the General Assembly on 30 September 1949, the Soviet member demanded the immediate abolition of the Commission. Both the Committee, however, and the full Assembly voted in favour of the Commission continuing in being and instructed it to pay special attention to

[1] Brookings Institution, *The Search for Peace Settlements*, by Redvers Opie and others (Washington, 1951), pp. 314–16.
[2] *NYT*, 7 October 1949.
[3] Council on Foreign Relations, *The United States in World Affairs, 1950*, ed. by R. P. Stebbins (New York, Harper, 1951), p. 200. On 2 November 1952 President Truman made public a memorandum of the Joint Chiefs of Staff of 26 September 1947 expressing the view that the United States had 'little strategic interest in maintaining' the existing 'troops and bases in Korea', which would be a liability in the event of a Far Eastern war in which a mainland offensive operation would by-pass Korea.
[4] *NYT*, 12 and 15 February 1949.   [5] See e.g. *Izvestia*, 12 August 1949.

developments that might lead to military conflict in Korea.[1] But when the reconstituted Commission returned to Seoul on 26 November it was not only ignored by the North Koreans but virtually boycotted by the South. South Koreans were prohibited by their Government from approaching the Commission except through the South Korean Foreign Ministry.[2]

After the end of 1949 news from Korea did not occupy much space in the Soviet press though there were reports of extensive guerrilla fighting, and *Pravda* reprinted the Cominform Journal's article by Pak Heun Yong on 'The Heroic Struggle for Unity and Independence of the Country of the People of South Korea'.[3] While the South Korean army announced successes in March and April against the guerrillas which had allegedly infiltrated from North Korea, *Pravda* announced the collapse of the anti-guerrilla campaign and stated that the army's actions were arousing the indignation of the peasants. The South Korean Government retained its aggressive attitude towards the North, and in a speech on 1 March Syngman Rhee declared that despite advice given by friends from across the seas not to attack the 'foreign puppets', the cries of their 'brothers in distress' in North Korea could not be ignored; and he renewed a plea for heavy weapons.[4]

After some hesitation, the elections due in May under the South Korean Constitution were duly held and, according to the United Nations Commission, properly conducted.[5] The Soviet press took a very different point of view; though its comments lacked consistency since they emphasized both the extent of the terror exercised by the Government's supporters and the fact that the latter had won only 48 seats against 120 which went to independents.[6]

Immediately after these elections the Central Committee of the UDFF met, and on 7 June published an appeal to the Korean people dismissing the elections as unfree, and making the following new proposals:

[1] *Soviet News*, 4, 5, 7, and 26 October; *NYT*, 4 October; *Pravda*, 25 October 1949.
[2] *NYHT*, 27 November, *NYT*, 23 December 1949.
[3] *For a Lasting Peace*, 24 March; *Pravda*, 27 March 1950.
[4] *NYT*, 2 March 1950.   [5] ibid. 30 May and 1 June 1950.
[6] *Pravda*, 1, 2, and 3 June 1950. It appears to be true that arrests in anti-Communist raids before the elections included thirty candidates (*Manchester Guardian*, 30 May; *NYHT*, 31 May 1950).

(*a*) From 5 to 8 August general elections should be held throughout Korea for a unified supreme legislative organ.

(*b*) On 15 August, the fifth anniversary of the liberation of Korea, a session of this supreme legislative organ should be held at Seoul.

(*c*) Meanwhile from 15 to 17 June a conference of the representatives of the democratic political parties and public organizations of North and South Korea who desired the peaceful unification of the country should be convened immediately north or south of the 38th parallel in order to determine the conditions for the peaceful unification of Korea and the procedure for the general elections; and to choose a Central Committee to direct the elections. Those responsible for obstructing the peaceful unification of the country and 'national traitors' should be debarred, and interference by the United Nations Commission on Korea should not be tolerated. The authorities of North and South Korea should be responsible for the maintenance of public order during the conference and the elections.[1]

The South Korean authorities took all possible steps to prevent the dissemination of this appeal, and since no response was forthcoming, the Central Committee of the UDFF passed another resolution on 19 June. This proposed a new move towards unification by the merging of the two legislative bodies of North and South Korea into a single all-Korean legislature which should draw up a Constitution and prepare for general elections. 'National traitors' were to be arrested and freedom was to be restored in South Korea; a united Government was to reorganize, on democratic foundations, the army and the police force; the United Nations Commission was to be requested to leave the country immediately. All these measures were to be completed by 15 August.[2] The Soviet press gave much space to the activities of the UDFF and to this document which, by the naming of a date for unification, could almost be described as an ultimatum. But no editorial comment upon it gave any indication that the North Koreans intended to proceed to forcible measures. Thus when the North Koreans made a direct attack across the 38th parallel, there was nothing precise

---

[1] *Pravda*, 9 June 1950. The text of this appeal and other relevant documents of this period will be found in Tewksbury, ed., *Source Materials on Korean Politics*.

[2] Tewksbury, ed., *Source Materials on Korean Politics*, pp. 156–7.

that could be pointed to as indicating Soviet responsibility or even foreknowledge. Later on, however, the North Korean successes led some students to take the view that the Soviet Government had deliberately planned the attack.

It is of course true that but for the help given by the Soviet Union in equipping and training the North Korean forces, the successes they gained would have been inconceivable, just as at a later stage in the war they depended on Chinese assistance. But the precise nature of the co-ordination existing between Moscow and the Chinese and North Korean Governments at the time remains obscure.

THE DIPLOMACY OF THE KOREAN WAR

The attack on South Korea by North Korean forces across the 38th parallel was made without warning in the early morning of 25 June 1950. The Soviet press, however, immediately accepted as correct the declarations of the North Korean radio which alleged that the attack had come from the South and that the North Korean army had been instructed to repel it.[1] Subsequently the Soviet press attempted to justify the accusation that the South Koreans had been urged on to the attack by the United States Government. Particular attention was given to the recent visit of Mr. John Foster Dulles and to the alleged activities of Brigadier-General W. L. Roberts, the chief of the United States Military Advisory Group in Korea.[2] The various bellicose speeches of South Korean political leaders were also recalled, but no details of the alleged attack were offered.

When the Security Council met on 25 June to consider the United States complaint of aggression against the Republic of

---

[1] *Pravda*, 26 June 1950. The Peking propaganda department seems not to have been prepared for the invasion or for the first twenty-four hours of the war, and the Chinese press was in disarray (Fitzgerald, *Revolution in China*, p. 220).

[2] In January 1950 General Roberts had told members of the United Nations Commission on Korea that the Government of the Republic of Korea had been informed that if it launched an attack against the North, all military and economic aid from the United States would cease. He also said that the fact that only defensive weapons were left behind when the United States forces were withdrawn from South Korea was due to the intention of making it impossible for South Korea 'even to contemplate launching a war for the unification of the country' (UN, *Report of the United Nations Commission on Korea*, General Assembly, 5th Session, 1950, Supplement 16, p. 10).

Korea, the Soviet Union was not represented since, as has been seen, the Soviet Union was at that time boycotting the organs of the United Nations owing to their continued exclusion of representatives of Communist China.[1] In the first couple of days the Soviet press had given relatively little attention to the Korean fighting. The Tass dispatch on the meeting of the Security Council on 25 June, published on 27 June, gave an outline report of the resolution of the Council calling upon the North Koreans to withdraw, and concluded with the following note:

Attention is drawn here to the fact that the representative of the Soviet Union was absent from the meeting of the members of the Security Council on 25 June. The lawful representative of China, a second permanent member of the Security Council, was also absent. Inasmuch as any decision on the substance of an issue in the Security Council requires the unanimity of the permanent members of the Council, in order that this decision should accord with the United Nations Charter, it is clear that . . . the meeting of the members of the Security Council could not on 25 June take any decisions having legal force.[2]

This argument remained the basis of the subsequent Soviet attitude towards the activities of the United Nations concerning Korea.

At the same time the Soviet press published the message of Kim Il Sung to the Korean people, which announced the advance of the North Korean forces south of the parallel and which made it clear that the object of the campaign was to unify the whole country.

Since the North Korean Government had taken no notice of the Security Council's resolution of 25 June President Truman made a statement on the 27th at noon noting that the resolution called on members of the United Nations to render assistance to the United Nations in its execution and announcing that he had ordered American naval and air forces 'to give the Korean Government troops cover and support'. Taking the attack on South Korea as a proof that Communism had adopted the tactics of armed invasion he had ordered the American Seventh

---

[1] A useful account of the early months of the Korean crisis is given in Council on Foreign Relations, *The United States in World Affairs, 1950*, ch. 5.

[2] *Pravda* and *Izvestia*, 27 June 1950.

Fleet to prevent any attack on Formosa, while calling on the Chinese Nationalists to refrain from attacking the mainland. He had also directed the strengthening of the United States forces in the Philippines, and the acceleration of military assistance to the forces of France and the Associated States of Indo-China.[1] A few hours later, the Americans secured a new Security Council resolution recommending the furnishing of assistance to the South Koreans.[2] The North Korean reply to the original message of 25 June from the Security Council was sent on the 29th, and declared that the North Korean Government did not recognize the decision of the Security Council, since it had not been consulted and since the Soviet Union and China had not been present at the meeting.

On 27 June the Soviet Government had received two communications, one from the Secretary-General of the United Nations informing them of the Security Council's decision, and the other from the American Ambassador to Moscow. The latter stated that since the Soviet representative had not been present at the meeting on 25 June, the United States Government found it necessary to call the attention of the Soviet Government to the North Korean aggression:

> In view of the universally known fact of the close relations between the Union of Soviet Socialist Republics and the North Korean regime, the United States Government asks an assurance that the Union of Soviet Socialist Republics disavows responsibility for this unprovoked and unwarranted attack, and that it will use its influence with the North Korean authorities to withdraw their invading forces immediately.[3]

Soviet replies to both communications repeated the legal argument about the decisions of the Security Council. The United States note also stated that the Soviet Government had alleged that the events in Korea had been the result of an attack by the South Korean troops and that the responsibility therefore rested with them. The Soviet Union had withdrawn its

[1] US Department of State, *United States Policy in the Korean Crisis* (Washington, USGPO, 1950), p. 18.

[2] On the first steps taken by the United Nations on the Korean crisis and the divergent views revealed, see Council on Foreign Relations, *United States in World Affairs, 1950*, pp. 202–7.

[3] US Department of State, *United States Policy in the Korean Crisis*, pp. 63–64.

forces from Korea before the United States and had thereby confirmed its adherence to the policy of non-intervention, to which it still continued to adhere.[1]

The Soviet press continued to report the Korean war without giving it particular attention or allowing it to displace the main propaganda line, which was at that time centred on the 'peace campaign'. In its reports of the war it stressed the participation of Americans, American losses, and also the atrocities allegedly committed by the South Korean forces. At public meetings called in the Moscow factories in connexion with the Stockholm Peace Appeal, American aggression against Korea was loudly condemned.[2] An editorial comment in *Pravda* stressed the demand of the Soviet people that the aggressors should be restrained.[3]

This propaganda formed the background to the first full official statement of the Soviet attitude to the crisis by Gromyko, the Deputy Minister of Foreign Affairs, on 4 July, which was circulated as an official document of the Security Council. He declared that the United States had resorted to direct intervention in Korea, 'ordering its air, naval, and subsequently its ground forces to take action on the side of the south Korean authorities against the Korean people'. This intervention had not for long been confined to South Korea since American planes had bombed North Korean targets. Furthermore, it had started before the convening of the Security Council on 27 June and could not be legalized by its resolution, which was anyhow invalid. At this point, in addition to repeating the customary argument about the absence of Russian and of properly qualified Chinese delegates, Gromyko developed a new theory. The conflict in Korea, he stated, was a civil war among the Koreans, and he compared the action of the United States in intervening to that of Great Britain during the American civil war, and to that of the Great Powers which had intervened in Russia after the October revolution. His statement also directly attacked the Secretary-General of the United Nations for permitting an illegal procedure to be used. It also declared that the Soviet Government continued to support the principles of strengthening world peace and of non-interference in the

---

[1] USSR, *The Soviet Union and the Korean Question*, pp. 89–92.
[2] *Soviet Monitor*, 29 June 1950.   [3] 3 July 1950.

domestic affairs of other nations, and expressed the hope that the United Nations would fulfil its duty and stop American aggression. On the other hand it gave no indication that the Soviet Union proposed to take any action with regard to the war.[1]

On 29 June the British Ambassador in Moscow, Sir David Kelly, had requested the Soviet Government to use its influence with the North Korean authorities to induce them to withdraw their forces. But on 6 July Tass denied reports that the British Government had made any specific proposals, stating that it had only expressed the hope that the conflict would be settled. The statement made by Sir David Kelly did not therefore require a reply. On the same day Gromyko invited the Ambassador to call upon him so as to give a fuller explanation of the British proposals.[2]

Meanwhile the Soviet Union had extended its propaganda through the world movement of the 'partisans of peace'; and by the end of the first fortnight of the fighting the Soviet press was able to refer to resolutions of various Communist-sponsored bodies, echoing its own views on the Korean conflict.

Despite the support given by the Americans, the South Korean forces continued to lose ground. On 4 July the American Ambassador notified the Soviet Government of the American blockade of the Korean coast. On 6 July the Soviet reply had reasserted its view that the Security Council decision had no legal force, and therefore could not serve as a basis for a blockade.[3]

On 7 July the Security Council adopted a resolution on a unified command under the United States for the United Nations forces in Korea, and General MacArthur was appointed to the post by President Truman on the following day. In reply to a communication from the Secretary-General, the Soviet Government repeated its view about the illegality of the Security Council's proceedings. *Pravda* commented:

By this resolution the command of the American interventionist troops will operate under the cloak of the United Nations and will be supposed to be acting under the authorization of the United Nations. For this purpose the troops of the American interventionists

---

[1] Security Council, 5th year, *Supplement for June, July and August 1950*, pp. 83–89.
[2] *Manchester Guardian*, 7 and 8 July 1950.
[3] US Department of State, *United States Policy in the Korean Crisis*, pp. 64–65.

are to be supplemented by military formations from certain other countries. .... Thus under the flag of the United Nations an attempt is being made to form a coalition of plunderers for the bloody suppression of the Korean people.[1]

An attempt was made by the Indian Government to bring about a peaceful solution of the Korean problem, a matter of considerable importance to that Government, which had made consistent efforts to remain on good terms with Communist China. On or about 5 July the Indian Ambassador in Peking, Sardar K. M. Pannikar, secured from the Chinese Government a statement of its attitude towards the conflict. On 13 July Nehru sent personal messages to Stalin and Acheson.

India's purpose [he wrote] is to localize the conflict and to facilitate an early peaceful settlement by breaking the present deadlock in the Security Council so that representatives of the People's Government of China can take a seat in the Council, the Union of Soviet Socialist Republics can return to it, and, whether within or through informal contacts outside the Council, the United States of America, the Union of Soviet Socialist Republics, and China, with the help and cooperation of other peace-loving nations, can find a basis for terminating the conflict and for a permanent solution of the Korean problem.

He concluded his message with the following words:

In full confidence of Your Excellency's determination to maintain peace and thus to preserve the solidarity of the United Nations, I venture to address this personal appeal to you to exert your great authority and influence for the achievement of this common purpose on which the well-being of mankind depends.

On 15 July Stalin replied, welcoming the Indian suggestion that the problem should be solved in the Security Council with the participation of the Chinese People's Republic, and added that it would be useful to give a hearing to the [North] Korean people. Nehru sent his thanks for the immediate reply and said that he was entering into negotiations with the other Powers.[2] The publication by the Russians on 18 July of what were meant to be the private exchanges between Nehru and Stalin frustrated any hope of progress along these lines, since

---

[1] 10 July 1950.   [2] *Department of State Bulletin*, 31 July 1950.

it was clear that the Soviet Government was chiefly concerned with making the Security Council's refusal to admit Communist China appear to be the main obstacle to a restoration of peace. The Soviet Government also maintained its direct contact with the British Government which was known to differ from Washington on the issue of Chinese representation. Sir David Kelly saw Gromyko on 11 and 17 July. On the latter occasion, Gromyko proposed that a procedure for settling the question should be followed similar to that suggested by Nehru, and did not conceal his view that the hostilities in Korea would have to continue until the Security Council was convened on these conditions. The British Government declined, however, to extend the discussions to matters not directly affecting Korea. On 20 July a Soviet version of these talks was published.[1] But as Attlee pointed out in the House of Commons on the same day, the Soviet account omitted all reference to the British request that Soviet influence should be exercised to have the North Korean forces withdrawn to the 38th parallel as an essential precondition of any attempt at a peaceful settlement.

Soviet press comment on the war followed familiar lines, contrasting the alleged atrocities of the Americans and the South Koreans with the welcome said to be given to the North Koreans in the 'liberated areas'. It was also indicated that the United States was rapidly becoming isolated in its attitude to the war, and there were comments on the lack of an immediate response to the appeal to other countries to allot forces for Korea. The news that the Turkish Government had offered a contingent was printed under the ironical headline: 'A Marlborough from Istanbul'.

On 1 August the normal rotation in the presidency of the Security Council was due to bring the Soviet representative into the chair, and Malik announced on 27 July that he proposed to return to the Council.[2] He submitted a provisional two-point agenda: the recognition of the representative of the Central People's Government of China as the delegate from that country; and peaceful settlement of the Korean question. The American delegate proposed that the more urgent problem, the

---

[1] UN, Department of Public Information, *Korea and the United Nations* (pamphlet, 1950), p. 29.

[2] ibid. p. 29.

complaint of aggression against the South Korean Republic, should be dealt with first. Malik, in a speech on 3 August, developed Gromyko's argument that the conflict in Korea was a civil war and that consequently the intervention of the United States was an act of aggression. On 6 August, a leading article in *Izvestia*, 'Ignorance in Questions of International Law', recalled, among other historical instances of intervention, the American protest against French intervention in Mexico in the eighteen-sixties. This legal argument was stressed in lengthy articles by eminent Soviet jurists and historians.[1] Malik also made repeated attempts to get a hearing for a North Korean representative. On 8 August Malik read to the Security Council a telegram from the North Korean Government, which stated that it had proof that the 'American interventionists' were resorting to 'inhuman and barbarous' methods of warfare, 'ruthlessly violating the rules of international law and the standards of human morality'.[2] In a speech on 22 August Malik concentrated on the general theme of the exploitation of Asia by the imperialist Powers.[3] It was obvious that no arguments of his were going to convince the Security Council to accept his point of view, and the purpose of his speech could only have been its general utility to Communist propaganda in Asia. When on 1 September the British representative took his turn as chairman, he invited the representative of the Republic of Korea to take his place at the table in accordance with the resolution of 25 June, despite Soviet protests. On 6 and 7 September the Security Council discussed a Soviet draft resolution about American bombing in Korea, but the American representative declared that the accusations were merely intended to divert their attention from the fact of North Korean aggression, and that the United States air forces had exercised particular care to limit their attacks to military objectives.[4]

During September the space devoted to comments on the Korean war in the Soviet press gradually decreased and the

[1] *Izvestia*, 6, 9, 13, and 15 August 1950; cf. V. H. Dudenevsky and A. M. Dalizhensky, 'Aggression and Intervention in the Far East', *Sovetskoe Gosudarstvo i Pravo*, no. 2, 1951.

[2] UN, Department of Public Information, *Korea and the United Nations*, p. 39.

[3] ibid. p. 59.

[4] *Korea and the United Nations*, pp. 65–66.

communiqués were usually restricted to those emanating from North Korea. The successful landing of the United Nations forces at Inchon, on 15 September, was not in line with the previous Soviet forecasts of an early and total defeat for the United Nations forces, and there was some delay before the Soviet press admitted the severe setback to North Korean hopes. When the rapidity of the United Nations advance in October could no longer be concealed, the Soviet press consoled itself by referring to increasing guerrilla activities behind the United Nations lines. Reports that the United Nations forces were making use of Japanese troops led to a Soviet protest to the Security Council.[1]

During their advances the United Nations forces captured a good deal of equipment, much of it of Soviet manufacture.[2] The Soviet representative in the Security Council denied that any Russian weapons had been supplied to the North Koreans and the Soviet press stressed that all the support given to them was of a purely moral character.[3]

Since no unanimity could be reached in the Security Council once the Soviet delegate had returned, the urgent question of what should be the United Nations policy after the repulse of the original attack was discussed in the General Assembly. An eight-Power draft resolution was prepared. This provided for the taking of appropriate steps to ensure conditions of stability throughout Korea, elections under United Nations auspices for the establishment of a 'unified, independent, and democratic Government' for the whole of Korea, measures of economic rehabilitation and the establishment of a new United Nations Commission to assist in the unification and rehabilitation of the country. The references to reuniting Korea appeared to give tacit assent to the crossing of the 38th parallel by the pursuing United Nations forces. The resolution also called for the setting up of an interim committee of the Assembly to advise the

---

[1] On 4 September a Soviet plane was shot down by an American naval force near the 38th parallel. The United States report on the incident stated that the bomber had acted in a hostile fashion over the ship. A Soviet report that it had been out on a peaceful training mission was issued. The American Ambassador refused to accept the note of protest on the ground that the matter was exclusively one for the United Nations (*Korea and the United Nations*, pp. 38–80; *NYHT*, 8 September 1950; *Pravda*, 22 October; *Soviet News*, 6 November 1950).

[2] *The Times*, 3 October; *Manchester Guardian*, 9 October 1950.

[3] See e.g. *Literaturnaya Gazeta*, 21 September 1950.

United Nations Command pending the new Commission's arrival in Korea.[1]

An alternative Soviet resolution called for the immediate cessation of hostilities, the withdrawal of foreign troops and the setting up of an interim all-Korean Government chosen by the two existing Korean legislatures which should conduct nation-wide elections under the supervision of the United Nations, including the Soviet Union and the Chinese People's Republic. The Soviet proposals were rejected and the eight-Power draft resolution was carried by the Assembly on 7 October. On 12 October after the 38th parallel had been crossed, the Interim Committee—which consisted of seven small Powers, four of them Asian—decided that the authority of the Republic of Korea was limited to South Korea only. In the North the United Nations Command would be responsible for civil administration.[2]

The second anniversary of the establishment of diplomatic relations between the Soviet Union and North Korea was marked by the customary exchange of telegrams, but Stalin's was very brief and non-committal. He merely acknowledged the greetings of Kim Il Sung and added: 'I wish the Korean people, who are heroically defending the independence of their country, the successful completion of their long years of struggle for the establishment of a united, independent, democratic Korea.'[3] The Soviet press did not comment editorially on this anniversary. In publishing also the report of Kim Il Sung's appeal to the Korean people, the Soviet press did not dwell on his reference to Soviet and Chinese support, but merely said that he had noted that the Korean people's struggle had the sympathy of all progressive mankind. The Chinese Government was not so reserved about its sympathies in the dispute, and on 24 August a complaint had been sent to the Security Council charging the United States with direct aggression against Chinese territory. On 30 September Chou En-lai made a speech proclaiming the Chinese conviction that the North Koreans would win the final victory, and declaring that although the Chinese nation loved peace, it would never be

[1] Opie, *The Search for Peace Settlements*, pp. 321–2.
[2] *NYT*, 14 October 1950.
[3] *Pravda* and *Izvestia*, 12 October 1950.

afraid to resist an aggressor for the sake of defending it: 'The Chinese nation will by no means suffer foreign aggression and cannot remain indifferent to the fate of its neighbours, subject to aggression from the side of imperialists.'[1]

Unwilling to commit themselves to more than moral support of the North Korean cause, the Russians rebuffed further American attempts to have the matter settled through direct Soviet-American negotiations. On 4 October Harold E. Stassen publicly proposed a meeting between President Truman and Marshal Stalin, but the suggestion was curtly dismissed by the Soviet press.[2] Truman's speech at San Francisco, after his return from conferring with MacArthur, was called 'insolent and ridiculous', and his suggestion that the Soviet Union should change its policy was met by a string of invectives.[3]

The rapid advance of the United Nations troops during October brought them close to the Manchurian border and to the important hydro-electric works on the Yalu river, which are situated on the Korean side, but supply power to the industries of both Korea and Manchuria. The Chinese press reported numerous violations of the Chinese border here by United Nations aircraft. During this month the presence of large-scale Chinese forces was reported in North Korea. By 25 October the support received was sufficient for the North Korean army to launch a counter-offensive. The first Soviet hint of the presence of these Chinese troops was given in *Pravda* on 4 November, in the form of a joint declaration by China's 'democratic' parties. The declaration stated that the Chinese nation not only had the moral obligation to help the Koreans but was compelled to do so in its own interests, owing to the strategic importance of Korea and to the extension of American aggression which could only be halted by force. This declaration did not specify in what way aid was being given, but on 5 November the crossing of Chinese forces into Korea was reported to the Security Council by the United Nations Supreme Commander, General MacArthur.[4] On 7 November Vyshinsky was asked at New York about this report and said that there were perhaps

[1] *Pravda*, 1 October 1950.
[2] ibid. 20 October 1950.
[3] ibid. 22 October 1950; *Trud*, 22 October 1950.
[4] Opie, *The Search for Peace Settlements*, p. 323.

some Chinese volunteers in Korea but that he had no information on the subject.[1]

The Security Council began its consideration of MacArthur's report on 8 November. The Soviet delegate argued that the matter should not be discussed by the Security Council and when defeated on this point insisted that a representative of the Chinese People's Government be given a hearing.[2] It was agreed that it should be invited to send a representative to be present during the discussion of the charges of Chinese intervention. On 10 November a resolution was proposed calling on Communist China to withdraw its forces but adding that it was the 'policy of the United Nations to hold the Chinese frontier inviolate and fully to protect legitimate Chinese and Korean interests in the frontier zone'. Debate on this draft resolution was interrupted when it became known that a delegation from the Chinese People's Republic, invited earlier in connexion with the Formosan dispute, was on its way to New York.[3]

The first direct acknowledgement of Chinese intervention in Korea in the Soviet press was made in the usual roundabout fashion. It consisted of a Tass report from Shanghai, printed in *Pravda* on 11 November, which quoted Manchurian papers about the large-scale assistance that the Korean people were receiving from Chinese 'volunteers'. Subsequently there were reports on the formation of the 'Chinese Committee for the Defence of Peace and the Struggle against American Aggression' and of the movement of 'volunteers' to Korea and of their military exploits. On 16 November the Soviet delegate to the Security Council announced that he would use the veto to bar a resolution calling on China to leave Korea. He stated that the advance of the American interventionist forces towards the Yalu river constituted a threat to China's frontiers.[4]

The Soviet press gave no indication that the Russians might join the Chinese in giving direct support to the North Koreans

[1] *NYT*, 8 November 1950.
[2] *Report of the Security Council to the General Assembly*, 1950–1, p. 23.
[3] Opie, *The Search for Peace Settlements*, pp. 323–4.
[4] During November Russian jet planes appeared in Korea for the first time and the numbers of armoured vehicles available to the North Koreans increased. General MacArthur estimated that the North Koreans had received between 900 and 1,000 of them (*NYT*, 16 October 1950). But rumours of the concentration of Soviet troops near Vladivostok remained unconfirmed (*Manchester Guardian, Daily Telegraph*, 7 November 1950).

or that the conflict might spread outside Korea. It was maintained that the Korean war had created dissension among the Western Powers and especially between the United States and Great Britain.[1] It was also said that the defeats suffered by the United Nations troops during November, after the Chinese intervention, had shaken the United States Government and people. This claim appeared first in a survey from New York of the American press printed in *Pravda* on 2 December. On the following day a changed and enlarged version of the article appeared in the paper above the signature 'Observer'. While the first version spoke of the reverses of the United States forces as having been due largely to the action of the 'Chinese volunteers', the second version did not use the word 'volunteers' and credited the Chinese, and not the North Koreans, with the recent victories. It spoke of the offensive as having been timed by Mao Tse-tung, and as being primarily a Chinese affair. More important still, the second version quoted American speculation about the possible involvement of the Soviet Union in the war. It referred to David Lawrence, a writer in the *New York Herald Tribune*, as saying on 30 November that if Russia did not wish to provoke a premature war, and was ready to settle the Far Eastern conflict, then there was the possibility of some sort of patched-up peace, and furthermore as saying that the Americans had not sufficient human reserves to conduct a war against the Chinese Communists and their Russian allies in Siberia. It also quoted an analysis of possible American policies by a Washington Associated Press correspondent, who had said that American official circles believed that the defeat of China would not solve the world problem of Communism, the centre of which was situated in the Soviet Union.[2]

Such a hint of the possibility of Soviet involvement even of this most indirect kind is so rare in Soviet comment upon international developments as to be worth recording. It is possible that the article was part of the Soviet reaction to the statement by President Truman at his press conference on 30 November when he declared that the United States was determined to continue with its mission in Korea and that he required further appropriations from Congress for the purpose,

[1] *Pravda*, 27 November and 4 December 1950.
[2] ibid. 3 December 1950.

which was itself briefly commented on on 3 December. Although *Pravda* and *Izvestia* severely criticized the aggressive plans which the President's statement was alleged to foreshadow, no more mention was made of the possible involvement of the Soviet Union, and the Chinese troops were again referred to as 'volunteers', a usage which was subsequently adhered to.

The expected delegation from Peking had meanwhile arrived in New York and appeared at the Security Council on 27 November. On 28 November its leader, Wu Hsiu-chuan, repeated the familiar charges that the United States had committed aggression against China, and enumerated alleged violations of Chinese territorial waters and alleged flights of American military aircraft over Chinese territory.[1]

In view of a further report from General MacArthur drawing attention to the extent of the Chinese intervention in the Korean war, a six-Power resolution was drafted calling for the Chinese forces to be withdrawn. Although this was accepted by an affirmative vote of nine to one, it was vetoed by the Soviet Union.[2] General Wu's speech was given publicity in the Soviet press and Soviet support for his point of view was made abundantly clear.[3]

At the request of the United States and other Governments, the matter was now taken up by the General Assembly and it was proposed that a draft resolution similar to that vetoed in the Security Council should be placed on the agenda. On 6 December Vyshinsky unsuccessfully opposed this move, repeating the substance of the Chinese case, and arguing that there were no proofs of Chinese intervention in Korea and that the Chinese fighting there were 'volunteers'.[4] Three days later, at a meeting of the First Committee, Vyshinsky made another speech of which the central point was that it was the American forces which were the real aggressors in Korea. He submitted a draft resolution of his own as follows:

The General Assembly, calling attention to the grave threat to the peace and security of the peoples represented by the continued intervention in Korea of the armed forces of the United States of

---

[1] *United Nations Bulletin*, 15 December 1950.
[2] Opie, *The Search for Peace Settlements*, p. 342.
[3] Text in *Soviet Monitor*, 1 December 1950.
[4] General Assembly, 5th Session, 319th Plenary Meeting, 6 December 1950.

America and of the armed forces of the other States taking part in that intervention, seeking a peaceful settlement of the Korean question and the operation of peace and security in the Far East, recommends: (1) that all foreign troops be withdrawn immediately from Korea; (2) that the decision on the Korean question be entrusted to the Korean people themselves.[1]

On 12 December in the First Committee thirteen Asian and Arab countries, for whom Sir Benegal Rau of India acted as spokesman, introduced a draft resolution requesting the President of the Assembly to constitute a group of three persons, including himself, to determine the basis on which a satisfactory cease-fire in Korea could be arranged; and also a second resolution calling for a meeting of certain Powers to consider the situation in the Far East and to make recommendations for a peaceful settlement of existing issues. The text of this draft resolution did not specify the countries who should participate in the proposed conference, but Sir Benegal Rau intimated that its sponsors had in mind: the Chinese People's Republic, France, Great Britain, the United States, the Soviet Union, Egypt, and India. In the debate on the suggestion of Sir Benegal Rau that his first draft resolution should be given priority over others before the Committee, the representatives of the Soviet bloc unsuccessfully opposed him.[2] On the following day Malik, who by now had no doubt received instructions from Moscow, spoke against the thirteen-Power draft resolution. He dismissed the proposed cease-fire as merely a device to enable the Americans to regroup their defeated troops, arguing that the only path to peace in Korea was the withdrawal of all foreign troops. One of the hidden intentions of the proposal was to exclude the Chinese People's Republic from participating in a solution of the Korean problem.[3] The draft resolution was approved the same afternoon against the votes of the Soviet bloc.[4]

On 15 December the Group on Cease-Fire in Korea, which had been set up under the resolution, got into touch with the Peking delegation, who refused to meet with them. When this

[1] General Assembly, 5th Session, First Committee, 412th meeting, 9 December 1950.
[2] ibid. 415th meeting, 12 December 1950.
[3] ibid. 416th meeting, 13 December 1950.
[4] ibid. 417th meeting, 13 December 1950.

was reported to the First Committee, Malik said that if the Group had in mind merely a cease-fire, and not a broader idea including the withdrawal of foreign troops, their efforts would fail.[1]

Wu Hsiu-chuan at a press conference in New York on 16 December read to the correspondents the speech which he claimed he had been prevented from making to the General Assembly. It reiterated the Chinese allegations of American aggression, rejected the proposals of the General Assembly for settling the Korean dispute, and announced that the Chinese 'volunteers' would continue fighting in Korea until the withdrawal of United States forces from Korea and Formosa.[2] On 19 December, despite the efforts of the cease-fire group to have his departure deferred, Wu left for Peking.[3] On 22 December a broadcast statement by Chou En-lai repeated in strong terms the Chinese rejection of the cease-fire proposal: the cease-fire group was illegal because China had not participated in setting it up; the United States was committing aggression in Korea, Manchuria, and Formosa; all foreign troops should be withdrawn from Korea, United States forces should be withdrawn from Formosa, and the Chinese People's Republic should be admitted to the United Nations.[4] The Chinese position was set forth in similar terms in a cable to the President of the Security Council from Chou En-lai on 23 December. And this position received full support from Malik at a meeting of the First Committee on 3 January.

On 11 January the United Nations Group on Cease-fire in Korea presented a new proposal to the effect that after a cease-fire had been declared arrangements should be made for the gradual withdrawal of all non-Korean armed forces, and that the United Nations should then supervise arrangements through which the Korean people might freely choose their future Government. As soon as a cease-fire agreement had been reached the General Assembly should set up a representative body, including representatives of the United States, Great Britain, the Soviet Union, and the Chinese People's Republic,

[1] General Assembly, 5th Session, First Committee, 418th meeting, 18 December 1950.   [2] *Pravda*, 19 December 1950.
[3] Council on Foreign Relations, *United States in World Affairs, 1950*, p. 423.
[4] *NCNA*, Supplement, 9 January 1951.

to settle general Far Eastern problems including that of Formosa and of the representation of China in the United Nations.[1]
This proposal was endorsed by the United States, which constituted a major concession on her part since it meant that she
was willing to enter into discussions with the Chinese People's
Republic and to include in the scope of such discussions the
questions of Formosa and of Chinese representation in the
United Nations.

Malik, however, in preliminary remarks on 11 January complained that the Chinese People's Government had been
branded as an aggressor without being given an opportunity
to state its case. The proposal on a cease-fire was clear but the
remainder of the proposals were ambiguous. The provision for
a gradual withdrawal of foreign troops would enable the United
States to retain her forces in Korea as long as she wished. The
Soviet Union could not support the proposals, which contained
nothing new and which were being presented to the Chinese
Government in a form which indicated them to be an ultimatum. The participation of Chinese volunteers could not be
regarded as constituting aggression.[2]

When a vote was taken on the proposals on 13 January, the
Soviet Union's was one of the seven cast in the negative. After
it had been taken Malik

explained that, in order to settle an issue similar to that on which a
vote had just been taken, it would indeed have been necessary to
invite both the representatives of the People's Democratic Republic
of Korea and of the People's Republic of China. Since those representatives had not taken part in the decision on the question
under discussion, the delegation of the USSR had voted against
approval of the proposals.[3]

Soviet press comments on the proposals were extremely
unfavourable, and again referred to the dominant American
need to secure a breathing-space for the American forces in
Korea.[4] The Chinese reply on 17 January was a final negation.[5]
On 20 January the United States Government introduced
a draft resolution in the First Committee under which the

[1] UN Document A/C.1/645, 11 January 1951.
[2] General Assembly, 5th Session, First Committee, 422nd meeting, 11 January
1951.
[3] ibid. 425th meeting, 13 January 1951.
[4] *Soviet News*, 23 January 1951.   [5] UN Document A/C.1/653.

Assembly would find that the Chinese Communists had 'en-gaged in aggression' and call upon them 'to cease hostilities against the United Nations forces and to withdraw from Korea'. A committee composed of members of the recently established Collective Measures Committee would consider 'additional measures to be employed to meet this aggression'.[1] This resolution was not supported by Great Britain or the Asian countries. On 22 January Sir Benegal Rau made known the substance of the position of the Chinese People's Government as it had been ascertained by the Indian Ambassador at Peking. If the principle of the withdrawal of all foreign troops from Korea were accepted and put into practice, the Chinese People's Government 'would assume the responsibility of advising the Chinese volunteers to return to China'. After a cease-fire for a limited period had been agreed on during which negotiations could proceed, then in order that the war should end and peace be assured, conditions for the conclusion of hostilities would have to be discussed in connexion with the political problems upon which agreement would have to be reached:

Steps and measures for the withdrawal of all foreign troops from Korea; proposals to the Korean people on the steps and measures to effect the settlement of the internal affairs of Korea by the Korean people themselves; withdrawal of United States armed forces from Taiwan and the Straits of Taiwan in accordance with the Cairo and Potsdam Declarations; other Far Eastern problems. . . . The definite affirmation of the legitimate status of the People's Republic of China in the United Nations had to be ensured.[2]

In his speech in the subsequent discussion, the Soviet delegate Tsarapkin made no reference to the suggestions contained in Sir Benegal Rau's communication and confined himself to a bitter attack on the United States draft resolution along familiar lines.[3] On 24 January, however, the Czechoslovak delegate announced his Government's full support of the proposals of the Chinese People's Government as clarified in Sir Benegal Rau's statement.[4] On 25 January Sir Benegal Rau, having received the text of the Peking Government's reply to questions

---

[1] UN Document A/C.1/654.
[2] General Assembly, 5th Session, First Committee, 429th meeting, 22 January 1951.
[3] ibid.   [4] ibid. 430th meeting, 24 January 1951.

put to it by the Indian Ambassador, presented a revised version
of the Asian countries' draft resolution of 12 December 1950.[1]
This draft resolution recommended that representatives of
France, the United States, Great Britain, the Soviet Union,
Egypt, India, and the Chinese People's Government should
meet as soon as possible to obtain all necessary elucidation of
the Chinese reply and to make arrangements for the peaceful
settlement of the Korean and other Far Eastern questions. The
United Kingdom delegate said that soundings undertaken at
Peking had revealed that Peking did not entirely reject the
principle of a cease-fire before negotiations and that the withdrawal of foreign troops from Korea had been meant to include
the Chinese 'volunteers'.[2]

Tsarapkin described the revised draft resolution as inadequate
but was willing to see it adopted. He proposed two amendments: the first would delete the reference in the heading of
the resolution to intervention in Korea by the Chinese
People's Republic. The second amendment made it necessary
for the President of the Assembly to secure agreement from the
Powers concerned before arranging for the proposed meeting.[3]

A further revised version of the Arab and Asian Powers' draft
resolution was put forward on 29 January which added the
provision that the proposed conference would at its first meeting
'agree upon an appropriate cease-fire arrangement in Korea'
and would proceed with their deliberations after it had been
put into effect.[4] In commending it Sir Benegal Rau warned the
Committee that the Indian Government had been informed on
the highest authority that once a resolution condemning the
Peking Government as an aggressor had been adopted there
would be no further hope of negotiation.[5] The Soviet and
Polish delegates asked for time to consider the revised draft,
and repeated this request at the meeting on the following day,
and when it was refused the Polish delegate made a rambling
statement which brought matters no further forward.[6] On the
same afternoon Tsarapkin, having received his instructions,

[1] UN Document A/C.1/642. Rev. 1.
[2] General Assembly, 5th Session, First Committee, 431st meeting, 25 January
1951.
[3] ibid.   [4] UN Document A/C.1/642. Rev. 2.
[5] General Assembly, 5th Session, 435th meeting, 29 January 1951.
[6] First Committee, 436th meeting, 30 January 1951.

announced that the revised version was even more unsatisfactory than the former one. He submitted a new amendment which eliminated the existing reference to a cease-fire and proposed instead the insertion of the following paragraph:

As the first step towards this end, the representatives of the aforesaid seven countries will, at their first meeting, agree upon an appropriate arrangement for a provisional cease-fire in Korea. After the said arrangement has been put into effect, the representatives of the seven countries will proceed to the second step; that is, they will give consideration to appropriate arrangements and methods for the withdrawal of all foreign forces from Korea, to ways and means to be recommended to the Korean people with a view to the free settlement of the domestic affairs of Korea by the Korean people themselves, to the question of the withdrawal of United States armed forces from Taiwan and the Taiwan Straits in conformity with the Cairo and Potsdam Declarations, and to questions relating to the Far East.[1]

The Soviet amendment and the two earlier ones were both rejected, as was an oral amendment to qualify the cease-fire as 'temporary'. The Soviet bloc abstained when the Asian Powers' resolution was finally rejected.[2] On 31 January the Security Council removed the Korean dispute from its agenda; the Soviet representative accepted this without difficulty since his Government had always held the matter to be outside the Council's competence.

On 1 February the Soviet delegate repeated the arguments against the branding of China as an aggressor but the United States draft resolution to that effect, in an amended and softened version, was passed by 44 votes (including that of Britain) to 7, with 9 abstentions, in a Plenary Session of the Assembly. Two new committees were set up simultaneously: an Additional Measures Committee to consider extending the scope of the United Nations support for South Korea, and a Good Offices Committee to seek for further opportunities for conciliation. On 4 February a telegram from the Chinese People's Government denounced the resolution and announced that it would ignore the Good Offices Committee.[3] On 6 February

[1] General Assembly, 5th Session, 437th meeting, 30 January 1951.
[2] ibid. 438th meeting, 30 January 1951; *The Times*, 31 January 1951.
[3] *International Organisation*, May 1951, pp. 319–20.

Pravda denounced the branding of China as an aggressor as a shameful decision. Despite the rather equivocal attitude of the Soviet delegates to the Asian Powers' plan for conciliation and what had appeared to be largely delaying tactics, the rejection of their move by the United States and its associated Governments and the subsequent passage of the resolution condemning China were used as evidence that the responsibility for prolonging the war rested wholly with the United States.

On 2 February the First Committee took up again the accusation of aggression in China brought against the United States by the Soviet Union in November 1950.[1] On 6 February after some discussion it was agreed to circulate to members of the Committee the statement made by General Wu Hsiu-chuan before his departure from New York.[2] On 7 February the Committee rejected the Soviet charges.[3]

In the latter part of January 1951 the United Nations forces in Korea launched a new offensive which rapidly brought them once more across the 38th parallel. At the end of March there were reports that these military successes had led certain delegates to the United Nations to sound the Soviet representatives as to whether the Soviet Union was in favour of a new effort at terminating the conflict. It was noted in this connexion that the Soviet Union was still not so committed to full support of the North Koreans as were the Chinese Communists.[4] But nothing came of these projects. In April 1951 there were reports of large concentrations of Soviet troops in Manchuria, but a Soviet denial was broadcast on the 6th of that month. On 12 April a short Tass communiqué announced MacArthur's removal from his position as Commander-in-Chief, and said that this had happened because of his inability to cope with the situation in Korea. Editorial comment was delayed until the 18th, when *Pravda* described the dismissal as the culmination of a crisis in American foreign policy. Truman had endeavoured to shift the blame for what had gone wrong on to MacArthur and was seeking credit for preventing the extension of the war,

---

[1] General Assembly, 5th Session, First Committee, 439th meeting, 2 February 1951.

[2] ibid. 440th meeting, 6 February 1951. The statement was circulated as document A/C.1/661.

[3] ibid. 441st meeting, 7 February 1951.

[4] *NYT*, 20 March; *Scotsman*, 26, 29 March 1951.

and for having stopped MacArthur from using Chinese Nationalist troops from Formosa. In fact, however, China's frontiers had already been repeatedly violated by American planes, and the Americans had long planned aggression against North Korea.[1] A new Chinese offensive in Korea was launched on 22 April, and the Soviet press again predicted the rapid defeat of United Nations forces.[2]

The course of the fighting showed that despite the large numbers of troops available to the Chinese, they were still inadequately supplied with modern weapons. The heavy losses inflicted upon them gave rise to rumours of Russian peace feelers through Sweden, but these were officially denied by Malik.[3]

New discussions took place in the United Nations on an American proposal for an embargo on the shipment of arms or strategic materials to areas controlled by China or the North Korean authorities. The Soviet delegate, Malik, now declared that the General Assembly was not competent to discuss such matters, since the responsibility for peace and security under the Charter lay with the Security Council, which was the only body able to impose an embargo under the provisions of Chapter VII of the United Nations Charter. In consequence, he did not participate in the voting, and on 18 May the American proposal was adopted unanimously.[4]

The first initiative taken by the Soviet Union in the whole Korean war crisis occurred without previous warning on 23 June, when in a broadcast by Malik, in a series of talks on the issues of war and peace, he made the familiar contrast between American aggressiveness and the Soviet devotion to peace, but added a section specifically devoted to Korea:

The Soviet peoples also believe that the armed conflict in Korea—the most acute issue of the present time—could also be settled. Readiness of the parties to take to the path of peaceful settlement of the Korean question is necessary for this. The Soviet peoples believe that as a first step the belligerents should negotiate a cease fire and an armistice with a mutual withdrawal of troops from the 38th parallel.

[1] *New Times*, 9 May 1951.
[2] cf. *Izvestia*, 20 April; *Literaturnaya Gazeta*, 21 April; *Pravda*, 13 May 1951.
[3] *NYT*, 24 May 1951.
[4] *United Nations Bulletin*, vol. 10, no. 11.

Is it possible to take such a step? I believe that it is, provided that there is the sincere desire to put an end to the sanguinary clashes in Korea. I believe that this is not too high a price for assuring peace in Korea.[1]

These proposals seemed to be in line with the American demand that a cease-fire should precede political negotiations and should itself be unconditional. Two days later Gromyko told the American Ambassador Kirk that the Soviet Government envisaged a meeting of the two commands to conclude a military armistice which would include a cease-fire but no political or territorial matters. The proposals were also endorsed by the Chinese. But naturally both Soviet and Chinese comment ignored the fact that by now the military position had been altered yet again to the advantage of the United Nations forces, who were established north of the 38th parallel. In fact there were bellicose broadcasts from Moscow and Peking, to the effect that if these proposals were rejected the Koreans and Chinese would certainly be able to complete the destruction of the enemy forces.

General Ridgway, the new Commander-in-Chief of the United Nations forces, was instructed to enter into talks on a cease-fire, and after some discussion of their location, these began on 10 July. At the first meeting the chief North Korean representative, General Nam Il, put forward the following proposals:

1. The immediate cessation of military activities of every kind;
2. the withdrawal of the forces of both sides beyond the 38th parallel for a distance of ten kilometres and simultaneous talks on the exchange of war prisoners;
3. that all foreign troops should be withdrawn in the shortest possible time. With the withdrawal of foreign troops the ending of the Korean war and the peaceful settlement of the Korean conflict could be basically assured.

The delegate of the headquarters of the Chinese 'volunteers', General Teng Hua, stated that the Chinese and North Korean aims were absolutely identical.[2] The United Nations delegation was instructed to limit the discussions to purely military questions, and to avoid being drawn into general political talks. In

[1] *Manchester Guardian*, 25 June 1951.
[2] *Soviet News*, 13 July 1951.

consequence of this and other difficulties the negotiations dragged on very slowly. The Soviet press published reports of them from Chinese and North Korean sources, declaring that the major stumbling-block was the refusal of the United Nations delegation to discuss the withdrawal of the United Nations forces to the 38th parallel, and of all foreign troops from Korea —a refusal designed to circumvent Malik's proposals. On 25 July the Communists agreed to drop their insistence that the wider question of withdrawing foreign troops should be considered with the cease-fire, and agreement on an agenda was reached on the 26th. But they insisted on the parallel as the line of demarcation for the cease-fire, while the United Nations negotiators demanded a line roughly following the position occupied by the two armies.[1] On 7 August various arguments in favour of the 38th parallel were printed in *Pravda*. It was pointed out that each side at present occupied a certain amount of territory on the other side of the parallel, and that to adjust a line along it would be fair to both, whereas the line proposed by the United Nations involved leaving a large area of territory north of the parallel under United Nations occupation. Finally the argument was renewed that the 38th parallel was the original line that Malik had suggested.[2]

The talks continued without much progress being made, and were marked by repeated Communist protests against alleged violations of the neutral zone set up for the talks by United Nations troops and planes. On 22 August the Communist negotiators suspended the negotiations, giving as their reason the alleged violation of the neutral zone, and there were subsequent accusations in the foreign Communist press and in the Cominform Journal that the Americans had been doing everything possible to drag out and frustrate the negotiations. Fighting had never completely stopped and after the suspension of the negotiations had increased in intensity. A new development was announced on 4 September by the Commander-in-Chief of the Eighth Army, General Van Fleet, namely, the presence of 'Caucasian' troops in the fighting area. This term was later clarified to mean not Russian but mainly East European, including East German, troops. On 8 September Tass issued an official denial of big concentrations of Soviet troops 'of white

[1] *Pravda*, 25 July 1951.   [2] cf. ibid. 9 August 1951.

race' in Korea. This of course would not cover either troops from the Soviet Union's European allies or troops drawn from the Asiatic peoples of the Soviet Union.

Nevertheless there was no evidence to support the suggestion made in some quarters that the talks in Korea had been suspended in order to enable the Soviet negotiators at the San Francisco Conference to use the possibility of a resumption of full-scale fighting as a threat. And after the conclusion of the Conference and signing of the Japanese Peace Treaty, talks were once again initiated with a view to bringing about the renewal of the cease-fire negotiations. At this time the major difference between the two sides was still the question of the 38th parallel, and pending the possible agreement on this or some other demarcation line, fairly stiff fighting continued. The general attitude of the Soviet press towards the whole Korean question showed little or no change.

VIII

Soviet Policy in South East Asia

By JOSEPH FRANKEL

LEFT-WING movements in most parts of South East Asia emerged from the war with a record of guerrilla and underground activities against the Japanese. They began the post-war period by taking part in popular fronts and adopted patriotic programmes omitting radical social goals; some of their leaders, like Sjarifuddin in Indonesia and Taruc in the Philippines, disguised their Communist allegiance. These Communist parties were subject to frequent inner differences, and splits between orthodox and 'Trotskyite' factions developed at a rate which varied in each separate country. But in all of them they assumed considerable political importance.

There is no evidence of any war-time liaison between Communist resistance formations in South East Asia and the USSR; the isolation of South East Asia under Japanese occupation and the Soviet preoccupation with the war against Germany made such liaison unlikely. After the war there were a few Russian-trained leaders holding prominent positions in the left-wing movements in Indonesia, Indo-China, and the Philippines, but there apparently were no such leaders in Burma or Thailand. Until the end of 1947 the Russians seem to have confined themselves to statements of support for the local nationalist movements and to the expression of criticism of colonial exploitation.[1]

A more active policy in South East Asia was inaugurated at the end of 1947 by Zhdanov's speech at the opening conference of the Cominform, which stressed, among other things, Communist support for the national liberation movements.[2] The theme was elaborated by Zhukov in his article, 'The Sharpening of the Crisis of the Colonial System', published in *Bolshevik*

[1] I. Lemin, 'Britain's Foreign Policy in the Post-war Period' (*Bolshevik*, 15 June 1947) and 'Post-war Tendencies of the United States Foreign Policy' (ibid. 22 November 1946).

[2] *For a Lasting Peace*, 10 November 1947.

on 15 December 1947, and was discussed at the Youth Conference of the countries of South East Asia, convened in February
1948 in Calcutta by the World Federation of Democratic Youth
and by the International Union of Students. The Conference
was of a broad international character, its 900 delegates including representatives of India, Pakistan, Burma, Malaya, Indonesia, Viet Nam, Ceylon, and the Philippines, together with
observers and guests from Europe, America, and Australasia.
The Soviet delegates and guests included representatives of the
Central Asian Republics.

The Communist New China News Agency referred to the
great importance of the Conference in a communiqué which
drew attention to the rising level of political consciousness of the
Asian people. The communiqué declared that the Conference
heralded 'the further broadening and consolidation of the
national democratic movements of South East Asia and of the
anti-imperialist front of the Western people'. The proceedings
and resolutions of the Conference were not divulged, but the
report of a Soviet delegate, A. Kharlamov, published in *Moscow
News* of 3 April 1948, mentioned that 'the Conference unanimously adopted a resolution supporting national liberation
struggle against imperialism, for national independence, and
for democracy and freedom for the peoples of the colonies and
dependencies'.[1] The Youth Conference was followed by the
Congress of the All-India Communist Party, which opened at
the end of February and was attended by 800 Indian delegates
and by fifteen 'fraternal' delegates from Burma, Australia, and
Yugoslavia.[2]

Within six months of these Conferences insurrections started
in Burma, Malaya, and Indonesia. Some Western journalists
attributed these risings to instructions received at Calcutta, but
there is no tangible evidence for this contention. The rising in
Indonesia took place as late as August and was preceded by
the return of the local leader, Muso, who had been trained in
the USSR. There can, however, be little doubt that during the
Conferences the representatives of the Communist movements

---

[1] V. Thompson and R. Adloff in *Left Wing in South East Asia* (New York, Sloane
for IPR, 1950), p. 153, speak of three separate conferences, convoked by the Indian
Communist Party, the South East Asia Students' Associations, and the New
Democratic Youth League, but in fact only one joint conference took place.

[2] *The Statesman* (Calcutta), 1 and 8 March 1948.

in South East Asia became acquainted with the new aggressive line of international Communism, which encouraged the resort to armed action, wherever conditions seemed favourable, even if it did not make it compulsory.

The rising in Indonesia failed completely. Insurgents in Burma and Malaya were equally unsuccessful in seizing power although they created grave disturbances and, in the case of Burma, established what amounted to a 'liberated area'. If, in the period of the Calcutta Conferences, India was intended to be the co-ordinating centre of the Communist movements in South East Asia, by mid-1949 any such plan seems to have been abandoned in favour of co-ordination through China, where the Communists were within reach of final victory.

The first indication of such a change was given by Zhukov, who strongly stressed the importance of the Chinese example in a report broadcast to South East Asia in June 1949, and also in an article published three months later. Zhukov developed the argument for colonial revolutions led by the working class and the Communist parties acting directly or through wider mass organizations. He claimed that dependent peoples were attracted to the 'democratic camp' for three reasons: the increasing aggressiveness of the United States, the successes of the 'People's Democracies' in China and North Korea, and the discredit into which bourgeois nationalism had fallen, the leaders of which, Nehru, Sjahrir, and Thakin Nu, had revealed their 'anti-popular' character.[1]

Co-ordination of the Communist movements in South East Asia was finally entrusted to the Permanent Liaison Bureau of the World Federation of Trade Unions, established at the Conference of Trade Unions of Asia and Australasia held in Peking in November 1949.[2] As appears from the report read at this Conference by the Secretary-General, the Federation had even before this date been an important medium of Communist activities in South East Asia. It had been active in Indonesia, Burma, Malaya, and (without success) in Viet Nam; and had also been engaged on the general welding together of the workers' movements in the Far East and in South East Asia. Further activities of the Federation in South East Asia were directed through China, and exhortations to the peoples of

[1] *NYT*, 28 June 1949.   [2] See above, p. 84.

South East Asia to follow the Chinese example and to imitate Chinese tactics became a standard feature of Communist propaganda. The Russians urged a united front of Asian peoples against the United States, whom they accused of designs to gain control of Asian markets through the elimination of competitors and through the subjugation of the people. The solidarity of the Asian Communist movements, they asserted, was finally cemented by the outbreak of the Korean war. The Cominform Journal described the United States as 'the gendarme and hangman of the peoples of South East Asia', which had mobilized the other colonial Powers as its 'junior partners'. The Journal declared that, following China's example, these peoples would prove invincible in the defence of their native lands against mercenary armies and would become 'an integral part of the national movements in defence of peace'.[1]

Communism in South East Asia was influenced throughout the period more by China than directly by the Soviet Union. The Chinese member of the Permanent Liaison Bureau apparently directed its activities, while the Chinese People's Government itself acquired considerable influence over the numerous and economically powerful Chinese groups residing in South East Asia. This influence was exercised through the Overseas Chinese Affairs Commission, a government department with manifold functions, and through diplomatic and consular representatives resident in the area. Consequently, Communism in South East Asia was affected by the racial antagonism between the indigenous peoples and the Chinese minorities residing among them. The predominantly mercantile character and outlook of these minorities was unfavourable to Communism; nevertheless, possibly because of a larger percentage of industrial workers among them, the Chinese were more prone than the indigenous peoples to adopt the Communist creed. After the establishment of the Chinese People's Republic this tendency was greatly strengthened by their patriotic sentiments and by their habit of supporting the Government in power in China. According to some observers, however, the Chinese mainly preferred to remain neutral in the conflict between Communism and democracy, and by 1951 there were some indications that Communism was losing ground

[1] *For a Lasting Peace,* 1 September 1950.

among them. In Malaya and in Thailand Communism became a predominantly Chinese movement, and the racial antagonism contributed to its rejection by the Malays and the Thai; while in Indonesia, Viet Nam, and Burma the movement found followers among the indigenous peoples. These racial complications were, however, ignored by the Russians who attributed them exclusively to the divide and rule policy adopted by the colonial Powers.

Soviet pronouncements on South East Asia were usually even vaguer than those on other parts of the world. It was difficult to fit the complicated local events into the rigid scheme of 'national liberation movements' opposing 'colonial exploitation'. The Russians were often compelled to reverse their judgement or to ignore facts, for example, when consistently describing as 'fictitious' the independence gained by South East Asian countries. The Soviet news items not only demonstrated the usual tendency to exaggerate the strength and successes of the Communists but, in some instances, showed such ignorance of the actual situation as to raise questions about the sources of the information available to the Russians. It is likely, though it cannot be verified, that the Russians exercised some direct influence through their diplomatic representatives who were established after the Second World War in Burma, Thailand, and with the so-called 'democratic republic of Viet Nam',[1] as well as through the local Communist parties, particularly their Russian-trained leaders. As regards the Permanent Liaison Bureau of the WFTU in China, it is difficult to estimate the degree of direct Russian control either through the Soviet member of the Bureau or through the central WFTU organization.

Apart from their concern with the political developments in South East Asia, the Russians showed interest in the raw materials of the area. They imported considerable quantities of Malayan rubber until 1951, when rubber exports from Malaya came under strict control.

[1] The Russians showed a marked reluctance to enter into diplomatic relations with South East Asian Governments. They did not recognize the Republic of the Philippines; despite recognition, they did not exchange representatives with Indonesia; in the case of Thailand, they delayed the dispatch of a representative to Bangkok by eighteen months; in that of Burma, they delayed the exchange by nearly a year and gave it no publicity.

INDONESIA[1]

When the Republic of Indonesia was proclaimed on 17 August 1945 the Indonesian Communist Party (Partai Kommunis Indonesia, PKI) was weak. Since the unsuccessful rising in Java in 1926–7 it had been outlawed and weakened by the secession of Tan Malakka, an able leader trained in Russia holding radical 'Trotskyite' views. After the war, Tan Malakka's movement was more influential than the PKI, but it opposed any understanding with the Dutch and plotted against the republican Government which finally arrested its chief leaders in 1947. The PKI by contrast at first fully supported the Government. Early in 1946 it was reorganized by its leaders who had returned from abroad, notably by the Russian-trained Alimin. Leadership was assumed by Sardjono who after years of imprisonment had been removed to Australia while the Japanese attacked.[2] While the PKI was consolidating its membership, organizing indoctrination centres at Madiun and later at Jogjakarta and establishing military formations, Alimin was in favour of an understanding with the Dutch, deeming it not only necessary for the preservation of the Republic from complete destruction, but also for securing the 'breathing space' necessary for the organization of the revolutionary movement.[3] According to some reports, Alimin was instrumental in persuading President Sukarno to appoint an additional 180 left-wing members to the House of Representatives in order to press through Parliament the Linggadjati Agreement reached with the Netherlands on 15 November 1946, which provided for the establishment of a Dutch-Indonesian Union. The Communist, Socialist, and Workers' Parties each had 35 members. Alimin became a member of the Central Committee of the House of Representatives and was in a position to bestow favours on the left-wing guerrilla bands and to facilitate Communist infiltration of the administration, the army, and the police force. In November 1945 he formed a united front of six leftist organizations under the name of Sajap Kiri (the Left Wing).

[1] See A. A. Guber, 'The Indonesian People in the Struggle for Independence', in *Krisis Kolonialni Sistema*.   [2] ibid. p. 151.
[3] 'De PKI, de Stem van Moskou', *Internationale Spectator* (The Hague), 30 May 1951; L. G. M. Jaquet, 'Tan Malakka's National Communism', ibid. no. 5, 7 March 1951.

The Linggadjati Agreement was finally signed on 25 March 1947, but by May the Sajap Kiri began openly to oppose the concessions granted to the Dutch. The moderate Sjahrir Cabinet, faced both with right-wing and with Communist opposition, was forced to resign at the end of June, and was replaced on 3 July by a Cabinet led by Sjarifuddin, who at the time was leader of the left wing of the Socialist Party, founded in December 1945, despite his having been a member of the Communist Party since before the war. His Cabinet of thirty-five included fourteen members of the Sajap Kiri.[1]

Serious military reverses during the Dutch 'police action', which started on 20 July 1947, economic difficulties resulting from the Dutch blockade of the Republic, and right-wing opposition were instrumental in causing the fall of the Sjarifuddin Cabinet in January 1948. This happened a week after the signing on 17 January, under the auspices of the United Nations, of the Renville Agreement, which provided for a cease-fire, and established the principles of a political settlement. Sjarifuddin's successor, Mohammed Hatta, invited the Sajap Kiri to participate in his Cabinet, but with a reduced representation, and the offer was declined.[2] The Communists now sought broad popular support. They already dominated the important trade union federation, SOBSI (Sentral Organisasi Buruh Seluruh Indonesia) which became affiliated to the World Federation of Trade Unions after its Congress in May 1947.[3] After Sjarifuddin's fall, they reorganized the Sajap Kiri on a broader basis into the 'People's Democratic Front'. In March 1948 the right-wing parties formed, in opposition, a 'National Front', but later they endeavoured to re-establish unity with the forces of the Left. Negotiations were apparently successful since on 27 May

---

[1] *Internationale Spectator*, 30 May 1951. One Communist at least was included though not as such. See also Guber in *Krisis Kolonialni Sistema*, p. 162.

[2] In November 1950 the Communists themselves analysed this move as a major blunder since it left the State power in the hands of the bourgeoisie which could use it to subdue the radicals (ibid.). Possibly already at this stage the PKI conceived a plan for revolutionary action (see G. McT. Cahin, 'The Crisis and its Aftermath', *FES*, 17 November 1948, vol. 17, p. 264; and V. Thompson and R. Adloff, 'The Communist Revolt in Java', ibid. p. 259).

[3] Guber in *Krisis Kolonialni Sistema*, p. 153. It was represented at the WFTU by Setiadjid, a Communist who had taken part in the Resistance in Holland during the war, had founded the Workers' Party in Indonesia at the end of 1945, and became Vice-Premier in Sjarifuddin's Cabinet.

Alimin declared that he would re-enter the Cabinet. On the same day, however, agreement was finally frustrated by the news received from Prague that the Indonesian representative there, the Communist Soeripno, had concluded an agreement with the USSR for the exchange of consular representatives, which was contrary to the Renville Agreement and was strenuously opposed by the right-wing parties.[1]

These developments received considerable attention in the Soviet press, which had traditionally given more prominence to Indonesia than to other parts of South East Asia. Soviet commentators noted that the Communists in Indonesia were not very influential, and described the nationalist movement as broadly popular, supported not only by socialists but also by peasants. They had some reservations about Sukarno's 'petty-bourgeois outlook' and his opposition to violence, but they expressed approval of Hatta. They also applauded the Republic's economic plans and excused its neglect of genuine agrarian reform on the grounds that it had had no breathing space.[2]

On the international scene, the Russians assumed the role of champions of Indonesian nationalism. Immediately after the landing of the British troops in Indonesia at the end of the war, they accused the British of forcibly suppressing the Indonesians with the assistance of Japanese. They ascribed British intervention to two motives: fear of the repercussions of Indonesian nationalism in British possessions, and the desire to preserve British investments in Indonesia. They maintained that only when confronted with determined Indonesian opposition did the British decide in favour of a compromise solution which would retain a modified Dutch rule with the support of the moderate elements among the Indonesians.[3] In January 1946 the Ukrainian Republic lodged a formal complaint with the Security Council that the situation in Indonesia was endangering international peace and security. The complaint was, however, rejected.[4]

---

[1] Thompson and Adloff, *Left Wing in South East Asia*, p. 182.

[2] V. Vasilyeva, 'The Fight for the Democratic Development of the Indonesian Republic', *Voprosy Istorii*, no. 1, 1948; 'Indonesia's Ten-Year Plan of Reconstruction', *New Times*, 6 June 1947, p. 20.

[3] Guber in *Krisis Kolonialni Sistema*, pp. 158–9; I. Kopylov, 'The Events in Indonesia', *New Times*, 1 October 1946, pp. 11–12; *Pravda*, 7 August and 28 September 1946.

[4] *Yearbook of the United Nations, 1946–47* (New York, United Nations, 1947), pp.

The Russian press questioned the good faith of the Dutch and commented on the Linggadjati Agreement as the outcome of 'a policy of concessions forced upon the Dutch imperialists who, however, intend to give these concessions a purely formal character and to preserve the essential colonial dependence and imperialist exploitation of Indonesia'. They maintained that the Dutch had endeavoured to 'strangle' the Republic by armed action and by naval blockade, and that they had ratified the agreement only after these means had failed.[1]

From May 1947 attacks against the United States in connexion with Indonesia began to appear in the Soviet press. They ascribed American interest in Indonesia to economic motives—to the favourable field for capital investment and to the already enlarged hold of the American 'monopoly capital' on all the basic branches of Indonesian economy, which, one commentator stated, had reduced the Dutch to 'mere sales clerks'. The Russians maintained that the Security Council was acting as an instrument of Dutch, or rather American policy, and they strenuously opposed the establishment of the 'Committee of Good Offices'. A Soviet reporter went so far as to call it the 'Evil Offices Committee', and accused its American member of having caused the downfall of Sjarifuddin's Cabinet through 'back-stage machinations' and intrigue with the right-wing groups.[2] Soviet criticism of the Renville Agreement of January 1948 was equally strong.[3]

The Russians declared themselves to be fully in favour of establishing consular relations with the Indonesian Republic, deeming them desirable 'from the point of view of normal politics and common sense, from the point of view of the strengthening of peace and international co-operation.' They accused the Dutch of employing fictitious arguments against their permitting them.[4]

Although the Soviet press represented the 'democratic

338–40. British troops were finally withdrawn on 30 November 1946. See 'Nationalism in Indonesia', *The World Today*, February 1948, vol. 4, p. 56.

[1] See Guber in *Pravda*, 13 January 1947; 'Holland's Agreement with Indonesia', *New Times*, 4 April 1947, pp. 25–26.

[2] G. Afrin, 'In Indonesia', *New Times*, 3 November 1948, pp. 27–32.

[3] 'The Indonesian Question in the Security Council', *New Times*, 10 March 1948, pp. 1–2; Guber in *Krisis Kolonialni Sistema*, pp. 167–71.

[4] Yavorov in *Pravda*, 8 June 1948.

elements' in the Netherlands as being strongly opposed to the Indonesian war,[1] the Dutch Communist Party was itself distinctly weak, and supported the Dutch Catholic-Labour Coalition, which was in power from mid-1946. The Indonesian cause met with considerable sympathy among the non-Communist nations, particularly India, the United States, and Australia, but the only Communist-sponsored support from abroad came from the Communist-dominated Australian dock workers who refused to load ships with supplies for the Dutch.

Further developments were precipitated by the return to Indonesia on 12 August 1948, along with Soeripno, of the Moscow-trained Communist leader, Muso, who immediately took charge of the Communist movement. The Politburo of the PKI acknowledged its past mistakes and violently attacked the agreements with the Netherlands; Sjarifuddin dramatically announced at the end of August that he had been a Communist since 1935, and, using his experience gained as a previous Minister of Defence, assumed command of the military affairs of the PKI. Muso declared himself against further compromise with the Government and violently attacked Sukarno and Hatta. An agreement was reached in September for the fusion of the Communist, Socialist, and Workers' parties.[2] When the right-wing parties declined the 'invitation' to join the National Anti-Imperialist Front, the Communist leaders left for Madiun, in eastern Java. There, on 18 September, they staged a coup and seized the city, but found little popular response. Using its loyal troops and the support of Tan Malakka, who was released from prison, the Government was able to subdue the insurrection without availing itself of the proffered Dutch assistance. By the end of the month Madiun was reoccupied, and Muso killed, while Sjarifuddin and other leaders, with between 30,000 and 35,000 followers, were taken prisoner. The leaders, including Sjarifuddin, were executed and, although the rank and file were later released, the PKI remained disorganized while Tan Malakka's followers, organized in Partai Murba, became an important political element.

Soviet reaction to the Madiun coup was extremely hesitant.

---

[1] *Pravda*, 13 January, and *Trud*, 13 June 1947.
[2] Guber in *Krisis Kolonialni Sistema*, p. 173. Muso is not mentioned in Guber's account, just as little prominence is given earlier to the role of Alimin.

On 22 August *Pravda* published a short communiqué based on Dutch sources and declared that the information available was insufficient for a clear understanding of the situation. On 24 August *Pravda* was still non-committal, although it spoke unfavourably of Hatta's actions. On the following day *Pravda* went so far as to style the insurgent authorities 'the new Government at Madiun'. When, however, the failure of the insurrection became certain, reports ceased to appear. Subsequent interpretation of the coup was inconsistent. In October 1948 it was described as the expression of popular sentiments favouring real independence, and opposing 'the policy of making deals with colonizers, pursued by the Hatta Government'. Early in 1949, however, the Communist press affirmed that the coup had been provoked by Hatta on American instigation, 'with the purpose of beheading the progressive movement and crushing the democratic organizations, especially the trade unions.' It described the period of co-operation between the PKI and the nationalists as faulty tactics, and stated that the Communists would 'wage the liberation struggle to a victorious end'.[1]

The Madiun coup was followed by the second Dutch 'police action' in December 1948. Within a week the major centres of the Republican territory were occupied and the Republican leaders were imprisoned. While the Security Council was discussing the issue, the Dutch were endeavouring to reach an understanding with the imprisoned Indonesian leaders. The Russians maintained their critical attitude to the Security Council's activities, and continued to accuse the Council of yielding to American influence. The Soviet representative refrained from voting on the Dutch proposal for a Dutch-Indonesian Round Table Conference, which was voted upon and accepted on 13 March 1949.[2]

The Republican leaders did not enjoy Soviet approval, even during the initial period of their imprisonment when they were rejecting the Dutch overtures. And the Russians regarded their later willingness to negotiate as conclusive proof of their subservience, and attacked the Round Table Agreement of 2 November 1949 which established an independent United States

[1] Pieter de Groot, 'National Liberation Movement in Indonesia', *For a Lasting Peace*, 14 February 1949.
[2] *United Nations Bulletin*, 15 April 1949.

of Indonesia within the Dutch-Indonesian Union. They affirmed that the negotiators had acted in bad faith, since Hatta was not really representative of the Indonesian people. The Dutch were striving in their view to preserve the colonial régime behind a 'smokescreen' of freedom and equality, while in the background the Americans were pushing their claims to the dismay of their Dutch and British competitors. (Accordingly, when the Round Table Agreement came before the Security Council, the Ukrainian delegate roundly denounced it. The PKI was equally emphatic in its rejection. But the transfer of sovereignty took place on 27 December 1949.[1])

At the beginning of 1950 the Soviet attitude to Hatta became somewhat less critical. Although on 18 January *Izvestia* again accused him of collaboration with the Dutch, the attack was couched in milder terms. At the end of the month the USSR accorded the Republic diplomatic recognition which Hatta immediately acknowledged, requesting at the same time that diplomatic relations should be established. The Indonesian Minister of Information announced that any ideology would be permitted in Indonesia, provided that its adherents did not disturb the peace. He thus clearly indicated the possibility of removing the legal ban on the Communist Party which still remained on the statute book from the period of Dutch rule before the war, although it was not enforced. During February the Indonesian request for the establishment of diplomatic relations received a reply from Vyshinsky, who suggested that either an Indonesian delegation should visit the USSR or that a Soviet delegation visit Indonesia. Negotiations proceeded very slowly, and in March the Soviet press repeatedly attacked the Republican Government and accused the United States of attempting to 'undermine' Indonesian relations with the USSR. In May an Indonesian delegation visited Moscow, and on 5 August Hatta announced that the Republic would soon appoint an Ambassador to the USSR.[2]

However, further violent attacks on Hatta soon appeared in the Soviet press in connexion with the conversion of the United States of Indonesia into a unitary State on 14 August 1950. While the Russians had rejected the previous federal solution as

[1] UN, Security Council, 455th meeting, 12 December 1949.
[2] *The Times*, 6 February 1950; *NYT*, 5 August.

being the result, in the main, of an Anglo-Dutch intrigue, they represented the new unification of the Republic as the outcome of American scheming. Subsequent Soviet comments on Indonesia reflected the belief that American influence on Hatta had become paramount both in the economic and in the political spheres. The Soviet press reported that the Americans had made plans for the establishment of military bases in Indonesia, and explained the controversy between the Dutch and the Indonesians over western New Guinea by United States pressure to retain that island under joint Dutch-Australian administration, as a link in the chain of American bases in the Pacific.[1] By December 1951 no exchange of diplomatic representatives had taken place.[2] Neither side explained the delay, but the Soviet attacks on the Indonesian Government indicate that the Russians were to blame.

Meanwhile, the PKI was being reorganized. The rank and file, taken prisoner during the Madiun coup, were released in the autumn of 1948 in order to take part in the guerrilla warfare against the Dutch, and the Communist Party was tolerated, although it was not legalized. Largely as a result of the coup, the trade union federation SOBSI split into three groups, but was reorganized early in 1951 and again claimed a large membership.

The PKI endeavoured to establish a 'United Front' with the Partai Murba. After long negotiations, on 30 March 1951 the two parties agreed on a common programme both on internal and on foreign affairs; but the 'United Front' did not materialize since no agreement was reached on the problem of leadership. From February 1951 the Partai Murba controlled a separate trade union federation.[3]

From its inception, the Indonesian Republic had to contend with internal opposition from Communists, right-wing extremists, former guerrillas, and some local communities. In mid-1951 disorders in which Communists participated became more serious in Java and Sumatra, and in August the Govern-

[1] *Pravda*, 17 and 21 November 1950; *Izvestia*, 2 February 1951.

[2] Orally confirmed by the Information Department of the Indonesian Embassy in London on 8 December 1951. Indonesia exchanged representatives with the Chinese People's Republic; and the first Chinese Ambassador to Indonesia presented his credentials on 14 August 1950.

[3] For a general discussion of the PKI of this period see 'De PKI, de Stem van Moskou', *Internationale Spectator*, 30 May 1951, pp. 1–5, and 11 July 1951, pp. 1–6.

ment retaliated by a security drive which involved the arrest of about 100 Communist suspects, including sixteen left-wing members of Parliament.[1]

The Russians commented severely on these developments. On 29 August 1951, the sixth anniversary of the proclamation of Indonesia's independence, the *New Times* complained that the slogans of 'freedom' prominently displayed during the anniversary were contradicted by the simultaneous police raids and arrests. It maintained that the disorders had been provoked by the Government, which was seeking an excuse for the repression of the democratic movements. On 27 August *Pravda* printed a Tass dispatch from The Hague which contended that the arrests in Java and Sumatra alone had amounted to 1,500, including many non-Communists, and that the Dutch right-wing press did not disguise the fact that the mass arrests had obviously been ordered by the United States.

VIET NAM

Communism in Viet Nam is indigenous but has strong international ties through its leader, Ho Chi Minh, who is the only South East Asian Communist of international stature; he has made several visits to Russia, was a foundation member of the French Communist Party, founded the Indo-Chinese Communist Party in 1930, and has carried out important organizing activities on behalf of the Comintern in China and in South East Asia.[2]

In May 1941 the Vietnames Communists under the leadership of Ho Chi Minh organized the Viet Nam Doc Lap Dong Minh Hoi (usually abbreviated as Viet Minh). This remained active underground during the period of Japanese occupation, but some of the leaders escaped to China. There they formed in 1942 the Viet Nam Cach Menh Dong Minh Hoi (abbreviated as Dong Minh), the League of Revolutionary Parties of Viet Nam. The core of this was the Viet Minh which had now adopted a purely patriotic programme omitting controversial social items. Ho Chi Minh, after a period of imprisonment by the Chinese

[1] *NYHT*, 17 August 1951.
[2] Article on Ho Chi Minh in *Diplomatischeskii Slovar*; Thompson and Adloff, *Left Wing in South East Asia*, p. 232. Until 1940 Ho Chi Minh was known under various names, usually as Nguyen Ai Quoc. See also 'The Nationalist Movement in Indo-China', *The World Today*, June 1947, vol. 3, pp. 268–77.

authorities, was released and was the dominant personality in the organization.

The Viet Minh increased its activities in Indo-China, and on the date of Japanese capitulation was sufficiently organized to replace the Government of the Emperor Bao Dai, established a short time before by the Japanese. The independence of the Democratic Republic of Viet Nam, comprising the Annamese lands of Tonkin, Annam, and Cochin China, was proclaimed by the Viet Minh on 22 August 1945.[1]

Cochin China was occupied by British troops, who landed at Saigon on 13 September, and later also by French troops. The local Viet Minh authorities came into conflict with them and were removed, but developments followed a different course in Tonkin and Northern Annam. Here the Chinese Nationalist troops, who occupied Indo-China north of the 16th parallel, supported, by preference, less radical and more pro-Chinese groups than the Viet Minh, but Ho Chi Minh employed considerable diplomatic skill and maintained himself in power. In November 1945 he formally dissolved the Communist Party and organized instead the Association for the Study of Marxism; he reshuffled his Government in December 1945 and (after elections held in January 1946) again in March 1946, and included representatives of right-wing groups.[2] Finally, on 6 March 1946, he concluded an agreement with the French at Hanoi, providing for the admission of French troops in exchange for a recognition of the independence of the State of Viet Nam within the framework of the Federation of Indo-China and of the French Union.[3]

[1] E. J. Hammer, 'Blueprinting a New Indochina', *Pacific Affairs*, September 1948, vol. 21, p. 253.

[2] For a Soviet view, see Vasilyeva, 'The People of Viet Nam in the Struggle for Independence and Democracy', in *Krisis Kolonialni Sistema*, p. 187.

[3] Institut Franco-Suisse d'Études Coloniales, *France et Viet-Nam* (Geneva, Milieu du Monde, 1947), p. 55. Little information is available on the January elections. The Russian comments mentioned their 'popular procedure' and Guber, in *Voprosy Istorii*, no. 10, 1949, maintained that over 90 per cent. of the voters cast their votes, 97 per cent. of them for the Viet Minh. In fact the Viet Minh clearly controlled the elections and no candidates could be put forward without its prior consent. They thus bore a closer relationship to the 'single-list' system of the Soviet Union than to the multi-party contests of the West. See the recent full-scale narrative of events at this period from a point of view highly critical of French policy: Philippe Devillers, *Histoire du Viêt-Nam de 1940 à 1952* (Paris, Editions du Seuil, 1952), pp. 200–1.

At first the Chinese adopted an ambiguous attitude towards the return of the French, but on 26 February 1946 a Sino-French treaty was signed at Chungking giving them political and economic concessions. As a result, the Chinese began to withdraw their troops. Nationalist parties, opposing the Viet Minh, were deprived of protection since the French did not continue the Chinese policy of supporting them. By employing violence, the Viet Minh soon reduced internal opposition in the Government to negligible proportions. The Viet Minh itself remained a nominal coalition united under its Communist leadership. Apart from political parties, it embraced the Vietnamese Confederation of Labour (TLD), the Union of Vietnamese Women, the Union of Youth, and several social and cultural societies. In May 1946 the Viet Minh combined with other parties and associations in a new organization, the Hoi Lien-Heap Quoc-Dan (or Quoc Gia) Viet-Nam (sometimes abbreviated as Lien Viet), which the French translate as 'Front National Populaire de Viet Nam', but which is also found referred to as the 'National Union of Lien Viet'.[1] The majority of the three hundred members of the National Assembly belonged to the Viet Minh, but a much smaller number were apparently members of the Association for the Study of Marxism.

During 1946 the French Government conducted protracted negotiations with the Viet Minh, both locally and in France, in order to determine the status of Viet Nam and its relation to Cochin China, which the Viet Nam leaders claimed as an integral part of the free State. Negotiations in France broke down in August, but before returning to Indo-China Ho Chi Minh signed a *modus vivendi* to come into force on 30 October. But at the end of November hostilities broke out at Haiphong and at Langson. On 19 December a surprise attack on the French was made in Hanoi; many were massacred. The intermittent fighting which followed secured for the French the command of the major part of the coastal zone but left considerable inland areas in the hands of the Viet Minh, which claimed to have undertaken in them ambitious economic and educational programmes.[2]

[1] J. R. Clémentin, 'The Nationalist Dilemma in Vietnam', *Pacific Affairs*, September 1950, vol. 23, pp. 303-4; *Izvestia*, 2 September 1950.
[2] See *The World Today*, June 1947, p. 275, which speaks of Ho Chi Minh having

In contrast to the interest exhibited in Indonesian affairs, the Soviet press scarcely commented on these events in Indo-China. It expressed general sympathy with the nationalist strivings and criticized General de Gaulle's declaration of March 1945, which envisaged the preservation of French sovereignty in Indo-China; it contended that the French people and, in particular, the French Communist Party held different views. In fact, however, the French Communist Party was quite vague and talked of Viet Nam achieving independence within the framework of the French Union. Similarly, the Soviet press did not interpret events in Indo-China in terms of a simple struggle for national liberation, aiming at complete independence, but as a question of reaching an understanding between the Vietnamese patriots and the French democratic forces, in opposition to the French 'banking and rubber interests' supported by native landowners.[1]

Throughout 1947 Soviet comments on Viet Nam were mild. They maintained that in France there existed a 'grave dissatisfaction of democratic public opinion' with the policy of suppression employed in Indo-China, and they publicized demands for a peaceful solution made by French 'democratic circles'. Towards the end of the year they began to express concern over the French designs to split the unity of the nationalist forces of Viet Nam by enlisting the services of the ex-Emperor Bao Dai. Since the French explained that their opposition to the Viet Minh was caused by its Communist leanings, a Tass communiqué issued in May 1948 emphatically stated that the Viet Minh 'was and still is a coalition of all patriotic parties and groups, and that the French are careful to omit all references to the formal dissolution of the Com-

---

lost control at this juncture to more extremist elements. In fact Ho Chi Minh's control of the Government seems to have been consolidated after his return (Devillers, *Viêt-Nam*, pp. 311–14).

[1] Some commentators explain the difference in Soviet attitudes to Indonesia and to Viet Nam by the considerable power and importance of the Communist Party of France which contrasted with the insignificance of the CP of the Netherlands. Possibly the Communist strategy aimed at the retention of Indo-China within the French orbit, since France showed some promise of becoming a Communist State. See M. Sacks, 'Communism and Regional Integration', in P. Talbot, ed., *South Asia in the World Today* (University of Chicago Press, 1950), pp. 212–13; Thompson and Adloff, *Left Wing in South East Asia*, p. 15. The Communists were finally dismissed from the Government coalition in France in May 1947.

munist Party and the holding of democratic elections in Viet
Nam'.[1]

From the beginning of 1948 the United States came under
attack for its alleged intervention in Viet Nam as part of a
wider plan to suppress national liberation movements in Asia,
and the protracted negotiations between the French Government and Bao Dai were ascribed to American inspiration.
When, on 8 March 1949, an agreement was finally signed under
which Viet Nam was described as an independent State within
the framework of the French Union, the Russians severely
criticized the important powers retained by the French and
referred to the agreement as a 'hollow farce'.[2] Throughout
1949 Soviet news from Viet Nam remained scanty, and occasions
like the anniversaries of the Viet Nam 'war of liberation' or of
the declaration of the Republic evoked little comment. Some
space, however, was devoted to the military operations and to
the Viet Minh successes, and also to the economic structure of
the Republic. On 9 August *Pravda* noted that the Republic had
completely severed its relations with the French Government
by recalling its resident secretary from France, but gave no
intimation of the impending diplomatic recognition of the
Republic by the USSR.[3]

Late in 1949 the existence of the Democratic Republic of Viet
Nam became acknowledged in Communist writings. The
French Communists engaged in a policy of strikes and sabotage,
aimed at preventing the dispatch of military supplies for Indo-
China.[4] Communist deputies in the French Parliament openly
incited French troops to mutiny and desertion.   Late in
November Ho Chi Minh exchanged telegrams with Chou En-
lai, and from that time they closely co-operated concerning
the Kuomintang troops which were crossing the Indo-Chinese
border in their retreat from the Chinese Communists. Although
the French were disarming these troops Chou En-lai protested
on 7 December against what he called 'underhand machinations of the . . . reactionaries and the French imperialists in
violating Vietnamese national sovereignty'. At the same time,

[1] I. Podkopayev, 'Viet-Nam Fights for Independence', *New Times*, 13 April
1949, pp. 11–13.
[2] ibid.; *Pravda*, 14 March; *Izvestia*, 17 August 1949.
[3] *Pravda*, 14 January, 9, 14, 17, and 22 August 1949.
[4] ibid. 26 December 1949, 4 January 1950; *For a Lasting Peace*, 6 January 1950.

the Viet Minh warned the French against harbouring the enemies of the New China, and declared that it would support the Chinese Liberation Army, should it deem it necessary to pursue its opponents into Viet Nam.[1]

On 14 January 1950 Ho Chi Minh declared that the Democratic Republic of Viet Nam was ready to establish diplomatic relations with other countries. On the following day his Minister for Foreign Affairs sent a formal telegram of recognition to the Central People's Government of China, and on 18 January he was notified in turn of China's willingness to establish diplomatic relations. According to French and to Chinese Nationalist sources the Chinese Communists had been giving considerable aid to the Viet Minh as early as the second half of 1949. After the recognition of Communist China, reports from Indo-China indicated an increase in supplies, and pointed to the existence of training camps in South China in which Viet Minh guerrillas were undergoing military training. Presumably existing communications were regarded as insufficient since, according to Chinese Communist sources, a direct railway from South China to the territory occupied by the Viet Minh was opened in November 1951.[2]

The Soviet Government recognized the Democratic Republic of Viet Nam on 31 January 1950 and incurred sharp criticism from the West for doing so. The Russians argued that this recognition was fully consistent with the Charter of the United Nations and with the Soviet policy of peace based on the principle of equality since, they said, the Republic commanded 90 per cent. of the country and had received French recognition by the agreement of 6 March 1946. There was no mention of the possibility of material assistance from the USSR, but the Soviet press prophesied the success of the Viet Minh offensive which began in 1950 and the impending defeat of the French. When the United States and the British Governments recognized the Bao Dai Government on 7 February 1950, the Soviet press attacked the 'American intrigues' and referred to Bao Dai

---

[1] M. Sacks, 'The Strategy of Communism in Southeast Asia', *Pacific Affairs*, September 1950, vol. 23, pp. 240–1. The Viet Minh supported also the Chinese protest against damage inflicted by the French on Chinese communities in Viet Nam.

[2] *The Times*, 31 July 1950; *Manchester Guardian*, 20 December 1951. The new railway was reported to be a 200-mile extension of the line from Hunan.

and to the American Minister in Indo-China in extremely abusive terms.[1]

In June 1950 relations between the USSR and the Democratic Republic of Viet Nam were further strengthened by the establishment of the Viet Nam–Soviet Friendship Society. On 2 September 1951 *Pravda* referred to the existence of diplomatic relations between the two countries, without specifying the date at which they had been established or mentioning the conclusion of any agreements.[2]

From 1950, especially after the beginning of the Korean war, the Soviet press intensified its attacks on American policy in Viet Nam, alleging that the Americans were continuing their economic penetration of the country with the ultimate aim of taking it over completely.[3] At the same time Soviet statements concerning the Republic gradually changed their character. On the occasion of the fifth anniversary of the foundation of the Republic, on 2 September 1950, the Soviet press represented the Viet Minh as completely independent of outside aid, maintaining that it was using exclusively Japanese, French, and locally-made weapons, without receiving Soviet or Chinese supplies. A year later, Viet Nam was described as an important part of the 'great universal democratic family', enjoying the support of friendly nations.[4]

The rise of the Democratic Republic of Viet Nam as a State recognized by other Communist States was accompanied by radical changes in the inner structure of the Viet Minh. These changes became evident from mid-1949 when moderate leaders were replaced by Communists throughout the country. In July the Communist Pham Van Dong was nominated Vice-President of the Upper Council of National Defence and of the Government. Shortly after his nomination he delivered a violently Communist speech, and the Vietnamese press redoubled its praise of the USSR and of the Chinese People's Republic.[5] After the Peking Conference of November 1949 the role of the organized working class was increasingly stressed. In

[1] *Pravda*, 6 and 9 February; *Izvestia*, 14 February and 7 June 1950.

[2] *Soviet News*, 9 June 1950; *Pravda*, 2 September 1951.

[3] S. Pogosov in *Voprosy Ekonomiki*, no. 3, 1950, p. 49; 'Imperialists in Indo-China', *New Times*, 25 July 1951, pp. 9–11.

[4] *Pravda*, 2 September 1950, 17 August and 2 September 1951.

[5] Clémentin in *Pacific Affairs*, September 1950, p. 310.

January 1950 the first national conference of trade unions was convened in order to carry out the decisions of the Peking Conference, and 'to map out plans for the consolidation of the Viet Nam working masses and making them a vanguard in the fight for national liberation and rebuilding a new economy'.[1]

Early in January 1950 Ho Chi Minh established an Inspection Committee with extremely wide powers; in February the immunity of the members of the National Assembly was cancelled and Pham Van Dong declared that the workers and peasants would take a greater share in the Government. Although by 1949 Moscow Radio had referred to the Communist Party of Viet Nam as leading the struggle, Ho Chi Minh was still speaking of its official dissolution of 1945, and the Viet Nam radio did not broadcast any official Communist statements.[2]

In February or March 1951 the Communist Party was officially reconstituted under the name of the Laodong, the Viet Nam Party of the Working People. Despite the new name, there can be little doubt as to the identity of the two parties. The new party was based on the principles of Marxism-Leninism and, in its organization, on the principle of democratic centralism. It proclaimed as its chief task the leadership of the working class and of all the Viet Nam people in their struggle for complete independence. Simultaneously the Viet Minh was merged in the Lien Viet.[3]

The Soviet press reported the formation of National United Fronts also in Laos and in Cambodia.[4] It referred to an all-Indo-China conference in November 1950 and to the emergence of a United National Front for the whole of Indo-China in March 1951.

MALAYA

In pre-war Malaya Communism was confined almost ex-

---

[1] According to a Soviet report, the 800 delegates who participated in the Conference represented 250,000 workers (Vasilyeva in *Bolshevik*, February 1950, p. 66). Reports mentioned the huge portraits of Communist leaders decorating the assembly hall, the Communist tone of the addresses, and the greetings sent to the Russian trade unions.

[2] M. Sacks in Talbot, *South Asia in the World Today*, p. 211.

[3] *Pravda*, 24 March 1951.

[4] V. Vasilyeva, 'People's Liberation Struggle in Laos and Cambodia', *New Times*, 28 February 1951, p. 12.

clusively to the Chinese community and received only sporadic support from some of the Malays and the Indians.[1] /

After the German attack on the USSR the Communists began to co-operate with the local Government. Before the fall of Singapore 200 Communists were trained and equipped for guerrilla warfare. Later the Communist Party organized about 3,000 members in guerrilla units which operated in the jungle. When contact with British forces was re-established in the summer of 1943, the guerrilla army undertook to co-operate with the Allied Command, to receive liaison officers in all units, and to accept tactical orders. In return, it was supplied with arms and equipment which arrived in quantities towards the end of the war. The Communist Party ostensibly abandoned the radical social items of its programme.

During the few weeks intervening between the Japanese surrender and the landing of the British, the guerrillas obtained undisputed power in the countryside. They did not oppose the British Military Administration and in December 1945 they were peacefully disbanded and surrendered their arms, or at least a considerable proportion of them.

The Communist Party, however, was generally uncooperative and concentrated on creating difficulties in the field of labour relations. Making use of the economic unrest, it organized hundreds of trade unions which were, in fact, Communist cells, and linked and controlled them through a General Labour Union.[2] On 29 January 1946 a general strike was staged. It was called off four days later for reasons which are not quite clear; another strike, proposed for 15 February, was successfully prevented by firm Government measures, including the arrest and deportation of its more important instigators.[3]

Although predominantly Chinese, the Communist trade union movement liked to stress its 'all-nationalities' character. In 1948 its federation—the All-Malayan Federation of Trade Unions—was admitted to the WFTU. From mid-1948, however, Communist influence in the labour movement began to be successfully countered.

[1] V. Purcell, *The Chinese in Southeast Asia* (London, Oxford University Press for RIIA, 1951), pp. 363–5.
[2] 'Communism in Malaya', *The World Today*, August 1949, vol. 5, pp. 346–54.
[3] Purcell, *Chinese in Southeast Asia*, pp. 378–9.

Following the findings of the mission of two British trade union experts, S. S. Awbery and F. W. Dalley, the Government amended the Trade Union Ordinance to restrict the political activities of trade unions. In June the All-Malayan Federation of Trade Unions was dissolved. The majority of the Communist organizers could not satisfy the new qualifications for trade union office; and general trade union federations going beyond a single industry were prohibited. The degree of the Communist penetration of the trade union movement was shown by the fact that by the end of September 1948 the estimated membership of the trade unions was more than halved.[1]

The Malayan Communist Party adopted a negative attitude to the post-war constitutional changes proposed by the British Government. It advocated the unification of Malaya in the form of a republic and therefore did not endorse the original Malayan Union proposals which were, on the whole, favourable to the Chinese community. It joined the Chinese protests against the subsequent Malayan Federation proposals, which were more favourable to the Malays.[2]

Until 1948 the Soviet press virtually ignored Malaya, devoting to it only casual communiqués. It appears that the Malayan Communist Party had little, if any, connexion with the outside world. Its leaders themselves admitted that they had been poorly educated and therefore had made mistakes in estimating the local situation and, even more, the international trend. According to press reports, only one Malayan delegate attended the Calcutta Conferences in February and March 1948, but the Australian delegate, L. Sharkey, visited Malaya on his way home and spent a full fortnight in conferences with the local Communist leaders.[3]

---

[1] S. S. Awbery and F. W. Dalley, *Labour and Trade Union Organisation in the Federation of Malaya and Singapore* (Kuala Lumpur, 1948); Gt. Britain, Colonial Office, *Annual Report on the Federation of Malaya, 1948*, pp. 12–14.

[2] Purcell, *Chinese in Southeast Asia*, p. 395.

[3] Thompson and Adloff, *Left Wing in South East Asia*, pp. 154–6. It seems likely therefore that armed action was ordered or advised from outside; this was the opinion of the Commissioner-General, Malcolm MacDonald. It is, however, possible that the Malayan Communist Party was governed more by requirements of local strategy and found it imperative to counter the Government's successful anti-Communist campaign among the trade unions. This reason was quoted by some Russian commentators, but the decision was clearly taken before the Government's move against the Communists in the unions.

It seems that in the spring of 1948 the Malayan Communists finally decided to stage an insurrection. There followed widespread labour unrest, causing intimidation and violence, and from mid-June the sporadic outrages intensified, inducing the Government to declare a state of emergency and in July to ban the Communist Party and affiliated organizations. Between 4,000 and 5,000 Communists took to the hills and jungles, and, aided by the difficult nature of the country and by the assistance received or extracted from isolated Chinese squatter communities, were successful in local attacks on mines and plantations, without, however, being able to disrupt Malaya's economic life or to seize enough territory to set up a People's Republic.[1] The Communist Party organized a considerable propaganda network.[2]

Despite the considerable military and police force deployed, Government action against the bandits was slow, but the efforts of the bandits to broaden the racial basis of the rebellion were unsuccessful. On 1 February 1949 they adopted the name of Malayan Races Liberation Army and formed the so-called Tenth Regiment of Malays in Pahang, but by the end of the year this regiment had been almost eliminated and the insurrection remained a Chinese movement.[3]

After the outbreak of the insurrection, Soviet comments on Malaya multiplied and referred also to previous events. They represented the British as the exploiters of the Malay workers and peasants, and contrasted the living conditions of the two races. They could not, however, decide on a consistent interpretation of American-British relations in Malaya. On the one hand, American capitalists were said to be seeking increased influence in Malaya and to be pressing for lower prices for rubber and tin, compelling the British to refuse the workers adequate wages; on the other hand, the 'colonial adventure in Malaya' was interpreted as part of joint aggressive American-British plans, apparently worked out in unison.[4]

[1] Purcell, *Chinese in Southeast Asia*, pp. 402–3.
[2] *The Economist*, 24 June 1950.
[3] Purcell, *Chinese in Southeast Asia*, p. 705.
[4] A. Guber, 'Malaya', *New Times*, 8 December 1948, pp. 18–25; Vasilyev in *Pravda*, 10 April 1950; Thompson and Adloff, *Left Wing in South East Asia*, pp. 159–60; G. L. Bondarevski, 'The National Liberation Struggle of the Peoples of Malaya', in *Krisis Kolonialni Sistema*, pp. 195 ff.

The Russians did not acknowledge the seriousness of the racial problem in Malaya and confined themselves to a general condemnation of a British 'divide and rule' policy. They scarcely commented on the Malayan Union plan, and stated that it had to be shelved 'to appease the rising tide of popular indignation', suggesting that the feeling was all-Malayan and not confined to the Malay community. The insurrection in Malaya was represented as a struggle of the broad masses against imperialism and its feudal allies, which had been provoked by the suppression of the labour movement and inspired by the liberation struggle in other Asian countries. The Russians emphatically rejected the British interpretation of the struggle as a campaign to restore law and order against bandits and terrorists, and endeavoured to disprove the Chinese character of the insurrection and to give proof of its Malay and Indian following.[1]

Soviet comment alleged that British troops were resorting to inhuman methods of warfare and condemned the emergency measures taken, especially the large-scale resettlement of Chinese squatters from isolated localities in which the bandits could intimidate them to furnish food and other supplies. British admissions of difficulty and the slow progress of the anti-bandit campaign were taken as proof of defeat.[2] On 13 April 1951 *Pravda* described the situation in Malaya as extremely critical and, despite the fact that the insurgents had never been successful in establishing a 'liberated area', maintained that 75 per cent. [*sic*] of the country was occupied by the People's Liberation Army.

Apart from political considerations, Soviet interest in Malaya was due to the importance of Soviet rubber imports from that country. These reached 67,898 tons in 1950. In 1951, however, rubber exports to the USSR were drastically curtailed. On 9 April export licensing was introduced and finally, on 22 May, regulations controlling the destination of rubber exports came into force. Under these Russia and China were allotted low monthly quotas. In July exports to the USSR amounted only to 422 tons.[3]

---

[1] O. Orestov, 'Two Years of the War in Malaya', *New Times*, 5 July 1950, p. 16; *Pravda*, 10 April 1950.

[2] Orestov in *New Times*, 5 July 1950; Vasilyev in *Pravda*, 5 October 1950.

[3] Federation of Malaya: Department of Statistics, *Rubber Statistics Handbook*

BURMA

While in Malaya Communism was confined to the Chinese, in Burma it was indigenous, and in 1945 and 1946 it played an important part in the Burmese nationalist movement. The Communist Party was a member of the Anti-Fascist People's Freedom League (AFPFL), formed in 1944 to oppose the Japanese. The League assumed a share in the government of Burma from the autumn of 1946 and successfully conducted the negotiations with the British Government which finally led to the declaration of Burma's independence. Moreover, Communist propaganda was purely nationalistic and discarded items offensive to popular feeling.

The Communist movement in Burma was divided, partly for ideological reasons and partly owing to personal rivalry between the leaders. In February 1946 one group, extremely orthodox in its Communism and therefore sometimes referred to as 'Trotskyite' or anarchist, seceded from the AFPFL and formed the Communist Party [Burma], or the Red Flags. It engaged in open revolt, especially in Arakan, where it was able to utilize the local separatist tendencies. A considerably larger group, organized under the name of Burma Communist Party or White Flags, remained in the League but clashed with its leaders over its demands for a stronger Communist representation in the Executive Council and for a less conciliatory policy towards Britain. In November 1946 the White Flags were expelled from the League, but they were not declared an illegal party and they took a limited part in the general election in April 1947.

In July 1947 the Prime Minister, Aung San, was assassinated. His successor, Thakin Nu, favoured rapprochement with the Communists and entered into negotiations with them; these, however, broke down in mid-November.[1]

The Soviet press devoted little attention to the situation in Burma and apparently had little information on it. It noted the importance of the Communist elements in the League and attributed the split which took place early in 1946 to 'forces of reaction', without favouring either section, despite the 'Trotsky-

1950 (Kuala Lumpur, Government Printer, 1951); *Malayan Statistics: External Trade of Malaya, July 1951* (Singapore, Government Printer, 1951); Sir Hartley Shawcross in the House of Commons, 31 May 1951, *Hansard*, vol. 488, coll. 390–1.
   [1] Thompson and Adloff, *Left Wing in South East Asia*, pp. 93–95.

ite' tendencies of the Red Flags.[1] As might be expected Great
Britain was the main target of Soviet attacks. She was accused
of having neglected the campaign against the Japanese and of
having failed to co-operate with the Americans and the Chinese,
in order to preserve her control over Burma. The Russians
maintained that the British were suppressing the Burmese
nationalists by a reign of terror and described as valueless the
basic British-Burmese agreement of January 1947, which provided for a free and independent Burma whether within or
without the British Commonwealth. They contended—without
further explanation—that this agreement did not satisfy a single
national demand of the Burmese people and alleged that the
mass demonstrations in Rangoon in January 1947 were a protest against it. Aung San was described as a British puppet who
had been induced to purge the League of its leftist elements.[2]

Russian comments became confused over the issue of the
Burmese elections of April 1947. On the one hand they admitted
that the elections had resulted from the struggle of the Burmese
people for their independence, on the other hand they dwelt on
the fact that there was no secret ballot, on the low percentage
of voting, on the presence of British forces, and on the 'terrorist
régime' of Aung San, which were said to have precluded really
free elections.[3]

In July 1947, immediately before Aung San's assassination,
the Russians were still styling him a British puppet, but two
months later they attributed his murder to Burmese right-
wingers supported by the British, who allegedly wished to
eliminate Aung San owing to his negotiations for the readmission
of the Communists into the League. From the perspective of
the autumn of 1948, Aung San had become a Burmese patriot
who had fallen 'for the British bait' and who had attempted
to win the confidence of the British and simultaneously to
secure a Burmese following by addressing emphatic nationalist
demands to Britain. A Soviet commentator emphatically stated
that Aung San 'was murdered . . . by British secret service

[1] A. Klimov in *Trud*, 3 July 1947; V. Vasilyeva in *Mirovoe Khoziaistvo i Mirovaya
Politika*, September 1947; Thompson and Adloff, *Left Wing in South East Asia*, pp.
111–13.

[2] ibid. pp. 115–16; *Izvestia*, 31 January 1947; *Pravda*, 18 January 1947.

[3] The British forces did not, in fact, take any part in supervising the elections.
The polling booths were guarded by AFPFL forces.

hirelings' and referred to a report in the *New Statesman and Nation*.[1]

The Russians considered the final British-Burmese agreement of 17 October 1947 as a further step towards the enslavement of Burma; they said that it granted 'fictitious independence while actually tightening the knots of colonial oppression', and regarded Thakin Nu as even more amenable to the British than his predecessor. The adverse comments centred on Burma's acceptance of debts due to Great Britain and to India, on the undertaking to compensate the owners of the nationalized industries, and on the 'military privileges' reserved for Britain. A Russian commentator described in detail the British commercial interests in Burma, and concluded that 'virtually speaking, all Burma is to this day the private domain of five British companies, which divide among themselves the lion's share of its natural wealth, transport facilities, trade and finances.'[2] Accordingly, the Russians considered as fictitious the declaration of Burma's independence on 4 January 1948. They repeated the argument that power had not, in reality, been handed over to the Burmese and that, in order to mislead the public, the British had sacrificed their hireling, Aung San's murderer, U Saw, and had allowed him to be sentenced to death.[3]

Meanwhile, from the latter part of 1947 the internal situation in Burma had been rapidly deteriorating. The Government was facing grave danger from the large Karen minority with a strong military tradition, as the Karen National Union was known to favour a separate Karen State although it did not rise in arms until the beginning of 1949. Moreover, after Aung San's assassination, the para-military People's Volunteer Organization (PVO), affiliated to the AFPFL, became increasingly disaffected and adopted part of the White Flags' programme, without, however, becoming allied to them.[4]

No information is available of any direct contacts between

[1] I. Alexandrov, 'Events in Burma', *New Times*, 6 October 1948, pp. 9–13. According to Thompson and Adloff (*Left Wing in South East Asia*, p. 93, n. 8), in an interview with them in April 1947 U Tin Tut stated that Aung San would not have forced the Burmese Communist Party out of the League had he not had firm evidence of that Party's strategy of boring from within.

[2] A. Leonidov, 'Labour Imperialism's Colonial Strategy in Burma', *New Times*, 9 February 1949, pp. 3–11.

[3] Alexandrov in *New Times*, 6 October 1948, p. 12.

[4] 'New Hope for Burma', *The World Today*, September 1950, vol. 6, pp. 381–2.

the Burmese Communists and the USSR and none of the prominent Burmese Communist leaders had been trained in Russia.
Before the Communist victory in China they had apparently no
direct contact with the Chinese Communists either. International contacts were established through India. A leading
member of the Burma Communist Party, H. N. Goshal, an
Indian by birth, visited India in December 1947 and, after his
return, violently attacked the 'reformist bourgeois leaders of the
AFPFL', and called for their overthrow by force. In February
the Burma Communist Party was represented by Goshal at the
Calcutta Conference of the South East Asia Youth Conference,
sponsored by the World Federation of Democratic Youth, and
was also strongly represented at the Conference in March of the
Indian Communist Party.[1]

There followed widespread strikes in preparation for a rising
planned for mid-April. The White Flags then struck suddenly
in several districts and scored initial successes, but were unable
to make a stand and were driven by Government troops to the
hills and the woods where they maintained guerrilla warfare
and terrorized the countryside. Through terrorism and expro-
priations the insurgents soon alienated the people's sympathy,[2]
and their popularity was further undermined by the reaction
against their Indian affiliations which were widely advertised
and exaggerated by the Government.[3] Thakin Nu evolved a
left-wing unity programme of his own which closely resembled
that of the PVO, but declined the demand for reconciliation
with the White Flags. Subsequently, part of the PVO rose in
arms. Despite the lack of co-ordination in their command, the
new rebels secured important initial successes. As has been
seen, the Karen National Defence Organization also rebelled, and
early in 1949 the position of the Government seemed desperate.
However, by mid-1950 it had achieved important success in
reducing the military danger.[4]

Communist influence persisted in the trade union movement.

[1] Thompson and Adloff, *Left Wing in South East Asia*, p. 110; 'Political Developments in Burma', *Current Notes on International Affairs* (Canberra), April 1950, vol.
21, pp. 248–9.
[2] *The World Today*, September 1950, p. 382.
[3] W. Wyatt, 'A Sea of Troubles', *New Statesman and Nation*, 12 February 1949,
p. 147.
[4] *The World Today*, September 1950, pp. 382–4.

After the All-Burma Trade Union Congress had been dissolved in March 1948, the Communists infiltrated the Socialist Burma Trade Union Congress which became affiliated to the AFPFL. A crisis was reached in the autumn of 1950 when the President and Vice-President of the new Congress were removed owing to their pro-Soviet declarations and to their praise of the World Federation of Trade Unions. Pending the replacement of these officers, the Congress was temporarily disaffiliated; in February 1951 it split.[1]

The Russian press devoted little attention to the insurrection in Burma, vaguely describing exaggerated successes of the rebels. By contrast, it abundantly discussed British policy in Burma. According to the Russians, the British endeavoured to reduce the Burmese to complete subservience through systematic dislocation of the country's economy and through the instigation to revolt of the Karen, Shan, and Kachin tribes. Thakin Nu was said to be threatened from one side by the British influence dominating Burma's economy, by the Karen and other pro-British elements in the army, and by the 'influential class of landlords, usurers, and compradores'; from the other side by workers and peasants rallying round the progressive camp. 'Chained by fear of its own people', Thakin Nu's Government was supposed to be under the sway of the British Military Mission, and the Government's anti-Communist policy and its willingness to receive foreign capital and aid from the Commonwealth were attributed to this dependence.[2]

From the beginning of 1949 the Russians began to accuse American capital of planning the 'Marshallizing' of all South East Asian countries and contended that, in order to consolidate their influence in Burma, the British were being obliged to transfer to the Americans a share of their profits.[3]

Thakin Nu followed his programme of establishing friendly relations with the Communist countries. In July 1949 Burma experienced some difficulties with a detachment of Chinese Nationalist troops who had crossed the Burmese border and

---

[1] UN, *Economic Survey of Asia and the Far East, 1950*, p. 99; S. B. Thomas, 'Burma' in L. K. Rosinger, ed., *The State of Asia*, p. 310, n. 14.

[2] Leonidov, in *New Times*, 9 February 1949, p. 10; *Izvestia*, 18 August 1950. In fact, during the period of the insurrections the British Military Mission was considerably reduced.

[3] Leonidov, loc. cit. p. 10.

refused to lay down arms, but the Burmese Government denied the rumours that Mao Tse-tung had threatened to intervene. In December 1949 the Burmese Government recognized the Chinese People's Government. Among the Chinese minority resident in Burma, estimated at 250,000 persons, a certain swing to the Left was noticeable, but probably their major interest remained in the preservation of the existing friendly relations with the Burmese.[1] China had previously maintained an Embassy and Consulates in Burma and, with the exception of the Ambassador and one other official, their personnel agreed to serve under the new Chinese Government.[2] Diplomatic relations with the USSR were established in the first half of 1951; on 28 February 1951 the Burmese Ambassador presented his credentials in Moscow, and on 16 May the Soviet Ambassador presented his at Rangoon. In July 1951 press reports spoke of a Burmese trade mission proposing to visit Eastern Europe, including the USSR.[3]

THAILAND (SIAM)

Communism in Thailand was confined almost entirely to the large Chinese minority. The strength of the Communist Party was variously estimated, but it is unlikely that it numbered very many militant members. After the Communist victory in China, membership probably increased,[4] but articles on Thailand published in *Izvestia* of 15 April 1951 and in *Trud* of 22 August 1951 made no mention of a Communist Party. They referred only to the Partisans of Peace movement, which was said to be persecuted by the Government. A report in October 1951 spoke of 152,531 signatories to the 'Stockholm peace appeal'.

Until June 1946 no collaboration existed between the Thai and the Chinese workers, who constituted about 60 per cent. of the non-agricultural labour force.[5] In January 1947 the Central

---

[1] The Chinese territorial claims in Upper Burma were strengthened by the fact that many of the Kachins live on their side of the frontier. The Chinese Communists have been making efforts to attract the Burmese Kachins (H. Hopkins, *New World Arising* (London, Hamilton, 1953), pp. 239–40).

[2] Purcell, *Chinese in Southeast Asia*, pp. 694–6.

[3] *Daily Telegraph*, 11 July 1951.

[4] Thompson and Adloff, *Left Wing in South East Asia*, pp. 58–59.

[5] V. Thompson, *Labour Problems in Southeast Asia* (New Haven, Yale University Press for IPR, 1947), p. 247.

Labour Organization was formed, which included both Thai and Chinese workers. At first this organization remained neutral in Chinese politics but by 1949 it was infiltrated by Chinese Communists and became a member of the World Federation of Trade Unions. In April 1948 the Government sponsored the establishment of the National Trade Union Congress, which later successfully removed the Thai workers from Communist influence. Although in February 1949 the Communist organization still claimed equal membership of both races, by the autumn of 1951 it was obviously overwhelmingly Chinese in composition.

Before the war Thailand had not maintained diplomatic relations with the USSR. Press reports affirmed that in 1941 the two countries had agreed to an exchange of diplomatic representatives, but the war had intervened. After the war Thailand was obliged to seek Soviet approval in order to avoid the possibility of a Soviet veto on its application for admission to the United Nations. Consequently, in a speech delivered in May 1946, the Siamese Prime Minister, Pridi Phanomyong, mentioned cautiously the desirability of establishing diplomatic relations with the USSR. In October 1946 the Thai Government repealed the 1933 law outlawing Communism, and in November its application for admission to the United Nations received the support of the Soviet representative. A formal approach for the exchange of diplomatic representatives was made on 26 December by the Thai Minister to Sweden, and five days later the Soviet Government gave its consent. The first Soviet Minister to Thailand, Sergei Nemchina, presented his credentials at Bangkok on 4 May 1948, nearly a year and a half later.[1] The Soviet Legation became an important propaganda centre; it published a Tass bulletin, opened an information centre, and introduced Russian films.[2]

Although immediately after the war the Russians expressed their sympathy with Thailand's territorial claims on Indo-China, and declared that the disputed provinces had been wrong-

---

[1] Thompson and Adloff, *Left Wing in South East Asia*, pp. 70–73; *Pravda*, 6 January 1947. The Soviet press did not explain the reasons for the long delay.

[2] *Straits Times*, 26 November 1948. Persistent rumours of espionage activities were officially denied by the Thai Government and were dismissed as exaggerated by some Western journalists. See A. Roth, 'Fact and Fiction in Siam', *The Nation*, 25 December 1948, vol. 167, p. 725.

fully annexed by France in the past,[1] they continued to treat Thailand as only nominally independent and as in reality controlled by foreign capital. A short time after the establishment of diplomatic relations between the Soviet Union and Thailand, the Soviet attitude to Thailand became pronouncedly unfriendly. The Russians complained of the rapid increase in American influence and criticized the royal family and Pibul Songgram's Government for suppressing the labour movement and for arresting Communists.[2]

In 1949 the Russians made an unsuccessful attempt to develop trade relations with Thailand through the Soviet representatives at Bangkok, offering prices above the market level for rubber and for non-ferrous metals. Owing to the high prices and the inferior quality of local products, they made only a few purchases through the agency of Chinese firms and did not conclude a general agreement.[3]

In 1950 Soviet criticisms of American penetration intensified. On 22 May *Pravda* reported the arrival of 100 American advisers and instructors, stating that they were to control the Thai forces. On 24 November *Pravda* announced that the United States was transforming Thailand into a military base for American aggression. It maintained that the technical and military agreements, concluded between Thailand and the United States after the visit of an American military mission in August, had established complete American military control.

The Russians devoted some comment to reports of commercial competition between the American and British traders in Thailand. When, however, in August 1951 Thailand adhered to the United Nations decision to restrict trade with Communist China, they contended that the American-British monopolies, apparently now working in unison, were artificially building up stocks of export goods in Thailand, forcing local producers to reduce prices, and causing unemployment.[4]

THE PHILIPPINES

During the war the left-wing resistance movement in the

---

[1] A. Guber, 'French Indo-China', *New Times*, 15 July 1946, p. 22.

[2] V. Tsvetkov, 'Siam', *New Times*, 25 August 1948, pp. 20–22.

[3] Thompson and Adloff, *Left Wing in South East Asia*, pp. 74–75.

[4] I. Kozlennikova, *Izvestia*, 15 April 1951; Belsky, *Trud* and *Soviet Monitor*, 22 August 1951.

Philippines was organized in the Hukbalahap (an abbreviation of *Hukbo ng Bayan Laban sa Hapon*, a Tagalog name for the People's Anti-Japanese Army), which successfully opposed the Japanese and organized its own administration in the 'rice bowl' of central Luzon.[1] It was based on peasant support secured by the confiscation and distribution of estates, and did not profess to be Communist, although its leadership was in fact drawn from experienced leaders of trade unions and of the United Socialist and Communist parties. It was headed by Luis Taruc, who at the time kept his Communist allegiance secret. The Chinese left-wingers were separately organized, but their fighting units joined the Huks.[2]

The Huks expected that, after liberation, their war-time co-operation with the United States Army would be followed by some sort of recognition of their organization. When the United States Army refused it, displaced Huk officials, and demanded the surrender of arms, the Huks began to resist by force, while Taruc, who had been arrested with other Huk leaders by the Americans early in 1945, entered into negotiations with the Philippine Government. The Huks also played an important part in the organization in June 1945 of the Democratic Alliance which, apart from the Communist Party (united with the Socialist Party since before the war), included the National Peasant Union of Luzon, the Committee of Labour Organization of Manila, and the Civil Liberties Union. The Democratic Alliance adopted a moderate social programme but included in it agrarian reform and the nationalization of public utilities. It denounced collaborators and was strongly anti-American, demanding immediate and unconditional independence and repudiating the Philippine Trade (Bell) Bill. In the general

[1] According to a Soviet source, the Hukbalahap was the fighting instrument of a United Front created on Communist initiative. See Zabozlaeva, 'The Struggle of the Philippine People for its Independence', *Krisis Kolonialni Sistema*, p. 211.

[2] R. H. Fifield, 'The Hukbalahap Today', *FES*, 24 January 1951, vol. 20, p. 16. According to a Soviet source, Taruc was trained by Pedro Abad Santos, the leader of the Philippine Socialist Party before it merged with the Communists in 1938. Santos, who died in 1944, had 'discerned' the similarity between the existing political and economic conditions in the Philippines and the situation in China, and had 'established contact with the teachers of the liberation struggle in China even before the war and borrowed their methods of partisan fighting and the organizational structure of the people's liberation army' (Zabozlaeva in *Krisis Kolonialni Sistema*, p. 218).

election in May 1946 the Democratic Alliance supported the candidature of Osmena who, however, lost the election to a former collaborationist, Roxas; it won seven seats in the House of Representatives but its members were deprived of them by the Government and some were arrested.[1] A Soviet comment suggests that this was necessary for Roxas to get a two-thirds majority for the Philippine Trade Bill.[2]

Negotiations between the Huks and the Government broke down over their refusal to disarm and eventually, in March 1948, President Roxas declared both the Huks and the Peasants' Union illegal organizations. After his death the following month his successor, President Quirino, reopened negotiations. Under a temporary truce agreement in June 1948 Taruc returned to Manila and was admitted to his elected seat in the House of Representatives while the President proclaimed an amnesty for the Huks, who were to surrender with their arms. It was now that Taruc publicly admitted that he had been a member of the Communist Party since 1939; both he and two other prominent Communist leaders, Mariano P. Balgos and Guillermo Capadocia, declared themselves in support of full Philippine independence and claimed that they were receiving no outside assistance.[3] Apparently, however, the Huks did not genuinely contemplate surrender. Despite two extensions of the time-limit, the last until 15 August, only few surrendered and practically none brought in their arms. By the end of August Huk concentrations assumed threatening proportions and a rupture seemed imminent.[4]

Developments in the Philippines received only scant notice in the Soviet press which scarcely mentioned the Huks but devoted some space to criticism of 'the landlords, fascists and collaborators.' These, according to the Russians, maintained their rule in order to oppose reforms, and were willing to accept an unequal trade agreement with the United States. The Soviet Government did not recognize the Philippine Republic, maintaining that it was not truly independent, and that the United States had granted it 'fictitious independence' as a nominal

---

[1] T. I. Moore, 'The Hukbalahap in the Philippines', *Australian Outlook*, June 1947, vol. 1, pp. 24–41.
[2] Zabozlaeva, loc. cit. p. 243.
[3] *NCDN*, 28 May 1948.   [4] ibid. 17 and 30 August 1948.

concession to the growth of the national movements in the Pacific and to the popular feelings of the Philippine people. In fact, the Russians argued, the Bell Act tightened United States economic control of the islands, while the agreement on military assistance in 1947 secured important privileges for the American forces.[1]

The Soviet press apparently wished to dispel the suspicion that the Huks might be receiving material assistance from the Soviet Union. On 16 March 1948 *Pravda* caustically commented on the statement made by President Roxas (which he later withdrew) that the Huks and the Peasants' Union had received Soviet support. The comment ended with the contention that Roxas was not in a position to deny concessions to the Americans since he was obliged to wipe out his record of collaboration with the Japanese.

Fighting flared up in the autumn of 1948, after the final breakdown of the negotiations between the Government and the Huks. In October the Department of Justice banned the Communist Party and a special Committee on Un-Filipino Activities began its hearings at the House of Representatives.[2]

The Filipino Communists began to stress their international connexions. Taruc, who had again fled to the hills, declared that the USSR was the only true ally of the Philippine people and that he would not sacrifice his life for the right of American imperialism to exploit the people.[3] Testifying before the Committee for Un-Filipino activities, Balgos denied any present connexion between the Philippine Communist Party and the Chinese People's Republic or the Cominform, but threatened that, if necessary, the party would resort to force to secure democracy, and that, in case of a world conflict, it would align itself with the USSR. There followed several announcements in the same vein by Taruc and by other Communist leaders.[4]

---

[1] *Pravda*, 26 April, 2 August 1946; I. Lapitsky, 'The Philippine Scene', *New Times*, 2 August 1950, pp. 12–15; cf. Zabozlaeva in *Krisis Kolonialni Sistema*.

[2] *NYT*, 17 and 21 October 1948.

[3] *Manila Times*, 5 September 1948, quoted by Zabozlaeva in *Krisis Kolonialni Sistema*, p. 247.

[4] *NCDN*, 18 December 1948. The Philippine authorities frequently alleged that the Huks were supported by Chinese agents, and, from the latter part of 1947, the likelihood of collaboration with the Chinese Communists was generally assumed, although it could not be proved.

Throughout 1949 clashes between the Huks and the Government forces continued. In October, on the eve of the general election, fighting intensified, and the President decided to entrust the conduct of the campaign to the army instead, as previously, to the constabulary. The Huks took part in the electoral campaign, supporting the candidature of Laurel, despite his record as a puppet President under the Japanese. They explained their support by the now predominantly popular following of Laurel, which was said to consist of 'workers, peasants, and anti-imperialist forces.' After Laurel's defeat, the armed struggle grew in intensity, and the Communists finally abandoned political activities within the framework of the Philippine Constitution. Early in January 1949 the Communist leaders, Balgos and Capadocia, joined the Huks and acquired a strong, if not predominant, position among them. The Communist alignment of the Huks was now openly divulged and by March 1950 they had changed their name to People's Liberation Army, abandoned their moderate programme of 1946, and stated as their aim a 'New Democracy' on the Chinese pattern.

The Government army scored some indecisive successes, but by mid-1950 fighting intensified again and in August Huk raids were reported over a wide area.[1] Apart from the military campaign, the Philippine Government adopted other repressive measures. In April 1951 it cancelled the registration permit of the Communist-dominated Congress of Labour Organizations, and inaugurated a campaign to purge the trade union movement of Communist influence. Communist leaders were tried and convicted.[2]

Soviet comments concentrated on reports of corruption and inefficiency in the Philippine Government and on its subservience to the Americans. In 1950 a particularly acid comment was evoked by the publication of the report by the American Bell Mission, which strongly criticized the Philippine Administration.[3] From July 1950 reports of the fighting became more frequent and dwelt on the difficulties of the Americans and the

[1] Fifield in *FES*, 24 January 1951; *NYT*, 26 August 1950.
[2] *SCMP*, 7 April; *NYT*, 12 May 1951.
[3] *Izvestia*, 4 November 1948, 29 April, 7 June, 1950; *Pravda*, 25 May, 1 November 1950.

successes of the Huks.[1] In 1951 Soviet approval of the Huks became even more pronounced. On 2 April *Pravda* represented the fighting in the Philippines as 'part of the struggle of the peoples of all countries against imperialist aggressors', and declared that 'the American imperialists and their puppets in Manila . . . will not succeed in bringing to their knees a people which has risen in the battle for liberation'.

Here, as elsewhere in South East Asia, the Russians thus increased the vehemence of their verbal support for the local independence movement, without, however, extending the promise of direct material assistance.

[1] e.g. *Izvestia*, 20 July and 29 August; *Pravda*, 17 and 27 September, 24 October 1950; Lapitsky in *New Times*, 2 August 1950, pp. 14–15.

IX

Conclusions

IN the light of the evidence presented in the foregoing chapters it is tempting to ask once more to what extent Soviet policy can be regarded as having followed a single clearly marked path during the period under review.

At the end of the war, the Soviet Union seemed to be justifying its policies and gains by the same considerations of national interest as had inspired the Governments of the Tsars. Stalin's declaration on 2 September 1945 that the turning of the tables on Japan in Manchuria was something for which Russians of the older generation had awaited for the entire forty years since the Russo-Japanese war, represents perhaps the extreme swing of the pendulum towards old-style nationalism. It was rendered even more striking by the historical fact that the revolutionaries of Stalin's generation had been utterly opposed to the expansionist policies which had led to the Russo-Japanese war and had looked upon Russia's defeat solely in the light of the opportunities it provided for revolutionary action at home.

Although this phase in Soviet sentiment was of short duration, and although there was in the post-war period a rapid return to at any rate the more orthodox language of Marxism, there was no indication that the legitimacy of the Soviet acquisitions in Manchuria was thought of as dependent in any way on the nature of China's internal régime, despite their limitation to a thirty-year period. The agreements with Communist China in February 1950, which made considerable concessions to the Chinese, at least on paper, and which fixed the end of 1952 as the terminal date for the special position of the Russians on the Changchun Railway and at Port Arthur, made it clear in so many words that a Communist China had got better terms. It was now possible to regard the territorial and other acquisitions of the Soviet Union in China as subordinate from the Soviet point of view to the progress of the Chinese revolution, or if preferred, as guarantees that this progress would be in the desired direction.

It has already been noted that there are good grounds for doubting whether the Russians expected at the time their armies invaded and stripped Manchuria that a Communist Government for the whole of China was a likely development in the near future. The matter has been examined recently once again in the context of the history of the Chinese revolution itself:

Two explanations of Russian policy in Manchuria are possible. It may be that the Russians were merely just as stupid and lacking in foresight as the Western powers. They had seized Manchuria from the Japanese; they could not keep it for themselves, but they could loot it to replace Russia's huge losses in industrial power. This plan would also deny such power to the Kuomintang, and so to an American ally; as for the Chinese Communists, the Russians believed them to be too weak and too deficient in technicians and skill either to hold Manchuria if it were given to them or to work its industries if they acquired them.[1]

The same writer offers as the other explanation:

By handing over the cities to the Kuomintang, but allowing the Communists to occupy the rural areas in Manchuria, the Russians induced Chiang Kai-shek to over-extend his military power and engage in a hopeless campaign in Manchuria which could not be supported by land communications. The Kuomintang strength was thus consumed in the far north-east and the Communist triumph in China proper made possible. By looting Manchuria of its potential, Stalin made sure that the triumphant Chinese Communists would be dependent on Russia and could not break away and stand on their own feet.[2]

Neither explanation, as the writer points out, contradicts any known facts; both probably put in too neat a form what was the result of experiment in a field in which many of the principal factors were genuinely unknown quantities. Soviet historians do not need to worry to explain much of this, since they do not refer either to their stripping of Manchurian industries or to their assistance to the Communists in getting control of the countryside—and of Japanese stocks of arms. On the other hand they have to find an explanation for their support of a coalition under Chiang Kai-shek's leadership, which is a matter

[1] Fitzgerald, *Revolution in China*, p. 94.
[2] ibid. p. 95.

on record in published documents, and which might, in the view of some authorities, have developed further had Chiang Kai-shek been willing to grant note concessions in Manchuria.

An explanation can be found, though only indirectly, in the form of a defence of the conduct of the Chinese Communist Party in carrying on discussions with the Kuomintang through the mediation of the United States:

This position came about because of the fact that the broad masses of the Chinese workers after the eight years of exhausting war with Japan desired peace and hoped that the democratic reconstruction of China and the improvement of the position of the masses might be achieved by means of an agreement between the Communist Party and the Kuomintang. And although it became clear to the leaders of the Communist Party soon after the beginning of the discussions that it was impossible to reach agreement with the Kuomintang reactionaries, struggling to retain their dictatorship, a change of programme at this time would have been an error for it would have meant a break with the masses. It was necessary to give the masses the opportunity of learning from their own experience that their hopes were unreal, and that the problem of the democratic recon-struction of China could not be solved by means of an agreement with reaction and American imperialism.[1]

But this too has an element of subsequent rationalization; could the Chinese Communists have got the independent position within the framework of a national Government to which they aspired with Soviet encouragement, it seems likely that they would have accepted it, and that in that sense the negotiations were not purely educative in purpose, as far as they were concerned.

It may be true that, as has been earlier suggested, it was not until the victories of 1948 that the Soviet Government finally realized that China could be and would be unified on the basis of Communist control and that all would depend upon the nature of the relationship between the Chinese and Soviet régimes that would now develop. The evidence on this point has not been easy to interpret. During the summer of 1951, for instance, there were some indications in the writings of the Chinese Communist leaders of a wish to assert their indepen-dent status.[2] This took the form of an emphasis on the achieve-

---

[1] G. V. Astafev in *Krisis Kolonialni Sistema*, pp. 58–59.
[2] See 'Chinese-Soviet Relations', *The Times*, 10 October 1951.

ments of the Chinese revolution, with a minimum of reference to the assistance and inspiration of the Soviet Union. In particular, there was none of that adulation of Stalin which was by this date common form among leaders of the Soviet Union's European satellites. There seemed indications indeed that Mao Tse-tung was being given the stature of an independent leader looking back directly to Marxist-Leninist teachings rather than that of a simple exponent of Stalinism as applied to China. The same note of independence was struck in a pamphlet published in China to commemorate the anniversary of the Chinese Revolution.[1] A speech by Chu Teh on the occasion of the anniversary of the Chinese Red Army mentioned that the Chinese army should avail itself of the military science of the Soviet Union, but stressed principally 'its own great tradition'.[2] The Commander of the Chinese volunteers in Korea was permitted to represent the Korean campaign in an article in *Pravda*, in terms which suggested that all the aid received by the North Koreans had come from China, and which contained no allusion to Russian help.[3]

The meeting in October 1951 of the National Committee of the Political Consultative Conference provided a platform for the restatement of China's position by her principal leaders. Both Mao Tse-tung and Chou En-lai emphasized China's allegiance to the 'world camp of peace and democracy' led by the Soviet Union, but did not picture China's relation to Russia as being in any sense one of subordination. According to Chou En-lai's report on 23 October, China's intervention in Korea had not merely safeguarded China but had encouraged the peoples in all the colonial and semi-colonial areas. China, however, needed peace and would not menace anyone, provided she were not the victim of aggression. The intention expressed by Chou En-lai to 'liberate Formosa from American aggression' was fully in line with current Soviet policies, but on the issue of the protection of the overseas Chinese a note was sounded that would have no particular meaning in a Soviet context.[4] China appeared in these speeches not as a satellite but as a

---

[1] See the leading article on Mao Tse-tung and Stalin in *Sotsialisticheski Vestnik* (*The Socialist Courier*), (New York), August 1951.

[2] *Pravda*, 2 August 1951.

[3] ibid. 5 August 1951.　　　　　　　　　　　[4] *NCNA*, 6 November 1951.

partner, even though a somewhat junior partner. In the Soviet press stress continued to be laid on the Chinese revolution's debt to Soviet inspiration and to the brilliant advice given by Stalin to its leaders.

It is perhaps true to say that even the necessity for the Chinese revolution to develop internally exactly along Soviet lines was more stressed in Russian than in Chinese statements. A lecture given at the Soviet Oriental Studies Institute included the statement that though Chinese agrarian reform had been a real gain for the Chinese peasantry because feudalism had been destroyed, the peasant problem was still unsolved. This could only be done by a socialist transformation of China's agricultural system; mere agrarian reform could not do away with the differentiation between the separate strata of the peasantry.[1] Chou En-lai in his report to the National Committee spoke, on the other hand, as though when agrarian reform was completed at the end of 1952 a period of relative stabilization on the land would follow. During this period, progress would be made only by the establishment of co-operatives on a voluntary basis.[2] But such differences were perhaps little more than tactical.

The extent to which the Soviet Union could influence the future course of China's internal development was bound up very largely with the question of its ability to give economic assistance on a scale commensurate with China's ambitious plans for industrialization. The speeches to the National Committee did not suggest that by the autumn of 1951 much assistance of this kind had been received, though the *New China Daily News* made frequent references to particular examples of Russian aid. The Russians again gave a different picture. In an article in the September number of *Bolshevik*, entitled 'On the successes of the Chinese People's Republic', many of these successes were attributed to Soviet help. China's State-owned industries were said to be using up-to-date Soviet machinery, help was being given in the struggle against plant and animal

[1] *Vestnik Akademii Nauk*, 1951, no. 3.
[2] A theoretical appraisal of the Chinese revolution in Soviet terms can be found in A. N. Kheifets, 'Problems of the Chinese Revolution', in the works of J. V. Stalin, *Voprosy Filosofii*, 1950, no. 3. A valuable series of studies by American experts on different aspects of the Chinese situation was collected in the *Annals* of the American Academy of Political and Social Science, September 1951, under the title 'Report on China'.

diseases, and so on. A statement quoted in this article, to the effect that under the credit agreement of 1950 China was able to import annually from the Soviet Union 65 per cent. more equipment than from all capitalist countries before the war, represents a typical Soviet use of the device of bare percentages to obscure rather than illuminate a problem. An article on China's foreign trade pointed out the extent to which it was now carried on mainly with the Soviet Union and other friendly countries: Poland, Hungary, Czechoslovakia, and Eastern Germany. But neither the real volume of trade nor the commodities dealt in were revealed in such a manner as to enable the reader to gauge to what extent China's vital needs were being met.[1]

On the other hand, all students agreed that Russian specialists and technicians in various fields continued to play an important if deliberately unobtrusive role:

Large numbers of Russian advisers had made their appearance in China in the winter of 1949–50, some thousands apparently, but it is difficult to check the figure. This however was in no sense a 'Russian occupation'. The most trustworthy accounts make it clear that these new arrivals were not political directors; that Russia did not impose them but sent them at China's request and that they do not work the controls but are essentially technicians generally of no exalted rank. They form various sorts of mobile auxiliary teams moving about in groups to attack definite tasks—railway repairing (very rapidly and remarkably completed in 1950), equipment of industry, medical aid, planning; and also military training, aeronautical instruction and the laying out of aerodromes.[2]

A year later a 'special correspondent lately in China' confirmed that there was 'certainly no obvious over-lordship', but went on to add:

China is too dependent on Russia for technical equipment and 'know-how' to be really independent. Moreover, circumstanced as China is, Mao is in no position to play off Russia against any other foreign factor; and since China also leans heavily on Russia for various kinds of military aid the sense of dependence is projected into other spheres.[3]

[1] *Vneshnaya Torgovlya* (Foreign Trade), September 1951.
[2] R. Guillain, 'The New China', *Manchester Guardian*, 7 May 1951.
[3] 'The Present China', *The Times*, 15 July 1952. On the supply of military equipment to China see 'Fighting Communists in South East Asia', *The Times*, 12 February 1952.

Decision between the rival interpretations of the Chinese revolution is impossible to reach because of the insufficiency of our information. It may be held that 'it remains true that the Chinese Revolution was at bottom a rallying of China to the Soviet Union and not an invasion of China by the Soviet Union.'[1] But this does not mean necessarily that the Soviet Union may not have come to exercise through force of circumstances a very considerable measure of control.

Compared with the complexities of China, the Soviet attitude to both Japan and Korea after the San Francisco Conference was not difficult to interpret. The Soviet Union's counter-proposals at San Francisco itself showed that with regard to a country which had shown itself largely resistant to Communist penetration, the Russians were still prepared to lay down terms not different in their essence from those that might have been demanded by any other ex-enemy country in a like strategic situation. It was not altogether unlikely that should all else fail, Soviet diplomacy would be prepared to hold out the bait of trade with the Communist mainland of Asia in order to detach Japan from its close links with the United States, or that Japan would not resist such temptation. On the other hand the Communist bloc could not supply certain vital raw materials.

In Korea, in the autumn of 1951, the Soviet Union, which had sponsored and equipped the Korean armies, was not apparently prepared to forward the North Korean cause, despite the approved revolutionary aspect of the war, except by purely conventional diplomatic means and, as it proved, the supply of arms.

Soviet comment on Asiatic countries is generally even less precise in regard to areas where no definite Russian interests exist. The general and unequivocal expressions of sympathy for revolutionary movements are framed in such a way as to make it clear that only those movements are meant which have Communism as well as national independence as their goal. References to the false independence of countries such as India, Burma, Pakistan, and the Philippines are common. But while foreign exploitation is given as the main source of the ills from which these and other countries suffer, nothing is said to indicate that the Soviet Union has an alternative solution to offer to

[1] Guillain, 'The New China', *Manchester Guardian*, 7 May 1951.

their problems except the abstract notion of socialism. The main political problem in so many of the countries of southern Asia—the existence of multi-racial, or 'plural', societies, is almost ignored. Malayan Communism, for instance, is discussed in terms which ignore the fact that its followers are drawn exclusively from a single element in that country's population and as if it were a national movement of the Malayan people. All this is perhaps understandable in the light of the general Communist antipathy to all elements of social cohesion, including religious and communal loyalties, and the general practice of building up the revolutionary movement on the basis of persons who for one reason or another are themselves emancipated from such allegiance. But even on the economic side where, if anywhere, one might expect some original contribution, nothing useful seems to be forthcoming. Indeed to refer to the gravest of all such problems, that of over-population, is to run the risk of being called a 'Malthusian', a term of abuse in current Soviet practice. The general agreement among Western economists that the provision of new capital and technical assistance, whether under the Point Four programme of President Truman or the Colombo Plan, are essential for these regions is not seemingly shared by the Russians. The conclusion must be that their unstated policy is that which has been followed in the Soviet Union and is being followed in China, namely the creation of capital out of the forced savings of the peasantry, despite the numerous obstacles which the already low level of consumption in these countries would seem to indicate.[1] The inability of the Soviet Government to make concrete proposals was made very obvious in the contribution by its representative Arkadyev to the discussion at the meeting of the United Nations Economic and Social Council on 12 September 1951. His speech combined complaints that nothing had been done in the past for the industrialization of the countries of southern Asia with denunciations of all forms in which capital had hitherto been invested in them.

When discussions under Soviet auspices are held on the

[1] One can verify the substance of these remarks by comparing any random selection of Soviet articles on such topics with a recent western survey of them such as that of Maurice Zinkin, *Asia and the West* (London, Chatto & Windus for IPR, 1951).

problems of the area, the Western student is bound to be struck
by the extreme scholasticism of the approach. The whole thing
seems to revolve around purely verbal definitions, and although
this Marxist hair-splitting no doubt conceals some real differences of opinion, it is not at all clear what these are. For instance the conference of the Institute of Oriental Studies of the
Soviet Academy of Sciences in November 1951 was devoted to
a discussion of the 'character and attributes of the system of
people's democracy in countries of the Orient'.[1] In his opening
address E. M. Zhukov explained that the

principal distinction between the Oriental countries of people's
democracy and the European countries of people's democracy lies
in the fact that in China, Mongolia, Korea, and Viet Nam the
people's democracy at the present stage is resolving the national-
liberation and anti-feudal tasks of the bourgeois-democratic revolution, does not set as its near prospect the task of building socialism,
and consequently does not perform the functions of the dictatorship
of the proletariat.

The discussion tended to ignore the frequent appeals made to
take account of the necessity of differentiating between the
concrete situations in each particular case and to resolve itself
into discussing merely how far this terminology was apt. Much
time seemingly was devoted to arguing as to whether the concept of people's democracy as a dictatorship of the proletariat
and peasantry was applicable to a country like Outer Mongolia,
in which no proletariat existed, and whether, thanks to the
existence of the Soviet Union, Outer Mongolia could pass from
the bourgeois to the socialist phase of the revolution without
first becoming industrialized. Whereas some speakers saw
Outer Mongolia as already in the stage of socialist construction
and therefore beyond the stage reached by the other Oriental
People's Democracies and comparable with the People's Democracies of Eastern Europe, others held that since the dominant
element in the country's economy is still 'small-scale peasant
production based on the most backward pasture-nomadic
stock-raising', it could hardly be said that the anti-feudal
bourgeois-democratic revolution had been accomplished there.
Little of this would seem to the non-Marxist a very positive

[1] *Izvestia Akademii Nauk* (Proceedings of the Academy of Sciences), History and
Philosophy series, no. 1, January–February 1952.

contribution to the problems of Outer Mongolia; nor did it cast any real light upon what was actually taking place there.

On the general question of the revolutionary social developments of the area, Soviet information is thus disappointingly vague. It is not surprising that on more precise questions relating to possible direct responsibilities of the Soviet Government itself, information is even harder to obtain. It has been seen that there are a number of important events for which such Soviet responsibility cannot be proved—among them the outbreak of the Korean war.

Some Western observers appear indeed to have no doubt of the Soviet Union's direct responsibility not merely for the arming of North Korea but for the timing of the war.

This war [writes the military correspondent of *The Times*] represented a fairly big Russian investment but it was one that paid a sensational dividend. The North Korean army was provided, it is believed, with 1,000 good tanks besides artillery and other equipment. It was given a long and thorough training. It was reinforced by Koreans domiciled in Russia who had gained experience in the world war. It came within measurable reach of complete victory in the Korean peninsula before Chinese intervention began.[1]

Others profess even more exact knowledge: that the Korean war had its origin in Moscow in the deliberations of Stalin and Mao Tse-tung in the winter of 1950–1.[2]

These hypotheses may well be correct, but cannot be accepted as proved historical fact. And they still leave unexplained the fact that the Russians should have chosen the precise juncture of the outbreak of war to be absent from the Security Council which was thus allowed to act without the obstacle of their veto, unless indeed they were convinced by previous American utterances that the United States would not intervene. By any calculation of *realpolitik* the Korean war doubly benefited the Russians: it locked up a large part of the available strength of the Western world in the remotest and least important of the threatened fronts, and it confirmed the breach between Communist China and the Western world, thus underlining, as has

[1] 'Fighting Communists in South East Asia', *The Times*, 12 February 1952.
[2] R. Guillain, *Manchester Guardian*, 26 November 1951. It also remains an open question whether a general Communist offensive was planned at the Calcutta Conference in February 1948.

been seen, its need of Soviet support. The drain on the resources of the Communist bloc, which was severe, fell mainly on China.

Meanwhile, neither in Indo-China nor in Malaya had Communism been mastered, and in the independent countries of South East Asia the position was almost equally encouraging to the Communists; the general situation at the beginning of 1952 was summed up as follows:

Siam is an anti-Communist country, but its future is tied up with that of Indo-China and its present complexion would not survive the complete triumph of Viet-Minh. If one were to go Communist, so would the other. Burma is racked by armed Communist revolt within and incapable of withstanding even a minor offensive from without, that is, over the frontier with the Chinese province of Yunnan. Guerrilla warfare, of which not much is heard, has been going on persistently in Java, the heart and the main source of the wealth of Indonesia. These States do not possess equal strategic importance, but they all have high economic importance. Weakness and confusion in them affect adversely the welfare of the world; collapse would involve famine over vast areas.[1]

From such reflections it would seem to follow that the opportunities afforded to Communism by the collapse of the European and Japanese empires in Asia have been fully exploited. The extension of the actual area of Sovietization has resulted, with the partial exception of Manchuria, rather from the weakness of the opposition to it than from positive contributions of strength from the Soviet Union. And even where Communism was still, at the time of writing, being held at bay, the resources required to resist it were an important drain upon the military strength and the economy of much of the rest of the world. Nor was it possible to disguise the fact that similar opportunities existed for Communist expansion in the Middle East and ultimately, perhaps, in Africa. The most novel and disturbing feature of the whole story from the point of view of the non-Communist world was the apparent ability of the Soviet Union to fight its Asiatic struggles almost entirely by proxy. This was as true of the actual large-scale warfare in Korea as of the minor conflicts in Indo-China, Burma, and Malaya.[2] The investment required from them to keep such

[1] 'Fighting Communists in South East Asia', *The Times*, 24 February 1952.

[2] On the Malayan background see 'Malayan Emergency', two articles in *The Times*, 11 and 12 August 1952. By this time there were signs in Malaya of a swing

hostilities going seemed much smaller than that required to check them.

The question remained open as to how long the Soviet Union would continue to enjoy this advantage, and how far indeed it could rely on controlling those movements that its example and encouragement had set in motion. The precise reasons for the Soviet initiative for truce talks in Korea in the summer of 1951 remain obscure, though the Chinese badly needed a pause for rest and re-equipment. In the subsequent long-drawn-out negotiations which were still in progress a year later it was China which acted for the Communist world (along with North Korea) albeit apparently with full Russian support, and it was Chinese intransigence which proved the barrier to agreement.

Presumably both the Russians and the Chinese preferred this relative stabilization of the Korean front to a continuation of all-out attempts at total victory; but one may legitimately inquire whether their motives were identical.

China, as has been seen, regarded herself throughout as principal, not as agent, in the Asiatic conflict. In the report by Chou En-lai already referred to he declared (with much greater assurance than China's industrial weakness justified) that 'the unity of the Chinese people and peoples of Asia will certainly create a powerful and matchless force in the Far East which will rapidly push forward the great wheel of history in the movement for independence and liberation of the peoples of the Asian countries'. If such statements mean that Peking regards itself as a primary source of inspiration at least where Asian countries are concerned, Soviet policy, which has rested on the absolute identification of world revolution and Soviet nationalism, would receive a blow more fundamental than any it has hitherto sustained. And there is some reason to believe that Peking for all the stridency of its leaders is inclined for the time being to limit its commitments.[1]

It is perhaps significant that in the paper read by Zhukov to the Institute of Oriental Studies at the meeting already re-

back from direct action by the Communists towards a new effort at political penetration.

[1] It has been noted that the Chinese were cautious about directly taking up the cause of the Chinese Communists in Malaya and it has been suggested that had they really wished to give active help, they could best have done so by implementing an exchange of diplomatic representatives with Great Britain which would have

ferred to, he pointed out that it would be risky to regard the Chinese revolution as some kind of 'stereotype' for the people's democratic revolutions in other countries of Asia, although the majority of those who spoke in the discussion emphasized the importance of Chinese experience. One speaker in particular, G. I. Levinson, pointed out that the reasons for this lay 'in the geographical proximity of these countries to China, in the age-old cultural ties with it, and in the presence in these countries of a substantial Chinese population (amounting to 45 per cent. of the total population in Malaya and 20 per cent. in Siam)'. He pointed out that these Chinese populations maintained close political ties with China and played an active political role in the countries in which they lived. All this promoted assimilation by South East Asia of the experience of the Chinese revolution, which was being intensively studied and spread by the Communist parties of these countries. On the other hand two experts on India agreed with Zhukov about the dangers of treating China as a stereotype.[1]

While all these nuances in the Soviet-Chinese partnership should be borne in mind, they afford no grounds for believing that Soviet-Chinese unity as it developed in this period was likely to be a superficial and transient phenomenon. Such a view was indeed held in some quarters in the West, but mainly by students of China alone who, having made an inadequate study of Communism in its original setting, were prepared to maintain that the Chinese variety owed much less than it did to the Soviet model.[2] More cautious students were content to note that Mao Tse-tung himself had the unique distinction of having been allowed to introduce elements of his own into Communist theory and to be, along with Stalin, the only Communist in the world to have enjoyed such a privilege since Lenin's death. They also suggested that if, as seemed probable, Mao were to outlive Stalin, he would have a personal prestige in the world Communist movement such as no Russian suc-

enabled them to station consuls in the principal Malayan centres (Fitzgerald, Revolution in China, p. 248).

[1] Izvestia Akademii Nauk, History and Philosophy series, no. 1, January–February 1952.

[2] See e.g. Jean-Jacques Brieux, La Chine du Nationalisme au Communisme (Paris, Éditions du Seuil, 1950): Robert Payne, Mao Tse-tung, Ruler of Red China (London, Secker & Warburg, 1951).

cessor to Stalin could hope to possess.[1] But even they did not take into account sufficiently the backwardness of China's economy and the consequent certainty that it would long continue to be subordinate in world politics as compared with the Soviet Union.

Besides these somewhat speculative considerations, there was the undeniable fact that in the summer of 1951 the Chinese régime began a move in the direction of an increasingly harsh and rigid totalitarianism.[2] This fact and the Chinese dependence on the Soviet Union for direct military supplies which, as has been noted, became considerable in the autumn of 1951, gave little encouragement to those who expected some kind of Chinese Titoism to develop, or blamed its absence upon the failings of Western diplomacy. It seems likely that those who held such views also overlooked the fact that the Russians had presumably learned from their experience with Yugoslavia how to avoid irritating national sentiment in handling foreign Communists. Finally, with the exception of the partially unresolved questions relating to the Soviet undertakings with regard to Manchuria, and the more obscure but relatively minor question of north-western Sinkiang, direct clashes of interest between the Soviet Union and China seemed unlikely. As long as China continued to look primarily towards South East Asia as a field for expansion, collision with the Russians seemed improbable. Statements on Chinese foreign policy, such as that of Chou En-lai on 19 November 1951 with reference to the disarmament discussions at the United Nations, were emphatic on the unity of views between China and the Soviet Union: and there is no reason to doubt their sincerity.

The history of Soviet policy in the Far East since the Second World War provides an apt illustration of the tensions between the Soviet Union as a centre of political power, and the Soviet Union as an agent of world revolution. Soviet statesmanship has as its major task the problem of their reconciliation. The region was one in which both successes and failures could be seen; but there was inadequate information for anyone to be able to say with confidence whether the task that the Russians had set themselves was too difficult or not.

[1] Fitzgerald, *Revolution in China*, pp. 254 ff.
[2] See e.g. Guillain's dispatches in the *Manchester Guardian*, November 1951.

APPENDIX

Texts of Treaties and Agreements

(The texts of the treaties are those of the English versions published by Tass at the time of their announcement)

TREATY OF FRIENDSHIP, ALLIANCE, AND MUTUAL ASSISTANCE BETWEEN THE USSR AND THE PEOPLE'S REPUBLIC OF CHINA

(14 *February* 1950)

THE Presidium of the Supreme Soviet of the Union of Soviet Socialist Republics and the Central People's Government of the People's Republic of China;

Filled with determination jointly to prevent, by the consolidation of friendship and co-operation between the Union of Soviet Socialist Republics and the People's Republic of China, the rebirth of Japanese imperialism, and a repetition of aggression on the part of Japan or any other State which should unite in any form with Japan in acts of aggression;

Imbued with the desire to consolidate lasting peace and universal security in the Far East and throughout the world in conformity with the aims and principles of the United Nations Organization;

Profoundly convinced that the consolidation of good-neighbourly relations and friendship between the Union of Soviet Socialist Republics and the People's Republic of China meets the fundamental interests of the peoples of the Soviet Union and China;

Resolved for this purpose to conclude the present Treaty and appointed as their plenipotentiary representatives:

The Presidium of the Supreme Soviet of the Union of Soviet Socialist Republics: Andrei Yanuarovich Vyshinsky, Minister of Foreign Affairs of the Union of Soviet Socialist Republics;

The Central People's Government of the People's Republic of China: Chou En-lai, Prime Minister of the State Administrative Council and Minister of Foreign Affairs of China;

Who, after exchange of their credentials, found in due form and good order, agreed upon the following:

ARTICLE I

Both High Contracting Parties undertake jointly to take all the necessary measures at their disposal for the purpose of preventing a repetition of aggression and violation of peace on the part of Japan or any other State which should unite with Japan, directly or indirectly, in acts of aggression. In the event of one of the High Contracting Parties being attacked by Japan or States allied with it, and thus being involved in a state of war, the other High Contracting Party will immediately render military and other assistance with all the means at its disposal.

The High Contracting Parties also declare their readiness in the spirit of sincere co-operation to participate in all international actions aimed at ensuring peace and security throughout the world, and will do all in their power to achieve the speediest implementation of these tasks.

ARTICLE II

Both the High Contracting Parties undertake by means of mutual agreement to strive for the earliest conclusion of a peace treaty with Japan, jointly with the other Powers which were allies during the Second World War.

ARTICLE III

Both High Contracting Parties undertake not to conclude any alliance directed against the other High Contracting Party, and not to take part in any coalition or in actions or measures directed against the other High Contracting Party.

ARTICLE IV

Both High Contracting Parties will consult each other in regard to all important international problems affecting the common interests of the Soviet Union and China, being guided by the interests of the consolidation of peace and universal security.

ARTICLE V

Both the High Contracting Parties undertake, in the spirit of friendship and co-operation and in conformity with the principles of equality, mutual interests, and also mutual respect for the State sovereignty and territorial integrity and non-interference in internal affairs of the other High Contracting Party—to develop and consolidate economic and cultural ties between the Soviet Union and China, to render each other every possible economic assistance, and to carry out the necessary economic co-operation.

ARTICLE VI

The present Treaty comes into force immediately upon its

ratification; the exchange of instruments of ratification will take place in Peking.

The present Treaty will be valid for thirty years. If neither of the High Contracting Parties gives notice one year before the expiration of this term of its desire to denounce the Treaty, it shall remain in force for another five years and will be extended in compliance with this rule.

Done in Moscow on 14 February 1950, in two copies, each in the Russian and Chinese languages, both texts having equal force.

Signed: *By Authorization of the Presidium of the Supreme Soviet of the Union of Soviet Socialist Republics*:

A. Y. VYSHINSKY

By Authorization of the Central People's Government of the People's Republic of China:

CHOU EN-LAI

AGREEMENT BETWEEN THE USSR AND THE PEOPLE'S REPUBLIC OF CHINA ON THE CHINESE CHANGCHUN RAILWAY, PORT ARTHUR, AND DALNY

The Presidium of the Supreme Soviet of the Union of Soviet Socialist Republics and the Central People's Government of the People's Republic of China state that since 1945 radical changes have occurred in the situation in the Far East, namely: Imperialist Japan suffered defeat; the reactionary Kuomintang Government was overthrown; China has become a People's Democratic Republic, and in China a new People's Government was formed which has united the whole of China, carried out a policy of friendship and co-operation with the Soviet Union, and proved its ability to defend the State independence and territorial integrity of China, the national honour and dignity of the Chinese people.

The Presidium of the Supreme Soviet of the Union of Soviet Socialist Republics and the Central People's Government of the People's Republic of China maintain that this new situation permits a new approach to the question of the Chinese Changchun Railway, Port Arthur, and Dalny.

In conformity with these new circumstances, the Presidium of the Supreme Soviet of the Union of Soviet Socialist Republics and the Central People's Government of the People's Republic of China have decided to conclude the present agreement on the Chinese Changchun Railway, Port Arthur, and Dalny.

ARTICLE I

Both High Contracting Parties have agreed that the Soviet Government transfers gratis to the Government of the People's Republic of China all its rights in the joint administration of the Chinese Changchun Railway, with all the property belonging to the Railway. The transfer will be effected immediately upon the conclusion of a peace treaty with Japan, but not later than the end of 1952.

Pending the transfer, the now existing position of the Soviet-Chinese joint administration of the Chinese Changchun Railway remains unchanged; however, the order of filling posts by representatives of the Soviet and Chinese sides, upon the coming into force of the present Agreement, will be changed, and there will be established an alternating filling of posts for a definite period of time (Director of the Railway, Chairman of the Central Board, and others).

As regards concrete methods of effecting the transfer, they will be agreed upon and determined by the Governments of both High Contracting Parties.

ARTICLE II

Both High Contracting Parties have agreed that Soviet troops will be withdrawn from the jointly utilized naval base of Port Arthur and that the installations in this area will be handed over to the Government of the People's Republic of China immediately upon the conclusion of a peace treaty with Japan, but not later than the end of 1952, with the Government of the People's Republic of China compensating the Soviet Union for expenses incurred in the restoration and construction of installations effected by the Soviet Union since 1945.

For the period pending the withdrawal of Soviet troops and the transfer of the above installations, the Governments of the Soviet Union and China will appoint an equal number of military representatives for organizing a joint Chinese-Soviet Military Commission which will be in charge of military affairs in the area of Port Arthur; concrete measures in this sphere will be determined by the joint Chinese-Soviet Military Commission within three months upon the coming into force of the present Agreement and shall be implemented upon the approval of these measures by the Governments of both countries.

The civil administration in the aforementioned area shall be in the direct charge of the Government of the People's Republic of China. Pending the withdrawal of Soviet troops, the zone of billeting of

Soviet troops in the area of Port Arthur will remain unaltered in conformity with the now existing frontiers.

In the event of either of the High Contracting Parties being subjected to aggression on the part of Japan or any State which should unite with Japan and as a result of this being involved in military operations, China and the Soviet Union may, on the proposal of the Government of the People's Republic of China and with the agreement of the Soviet Government, jointly use the naval base of Port Arthur in the interests of conducting joint military operations against the aggressor.

ARTICLE III

Both High Contracting Parties have agreed that the question of Port Dalny must be further considered upon the conclusion of a peace treaty with Japan.

As regards the administration in Dalny, it fully belongs to the Government of the People's Republic of China.

All property now existing in Dalny provisionally in charge of or under lease to the Soviet side, is to be taken over by the Government of the People's Republic of China. For carrying out work involved in the receipt of the aforementioned property, the Governments of the Soviet Union and China appoint three representatives from each side for organizing a joint commission which in the course of three months after the coming into force of the present agreement shall determine the concrete methods of transfer of property, and after approval of the proposals of the Joint Commission by the Governments of both countries will complete their implementation in the course of 1950.

ARTICLE IV

The present agreement comes into force on the day of its ratification. The exchange of instruments of ratification will take place in Peking.

Done in Moscow on 14 February 1950, in two copies, each in the Russian and Chinese languages, both texts having equal force.

Signed: *By Authorization of the Presidium of the Supreme Soviet of the Union of Soviet Socialist Republics*:

A. Y. VYSHINSKY

By Authorization of the Central People's Government of the People's Republic of China:

CHOU EN-LAI

EXCHANGE OF NOTES OF 15 SEPTEMBER 1952 AMENDING ARTICLE II OF THE SINO-SOVIET TREATY OF 14 FEBRUARY 1950[1]

From China to the USSR:

Most Esteemed Comrade Minister,

Following Japan's refusal to conclude an omnilateral peace treaty and the conclusion of a separate treaty with the United States and with certain other countries, in view of which Japan has not, and apparently does not wish to have, a peace treaty with the Chinese People's Republic and the Soviet Union, conditions have arisen which constitute a threat to the cause of peace and favour a recurrence of Japanese aggression.

In view of this and with the aim of preserving peace and likewise on the basis of the Treaty of Friendship, Alliance and Mutual Assistance between the Chinese People's Republic and the USSR, the Government of the Chinese People's Republic proposes, and requests the Soviet Government to agree to, prolonging the terms fixed by Article II of the Soviet-Chinese Treaty on Port Arthur for the withdrawal of Soviet troops from the jointly used Chinese naval base of Port Arthur, pending the conclusion of peace treaties between the Chinese People's Republic and Japan and the Soviet Union and Japan.

If the Soviet Government agrees to the aforesaid proposal of the Government of the Chinese People's Republic, the present Note and your Note of reply will be considered a component part of the Treaty of 14 February 1950 between the Chinese People's Republic and the USSR with regard to the naval base of Port Arthur, coming into force on the day of the exchange of Notes.

I ask you, Comrade Minister, to accept assurances of my most profound esteem.

Signed: CHOU EN-LAI, 15 *September* 1952

From the USSR to China:

Most Esteemed Comrade Premier and Minister. This is to acknowledge receipt of your Note of 15 September of this year.

The Soviet Government expresses its agreement with the proposal of the Government of the Chinese People's Republic and also to the proposal that your Note and the present reply thereto become a component part of the above-mentioned Treaty of 14 February 1950, on the naval base of Port Arthur as from the day of the exchange of the present Notes.

[1] *The Times*, 22 September 1952.

I ask you, Comrade Premier and Minister, to accept assurances of my most profound esteem.

Signed: A. VYSHINSKY, 15 *September* 1952

AGREEMENT BETWEEN THE USSR AND THE PEOPLE'S REPUBLIC OF CHINA ON GRANTING CREDITS TO THE PEOPLE'S REPUBLIC OF CHINA

In connexion with the consent of the Government of the Union of Soviet Socialist Republics to grant the request of the Central People's Government of the People's Republic of China on giving China credits for paying for equipment and other materials which the Soviet Union has agreed to deliver to China, both Governments have agreed upon the following:

ARTICLE I

The Government of the Union of Soviet Socialist Republics grants the Central People's Government of the People's Republic of China credits, calculated in dollars, amounting to 300 million American dollars, taking 35 American dollars to one ounce of fine gold.

In view of the extreme devastation of China as a result of prolonged hostilities on its territory, the Soviet Government has agreed to grant credits on favourable terms of 1 per cent. annual interest.

ARTICLE II

The credits mentioned in Article I will be granted in the course of five years, as from 1 January 1950, in equal portions of one-fifth of the credits in the course of each year, for payments for deliveries from the USSR of equipment and materials, including equipment for electric power stations, metallurgical and engineering plants, equipment for mines, for the production of coal and ores, railway and other transport equipment, rails and other material for the restoration and development of the national economy of China.

The assortment, quantities, prices and dates of deliveries of equipment and materials will be determined under a special agreement of the Parties; prices will be determined on the basis of prices obtaining on the world markets.

Any credits which remain unused in the course of one annual period may be used in subsequent annual periods.

ARTICLE III

The Central People's Government of the People's Republic of

China repays the credits mentioned in Article I, as well as interest on them, with deliveries of raw materials, tea, gold, American dollars. Prices for raw materials and tea, quantities and dates of deliveries will be determined on the basis of prices obtaining on the world markets.

Repayment of credits is effected in the course of ten years in equal annual parts—one-tenth yearly of the sum total of received credits not later than 31 December of every year. The first payment is effected not later than 31 December 1954, and the last on 31 December 1963.

Payment of interest on credits, calculated from the day of drawing the respective fraction of the credits, is effected every six months.

ARTICLE IV

For clearance with regard to the credits envisaged by the present agreement the State Bank of the USSR and National Bank of the People's Republic of China shall open special accounts and jointly establish the order of clearance and accounting under the present agreement.

ARTICLE V

The present agreement comes into force on the day of its signing and is subject to ratification. The exchange of instruments of ratification will take place in Peking.

Done in Moscow on 14 February 1950, in two copies, each in the Russian and Chinese languages, both texts having equal force.

Signed: *By Authorization of the Government of the Union of Soviet Socialist Republics*:

A. Y. VYSHINSKY

By Authorization of the Central People's Government of the People's Republic of China:

CHOU EN-LAI

SOVIET-MONGOLIAN TREATY OF FRIENDSHIP AND MUTUAL ASSISTANCE BETWEEN THE UNION OF SOVIET SOCIALIST REPUBLICS AND THE MONGOLIAN PEOPLE'S REPUBLIC

(27 *February* 1946)

In connexion with the ending of the ten-year term of the Protocol on Mutual Assistance concluded between the Union of Soviet

Socialist Republics and the Mongolian People's Republic, the Presidium of the Supreme Soviet of the USSR and the Presidium of the Little Khural of the Mongolian People's Republic decided to change the Protocol of 12 March 1936, quoted below, into a Treaty of Friendship and Mutual Assistance to be valid for ten years:

The Governments of the Union of Soviet Socialist Republics and the Mongolian People's Republic, proceeding from the relationship of consistent friendship which has existed between the two countries since the liberation with the aid of the Red Army of the territory of the Mongolian People's Republic in 1921 from the White Guard detachments which had contact with the troops that invaded the territory of the USSR;

and directed by the desire to secure peace in the Far East and to strengthen further the friendly relations existing between them;

hereby formulate in this Protocol the gentlemen's agreement existing between them since 27 November 1934, which provides for mutual support by all possible measures in averting and forestalling any threat of military attack as well as for mutual assistance and support in case of attack on the USSR or on the Mongolian People's Republic by any third party.

ARTICLE I

In the case of a menace of attack on the territory of the Union of Soviet Socialist Republics or on the Mongolian People's Republic by a third State, the Governments of the Union of Soviet Socialist Republics and the Mongolian People's Republic undertake immediately to discuss jointly the situation arising and to take all such measures as might be necessary to safeguard the security of their territory.

ARTICLE II

The Governments of the Union of Soviet Socialist Republics and the Mongolian People's Republic undertake in the case of military attack on one of the Contracting Parties to render each other every assistance including military assistance.

ARTICLE III

The Governments of the Union of Soviet Socialist Republics and the Mongolian People's Republic deem it self-understood that the troops of one of the Parties stationed by mutual agreement on the territory of the other Party, in fulfilment of the undertakings under Article I or II, will be withdrawn from the territory in question without delay when the necessity for this is over, as was the case in

1925 in regard to the withdrawal of Soviet troops from territory of the Mongolian People's Republic.

The present Treaty comes into force as from its ratification, which must be effected within as short a time as possible. The exchange of ratification instruments will take place in Ulan Bator.

Unless one of the High Contracting Parties one year prior to the expiration of the term of the present Treaty gives notice of its desire to denounce the Treaty, it will remain valid for the next ten years.

Done in Moscow, 27 February 1946, which corresponds to the 27th day of the Second Moon of the 36th year of the Mongolian Calendar, in two copies, each in the Russian and Mongolian languages, both texts being equally valid.

> Signed: *On the Authority of the Presidium of the Supreme Soviet of the Union of Soviet Socialist Republics*:
> V. M. MOLOTOV
>
> *On the Authority of the Presidium of the Little Khural of the Mongolian People's Republic*:
> MARSHAL CHOIBALSAN

AGREEMENT ON ECONOMIC AND CULTURAL COLLABORATION BETWEEN THE GOVERNMENT OF THE UNION OF SOVIET SOCIALIST RE- PUBLICS AND THE GOVERNMENT OF THE MONGOLIAN PEOPLE'S REPUBLIC

The Government of the Union of Soviet Socialist Republics and the Government of the Mongolian People's Republic, considering that economic and cultural collaboration between the Soviet Union and the Mongolian People's Republic, established since the time of the foundation of the Mongolian People's Republic, has proved extremely beneficial and to correspond with the interests of both countries, have decided to conclude an Agreement on the following:

ARTICLE I

The High Contracting Parties agree to develop and consolidate the collaboration in the fields of national economy, culture, and education existing between the Union of Soviet Socialist Republics and the Mongolian Republic.

ARTICLE II

On the basis of the present Agreement and in pursuance of it, separate agreements and contracts will be concluded between corresponding economic, scientific, and cultural-educational institutions and organizations of the USSR and the Mongolian People's Republic.

ARTICLE III

The present Agreement comes into force as from the moment of its signing and will be valid for ten years. Unless one of the Contracting Parties one year before the expiration of the term of the present Agreement gives notice of its desire to denounce the Agreement, it will remain in force for the subsequent ten years.

Done in Moscow, 27 February 1946, which corresponds to the 27th day of the Second Moon of the 36th year of the Mongolian Calendar, in two copies, each in the Russian and Mongolian languages, both texts being equally valid.

> Signed: *On the Authority of the Government of the Union of Soviet Socialist Republics:*
> V. M. MOLOTOV
>
> *On the Authority of the Government of the Mongolian People's Republic:*
> MARSHAL CHOIBALSAN

AGREEMENT ON ECONOMIC AND CULTURAL CO-OPERATION BETWEEN THE USSR AND THE KOREAN PEOPLE'S DEMOCRATIC REPUBLIC

(17 March 1949)

The Presidium of the Supreme Soviet of the Union of Soviet Socialist Republics and the Presidium of the Supreme National Assembly of the Korean People's Democratic Republic, striving for the further promotion and strengthening of economic and cultural relations between the USSR and the Korean People's Democratic Republic, convinced that the consolidation and promotion of these ties meets the vital interests of the peoples of both countries and will in the best way facilitate their economic and cultural development, have decided to conclude to these ends the present agreement and to appoint as their plenipotentiary representatives:

The Presidium of the Supreme Soviet of the Union of Soviet Socialist Republics: Andrei Yanuarovich Vyshinsky, Minister of Forgein Affairs of the USSR;

The Presidium of the Supreme National Assembly of the Korean People's Democratic Republic: Kim Ir Sen, Chairman of the Council of Ministers of the Korean People's Democratic Republic;

Who upon exchange of their credentials, found to be in proper order, have agreed upon the following:

ARTICLE I

The Contracting Parties will in every way promote and consolidate trade relations between them on the basis of co-operation, equality, and mutual benefit. The Governments of both Contracting Parties will from time to time conclude agreements determining the volume and composition of mutual deliveries of goods for yearly as well as longer periods and other conditions ensuring uninterrupted and increasing trade turnover between both countries in accordance with the requirements for developing the national economy of each of them.

ARTICLE II

The Contracting Parties shall grant each other the right to reciprocal most-favoured nation treatment with respect to all matters relating to commerce and navigation between both countries, as well as with regard to the activity of physical and juridical persons of one Contracting Party on the territory of the other Party.

ARTICLE III

The Contracting Parties shall in every way promote and consolidate the relations established between them in the fields of culture, science, and art.

Accordingly, the Governments of the Contracting Parties shall enter into negotiations with the object of concluding corresponding agreements. In so doing both Governments shall be guided by their aspirations further to consolidate these relations.

ARTICLE IV

The Contracting Parties shall facilitate the exchange between both countries of experience in the field of industry and agriculture through the dispatch of experts, the rendering of technical aid, the organization of exhibitions, the exchange of specimens of seeds and plants, as well as in other ways.

ARTICLE V

The present agreement is concluded for a period of ten years.

The agreement shall be ratified in the shortest possible time and shall come into force as from the day of the exchange of ratification instruments, which shall be effected in Phyeng-Yang.

Unless either of the Contracting Parties gives notice in writing one year prior to the expiration of the said ten-year term of its intention to renounce the agreement, the latter will remain in force for one year as from the day when the agreement may be renounced by either of the Contracting Parties.

In witness whereof the plenipotentiary representatives of both Contracting Parties have signed the present agreement and affixed their seals thereto.

Done in Moscow on 17 March 1949, in two copies, in the Russian and Korean languages, both texts being equally valid.

Signed: *Upon the Authorization of the Presidium of the Supreme Soviet of the Union of Soviet Socialist Republics:*

A. Y. VYSHINSKY

Upon the Authorization of the Presidium of the Supreme National Assembly of the Korean People's Democratic Republic:

KIM IR SEN

Index

PRINTED IN
GREAT BRITAIN
AT THE
UNIVERSITY PRESS
OXFORD
BY
CHARLES BATEY
PRINTER
TO THE
UNIVERSITY